Sci...

ℓ4

19/24

BATS

Biology and Behaviour

BATS

Biology and Behaviour

JOHN D. ALTRINGHAM

*Department of Biology,
The University of Leeds*

Drawings by Tom McOwat and Lucy Hammond

Myotis myotis

Oxford   New York   Tokyo
OXFORD UNIVERSITY PRESS
1996

Oxford University Press, Walton Street, Oxford OX2 6DP

Oxford   New York

Athens   Auckland   Bangkok   Bombay
Calcutta   Cape Town   Dar es Salaam   Delhi
Florence   Hong Kong   Istanbul   Karachi
Kuala Lumpur   Madras   Madrid   Melbourne
Mexico City   Nairobi   Paris   Singapore
Taipei   Tokyo   Toronto

and associated companies in
Berlin   Ibadan

Oxford is a trade mark of Oxford University Press

Published in the United States
by Oxford University Press Inc., New York

A catalogue record for this book is available from the British Library

Library of Congress Cataloging in Publication Data

Altringham, John.
Bats: biology and behaviour/John Altringham; drawings by Tom McOwat and Lucy Hammond.
Includes bibliographical reference (p.   ) and index.
1. Bats. 2. Bats—Behavior. I. Title.
QL737.C5A4 1996   599.4—dc20   95–49029 CIP

ISBN 0 19 854075 2

Typeset by EXPO Holdings, Malaysia
Printed in Great Britain by Biddles Ltd., Guildford

Preface

This book is aimed primarily at undergraduate and graduate students wishing to learn about bats, but also aims to show how a study of one group of animals can contribute to a wider understanding of the processes which shape the natural world. It therefore has two main objectives. The first is to give an account of the biology of the world's bats, emphasising those aspects which are unique or highly adapted, notably flight and echolocation. The second objective is to illustrate processes and concepts of broad biological relevance, many of which are major themes in current research. The coverage is broad, but by no means comprehensive. I have tried to make the book accessible to the growing number of bat enthusiasts in all walks of life, by giving some relevant background to what I imagine are the more difficult sections and by explaining terminology and principles that may be unfamiliar.

Taphozous mauritianus

Acknowledgements

I would like to thank the following people.

The final year students whose enthusiasm for my course on bats led me to write this book.

The many people who shared their data and thoughts, and gave me encouragement.

Gareth Jones, Brock Fenton, Geoff Welford, and Judith May for their valuable comments on the manuscript.

Tom McOwat and Lucy Hammond for the fine drawings which grace the book, and Merlin Tuttle of BCI and Brock Fenton for allowing the artists to use their photographs as source material.

David Bullock for introducing me to bats.

Kirsty Park for her enduring enthusiasm and good humour in our work on bats.

Kate, for her understanding and support during the many hours I worked on this book, and our kids, Sandy and Anne, for only once (at least that I remember) saying 'you're not going upstairs to write that book AGAIN are you dad?'

CREDITS

Fig. 4.4 is reprinted from *Comp. Biochem. Physiol.* **31**, McNab, B.K. The economics of temperature regulation in Neotropical bats, 227–268. © (1969), with kind permission from Elsevier Science Ltd, The Boulevard, Langford Lane, Kidlington, OX5 1GB, UK. Fig. 6.15 is reprinted with permission from *Nature*: Wilkinson, G.S. Reciprocal food sharing in the vampire bat. *Nature* **308**, 181–184. © (1985) Macmillan Magazines Limited. Fig. 6.18 is reprinted with permission from the University of Chicago Press, from Howell, D.J. and Hartl, D.L. (1980) Optimal foraging in Glossophagine bats: when to give up. *Am. Nat.* **115**, 696–704. 1980 University of Chicago. All rights reserved. Figs 1.6, 3.9, 3.17, 3.25 and 6.22 are printed with permission from Springer-Verlag from: Habersetzer, J. and Storch, G. (1992) Cochlea size in extant Chiroptera and middle Eocene Microchiropterans from Messel. *Naturwiss.* **79**, 462–466, Fig. 4. Simmons, J.A. and Stein, R.A. (1980) Acoustic imaging in bat sonar: echolocation signals and the evolution of echolocation. *J. Comp. Physiol.* **135**, 61–84, Figs 1 and 4. Schnitzler, H.-U., Menne, D., Kober, R. and Heblich, K. (1983) The acoustical image of fluttering insects in echolocating bats. In: *Neuroethology and behavioural physiology. Roots and growing points*. Edited by F. Huber and H. Markl. pp. 235–250, Fig. 2. Fleming, T.H., Nunez, R.A. and Sternberg, L. da S.L. (1993) Seasonal changes in the diets of migrant and non-migrant nectarivorous bats as revealed by carbon stable isotope analysis. *Oecologia* **94**, 72–75, Figs 1 and 2. © Springer-Verlag, Berlin/Heidelberg 1980, 1983, 1992, 1993.

Drawings on pages iii, 30, 31, 40 (top), 43, and 44 (top) by Lucy Hammond, all others by Tom McOwat.

Contents

Introduction—biology lessons from the bats

Bats are one of the most successful mammalian orders, and probably the most diverse. The 966 species (by the more optimistic estimates) provide an unparalleled exhibition of variations on the mammalian theme, and a broad lesson in biology. In the bats we see excellent illustrations of adaptive radiation, optimal foraging, co-evolution, reciprocal altruism, the consequences of continental drift, and the arms race between predator and prey, to name just a few examples. This is a book about bats, but it will also use them as a vehicle to show how these processes shape the natural world.

Rodents are the only mammalian order to outnumber bats with, by some estimates, about 1700 species, but they are certainly less diverse in their biology. One quarter of all mammals are bats—surprising, when you think that there are 21 mammalian orders, including animals as varied as primates, carnivores, cetaceans, rodents, insectivores, ungulates, seals, sloths, marsupials, etc. They are distributed all around the world: over 200 species are found in Africa and Madagascar, over 300 in South and Central America and the Caribbean, and a similar number in South East Asia and Australasia. They are also well represented in higher latitudes: about 40 species are resident in both North America and western and central Europe. Several vespertilionid bats (e.g. *Eptesicus* and *Lasiurus* and *Myotis* spp.) spend the summer north of the Arctic Circle. Other members of this very large family (e.g. *Dasypterus* spp.) forage in the chill and windy regions of southern Patagonia. Bats have found their way to most islands, however remote, where they may be the only native mammals. New Zealand has only two species of land mammal, both bats: one species from the endemic family Mystacinidae and a vespertilionid. The nearest relatives of *Mystacina tuberculata* are the fisherman bats (*Noctilio*) of South America—one of several possible examples of related families separated by the breaking up of Gondwanaland in the late Cretaceous. This is one of several bits of circumstantial evidence for the very early origin of microbats, which may go as far back as 70–100 million years—the microbats may have watched the demise of the dinosaurs in the mass extinction at the end of the Cretaceous.

Bats range in size from the smallest mammal (the bumblebee bat, *Craseonycteris thonglongyai*, 1.5–2 g) to 1 kg flying foxes (*Pteropus* spp.) with wingspans of over 1.5 m. They also come in a wide range of shapes and colours. Most bats are admittedly rather drab in colour, but there are exceptions, like the painted bats (*Kerivoula*), whose bright and cryptic patterning may camouflage them in their exposed tree roosts—some look like flowers and fruit. The tube-nosed fruit bat (*Nyctimene major*) has wing patterning to match the tree trunks to which it clings. The wonderfully grotesque hammer-headed bat (*Hypsignathus monstrosus*) has a nose of immense proportions. Males hang in the trees along rivers and call to passing females, who select the best (the most impressive callers?) for mating—one of the best documented examples of lekking in mammals—but more are now being found among bats. The noseleaves and varied facial protuberances of many bat families are often useful identification features. Some appear to have a functional role in echolocation, e.g. those of the horseshoe bats (Rhinolophidae), but the function of others has yet to be determined, if indeed they have one!

A complex and exciting story is unfolding around the very origins of bats. There are two sub-orders, the Old World, Megachiroptera or flying foxes, and the more widespread, more numerous, and more diverse Microchiroptera. The traditional and widely accepted view has been that these two sub-orders arose from a common ancestor. However, a substantial and broad-based body of evidence for independent origin, with subsequent convergent evolution, has been compiled over the last decade. The traditional viewpoint seemed to be shaking on its weak, and largely anatomical, foundations. But new evidence for the common origin of bats is emerging from the laboratories of molecular biologists and anatomists, and the controversy becomes more finely balanced and even more exciting. The resolution of this issue, and the arguments surrounding it, are important to all evolutionary biologists, not just those interested in bats. Some basic assumptions about evolutionary processes, and the methods used to study the inter-relationships between animals, are under the microscope.

The niche that many bats exploit as aerial, nocturnal hunters, is a demanding one. Flight places major anatomical and physiological restrictions on bats, but the rewards, evident in their success, are great. New theories on the aerodynamics of flapping flight have stimulated studies of the relationship between wing morphology, flight characteristics, and feeding ecology. Add to flight the ability to locate prey in the dark, and often to catch it on the wing, and you have in bats a highly adapted product of evolution, with many interesting biological stories to tell. We are only just beginning to understand the complexity, subtlety, and remarkable perceptual abilities of bat echolocation. Advances in technology, and some ingenious experimentation are uncovering dazzling feats—such as the ability of greater horseshoe bats (*Rhinolophus ferrumequinum*), at least under laboratory conditions, to identify prey species from the modulated echoes returned by flying insects. Like flight characteristics, the type of echolocation used is determined by environment and the prey sought. Some bats have rather stereotyped patterns of echolocation pulses, others such as the Mexican free-tailed bat (*Tadarida brasiliensis*) have a large and plastic repertoire which gives them considerable foraging flexibility. Broad-based taxonomic evidence, and a cladistic analysis of echolocation pulse patterns, indicate a more recent evolution for the echolocating strategy of bats such as *Tadarida*.

The success of bats in high latitudes is due in no small measure to their ability to reduce body temperature and save energy when insect availability is low. Torpor is the ability to reset body temperature to a level well below that required for normal activity, to actively regulate it within narrow limits, and to actively return to full operating temperature: few mammals perform this task as well as bats. We commonly think of torpor in the context of the long winter hibernation, but its use is an important part of a flexible, day to day, energy-saving strategy among many temperate bats—much studied, but still poorly understood.

Few potential roost sites have been overlooked by bats. Mexican free-tailed bats (*Tadarida brasiliensis*) in Central America and the southern United States form cave dwelling colonies of over 20 million individuals. The hoary bat (*Lasiurus cinereus*) is a solitary tree dweller, hanging (with its young) from high branches in the boreal forests (incidentally this species ranges all the way to South America, and is the only species found in Hawaii). A few species live in underground burrows, and in the case of the African slit-faced bats (*Nycteris* spp.), those of the aardvark! The short-tailed bat (*Mystacina tuberculata*) of New Zealand frequently forages on the ground, and burrows into fallen and decaying kauri trees, where they roost like peas in a pod. Adaptations for this unusual way of life include tough wings, which can be tucked away in pouches on the body, and strong talons on the thumb and toes. Several species (e.g. *Artibeus*, *Ectophylla*, and *Uroderma*) bite through the main supporting ribs of palm and *Heliconia* leaves to collapse them into tents, and in Gabon, *Myotis bocagei* roosts inside the flowers of the water arum. Two species of *Tylonycteris* roost inside bamboo shoots, gaining entry through the internodal emergence holes of a chrysomelid beetle. They have fleshy pads or 'suckers' on their wrists and ankles to grip the inside of the culm. Suckers are also present on bats of two other families (which roost in furled leaves) the Myzopoda of Madagascar, and the Thyroptera of Central and South America—another example of related species separated by the fragmentation of Gondwanaland, or of convergent evolution? The availability of some of the more unusual roosts may be a factor limiting the density and distribution of certain bats.

Bats feed on a wider variety of food than any other mammalian order. Most feed on insects and other arthropods—the pallid bat (*Antrozous pallidus*) of the south western United States, and some African slit-faced bats, have a liking for scorpions! One population of the fisherman bat (*Noctilio leporinus*) eats lots of fiddler crabs. Others feed on fish, amphibians, reptiles, birds, mammals (including other bats), fruit, nectar, pollen, and of course blood. Many are highly specialised in their diets, but others, e.g. some spear-nosed bats (Phyllostomidae) of South and Central America are omnivorous and will take insects, vertebrates, and fruit. The very diverse feeding ecologies of bats have been sources of many interesting and informative investigations. Evidence for optimal foraging in the feeding strategies of animals is constantly being sought. One excellent mammalian example involves the Mexican long-nosed bat, *Leptonycteris curasoae (sanborni)*, which feeds primarily on the saguaro cactus (*Carnegiea*) and the tequila agave (*Agave*). Careful field observations, outdoor experiments with glass flowers, and computer models, together suggest that the flock feeding behaviour of these bats is governed by a set of simple rules, which work to maximise energy intake. Very new work is uncovering possible examples of optimal foraging among insectivorous bats. Nectar and fruit eating bats also provide the biologist with some fascinating examples of co-evolution. Take, for example, the relationship between the tree *Oroxylum iridicum* and a small pteropodid, *Eonycteris spelaea*. The flowers of *Oroxylum* open 2.5 hours after dark—when the bats first reach them from their distant roosts. In the meantime, no other species can get in. The flowers fall before dawn. *Eonycteris* is just the right size to put its head in the flower, just the right weight to tip the flower and load a tuft of hairs with nectar, and has a tongue just the right length to reach the nectar. The flower releases just enough nectar to persuade the bat to move on to the next flower—and the next— maximising the chances of pollination.

Interactions between predator and prey have led to a continual 'arms race', with the prey evolving better means of escape, and the predator, of necessity, overcoming them in the fight for survival. This arms race is perhaps nowhere better illustrated than in the relationship between bats and their insect prey. Noctuid moths, for example, have evolved 'ears' to detect approaching bats and have stereotyped avoidance mechanisms hardwired into their nervous system. Some bats have evolved echolocation calls which are less audible to moths, or catch them without using echolocation. Incidentally, noctuids were about almost 70 million years ago, further indirect evidence for the very early evolution of microbats—in the absence of echolocating bats, noctuids would not need ears.

Few cited examples of reciprocal altruism are clear cut, and beyond explanation in terms of kin selection. One exception appears to be blood sharing in the common vampire bat (*Desmodus rotundus*). Vampires must have their 25 ml blood meals on a regular basis to survive, and in close-knit groups within a colony, bats will regurgitate some of their last meal to a 'buddy' who has been unable to feed. From studies of the behaviour of wild bats in the roost, and of captive bats whose degree of relatedness was known, it appears that the behaviour of vampire bats is truly altruistic, and cannot always be explained on the basis of kin selection. The system works because the donor will only give if the benefit to the recipient is far greater than its own loss, and because the favour is returned at a later date.

The Phyllostomidae (New World leaf- or spear-nosed bats) are the family to go to for a lesson in adaptive radiation. The family contains about 147 species in 51 genera. They are fewer and far less widespread than the Vespertilionidae or evening bats, but are unmatched in their range of foods. Many species are insectivorous, like all in the ancestral family, but there are now large numbers of fruit, flower, nectar and pollen-eaters, carnivores, and 3 species of vampire bat. This diversity of feeding habits is paralleled by a fine display of variations in form, physiology, and ecology—the long and bristly tongues of nectar feeders, the white tent-makers, the record-breaking kidneys of vampires, and the chin-flap-cum-night-cap of the wrinkle-faced bat. The Phyllostomidae are a taxonomic hotbed, and controversial new classification schemes are published at intervals creating a lively and thought provoking scientific debate. My hope is that this book will be a thought provoking biology lesson from the bats, a group about which we know remarkably little compared with many other mammals, but which has already given us some rewarding insights of broad biological significance.

Leptonycteris curasoae

1 The evolution and diversity of bats

Fossil bats—the evolutionary history of bats. The origins of flight and echolocation (covered in detail in later chapters). Megabats and microbats—a common ancestor or a stunning example of convergent evolution? The current controversy over the origin of bats, the methods being applied to the problem and their wider significance. A brief classification of modern bats. The sub-orders: mega- and micro-bats. Brief descriptions at family level. The Phyllostomidae—an example of adaptive radiation.

EVOLUTION

Fossil bats

Bats are currently placed in a single order, the Chiroptera. They are divided into two sub-orders, the Mega- and Microchiroptera, commonly referred to as the megabats and microbats. The megabats are the Old World fruit bats: large (for bats, 20–1500 g), exclusively plant-eating (i.e. they eat fruit, flowers, nectar, and pollen), and confined to Africa, tropical Asia, and Indo-Australasia. There are about 175 living species, all belonging to one family, the Pteropodidae. Microbats on the other hand are found on every continent except Antarctica, and on many isolated islands. They are, as their name implies, generally smaller than megabats (1.5–150 g), and they eat all sorts of things, as we'll discover later, although the ancestral microbat almost certainly ate insects and other arthropods. The approximately 790 species are distributed among 17 families. Figure 1.1 will fulfil our immediate needs as we look at the origins of bats, and the source of this diversity. It shows the known fossil bats in relation to a simplified evolutionary tree of extant bats.

It is generally said that bats are not well represented in the fossil record. There is no shortage of species, just a shortage of anything more than jaws for most of them. A decade ago, fossils of 132 species had been found: 92 of extant species, 40 extinct. The 40 extinct species are distributed through 30 genera and 11 families, and 8 living species are known for 8 of these families (Hill and Smith, 1984). The ratio of known extinct to living species is low for bats, in relation to other mammals, so the big question is whether this fossil record can provide some clues to the origins of bats. Recent, exciting discoveries in Australia of an extensive fossil bat fauna, dating back 55 million years, may prove to be very important.

The origins of microbats

What do the earliest fossils tell us about microbat evolution? The answer is, surprisingly little. The oldest fossil bat, *Icaronycteris index*, was found in the Polecat Bench formation

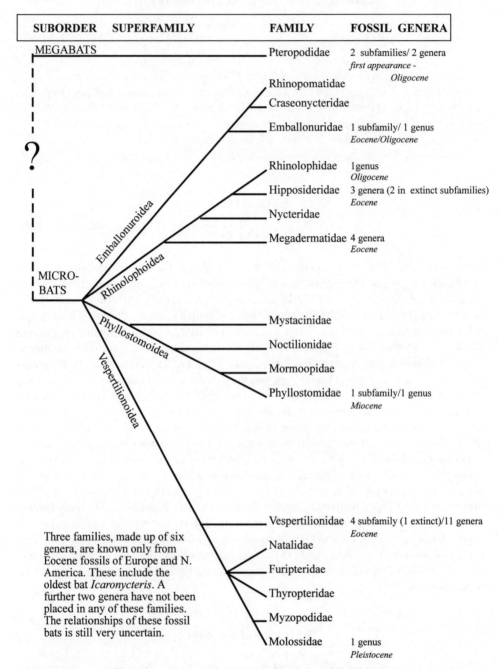

Fig. 1.1.   An evolutionary tree of modern and fossil bats.

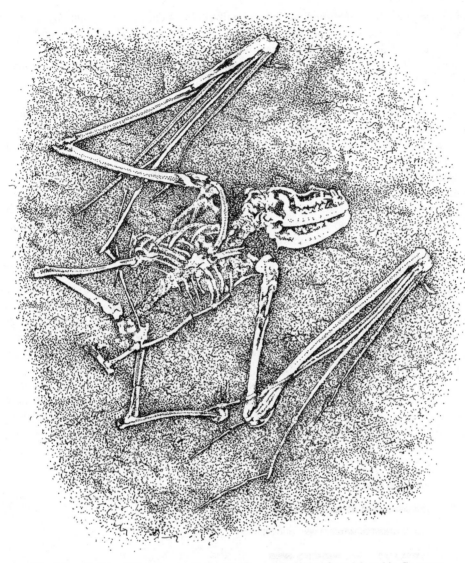

Fig. 1.2. *Palaeochiropteryx tupaiodon,* an Eocene fossil bat from Messel in Germany.

of Wyoming, not far from Yellowstone Park in the United States, and has been dated to
the early Eocene, 50 million years before the present (myr BP) (Jepson, 1966; 1970).
Icaronycteris looks remarkably like a modern microbat. The best European specimens
were found in the famous oil-shale pits at Messel, near Darmstadt in Germany—
Archaeonycteris, Palaeochiropteryx (Fig. 1.2), and *Hassianycteris* (Smith and Storch,
1981). Preservation is so good that recognisable insect remains can be seen in the gut of
some specimens. All date back about 45 million years, and all resemble modern microbats. A lavishly illustrated book has recently been published on the Messel beds, with
superb photographs of these bats (Schaal and Zeigler, 1992). No fossil bats are known

which are in any way intermediate in form between a modern microbat and some early tree-living ancestor which might have got around by jumping or gliding. Figure 1.3 shows the first appearance of bats in relation to some other mammals. Most mammalian groups began their big radiation (i.e. a dramatic increase in the number of species) around 50 myr BP, and bats are probably no exception.

If we allow time for the evolution of these sophisticated aerial insectivores, with an apparently advanced echolocating capability, then microbats may have made their appearance 65–100 M years ago, in the early Palaeocene (65–53 myr BP) or late Cretaceous (135–65 myr BP). If so, they shared the world with the dinosaurs, and watched their extinction at the end of the Cretaceous.

What evidence can we cite in support of this time scale? There is little evidence of real substance, but some of a persuasive, if circumstantial, nature. As we'll see a little later, microbats show no close affinities to any other mammalian order: the nearest, but still distant order, may be the Edentates—anteaters and sloths, themselves a very ancient group. These are unlikely ancestors for the bats, and they probably evolved from something similar to modern tree shrews. This inability to link bats to any known mammalian group in itself suggests a very early origin. Some moths, mantids, lacewings, and other insects have 'ears' whose main function appears to be to detect the echolocation calls of bats and trigger escape responses (Fullard, 1987; Bailey, 1991). Gall and Tiffney (1983), discovered the fossilised egg of a noctuid moth in deposits at Martha's Vineyard in Massachusetts which date back to about 75 myr BP. All known living and extinct noctuids are tympanate, and their ears are tuned to the ultrasonic frequency range used by many bats. If the moth that laid this egg was tympanate, then echolocating bats may already have been around for a while 75 million years ago. Finally, there are a number of cases where possibly closely related microbat species live on once adjacent, but now distant, fragments of Gondwanaland, the supercontinent which broke up into the fragments which now make up the land masses of the southern hemisphere. This process

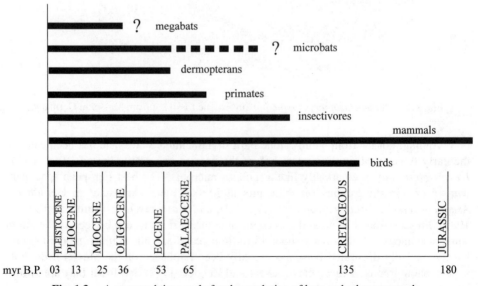

Fig. 1.3. A proposed time scale for the evolution of bats and other mammals.

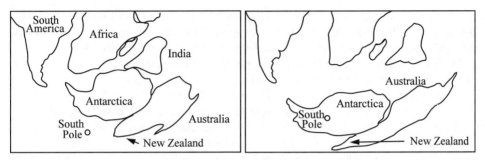

Fig. 1.4. The break-up of Gondwanaland. The fragments in the early (left) and late (right) Cretaceous. New Zealand broke away from the Australian plate shortly after the end of the Cretaceous.

went on right through the Cretaceous, starting with the separation of Antarctica/ Australasia from South America, and ending with the separation of Australia from Antarctica around 50 million years ago (Fig. 1.4).

New Zealand has just two endemic mammalian species, both bats. The closest living relatives of the short-tailed bat (*Mystacina tuberculata*) are the fisherman bats (*Noctilio*) of South America (Pierson *et al.*, 1986). The link is based on an immunological comparison of the proteins albumin and transferrin, supplemented by a number of morphological similarities. The ancestors of these bats either separated as much as 80 million years ago, when New Zealand drifted away from the Antarctic–Australian Plate, which connected it ultimately to South America (Griffiths and Varne, 1972), or an ancestral *Mystacina* somehow made the long journey to New Zealand via Antarctica with long ocean stretches. Pierson *et al.*, assuming that bats originated in the Palaeocene, 55–65 myr BP, suggest the separation occurred around 35 million years ago, but they confess to uncertainty about the speed of the molecular clock on which they base their estimate. On the basis of the unusual suckers on their wrists and ankles, and a number of skeletal characteristics Yalden and Morris (1975) suggest that the Myzopoda from Madagascar, and Thyroptera from South America may be related. Is this another case of related species isolated by the break up of Gondwanaland, as Pettigrew *et al.* (1989) propose, or an example of convergent evolution? Pettigrew and colleagues also argue that all of the more primitive microbats are restricted to fragments of Gondwanaland. The recently discovered bumblebee bat, *Craseonycteris thonglongyai* (Hill, 1974), at first appears to be something of a puzzle, in that it is primitive, but restricted to a tiny area of western Thailand. However, this spot happens to be part of the Indo-Australian plate, and one of a number of small limestone fragments of Gondwanaland in South East Asia (Audley-Charles, 1983).

Why did bats evolve? The evolution of new species is the product of the spontaneous generation of random genetic mutations, and the forces of natural selection—often a response to a changing environment. Change means a new physical environment, new sources of food, new habitats, new competitors, and new predators. At the time bats are thought to have been evolving, the flowering plants were in the first stages of their massive diversification. Müller (1981) conducted a review of the pollen record and demonstrated a proliferation of angiosperms at all taxonomic levels. They became dominant over more primitive plants in the Cenomanian period (100–95 myr BP), and modern families appeared in great numbers from the beginning of the Maastrichtian (69 myr BP). By the end of the Cretaceous the insects supported by these plants were abundant and insectivorous and frugivorous mammals were becoming well established (Lillegraven, 1974). These insects were a potential food source for proto-bats and other mammals, but they didn't have them to themselves. During the day, they would have had to compete with birds and other insect eaters. *Archaeopteryx*, the first bird, dates back to the early Cretaceous (135 myr BP), and birds were abundant by the time bats appeared on the scene. Birds were likely to be significant competitors, and predators, of small mammals by the late Cretaceous (65 myr BP). For these reasons, many early species (like their modern counterparts) were nocturnal, and it is presumed that bats evolved from one of these small, nocturnal, and arboreal (tree-dwelling) mammals.

Gliding and flying

What follows is largely informed speculation, but I think few biologists would question it. Over thousands of years of jumping around after insects, from branch to branch, and tree to tree, the ancestors of microbats probably evolved gliding membranes similar to those of modern mammals such as flying squirrels and sugar gliders (Fig. 1.5). We should not be surprised that this may have happened—gliding has evolved independently many times in the vertebrates, with living examples among the fish, amphibia, reptiles, marsupials, and eutherian mammals (see e.g. Rayner, 1981).

Before going any further, we ought to ask the question why did flight evolve? Two very powerful reasons come quickly to mind. Less energy is expended gliding from tree to tree than running down the trunk, running across the ground, and running up the trunk of the next tree. If the animal doesn't come down to the ground, it doesn't have to face terrestrial predators either. Controlled, flapping flight brings other advantages, discussed in Chapter 2.

Let's go back to the evolution of gliding. A narrow extension of the skin between front and hind legs probably became more extensive, and extended to the spaces between hind legs and tail. With the appearance of webbing between the fingers and toes, the fingers could elongate, carrying the webbing with them, dramatically increasing the wing area. This also gave the ancestral bat control over its wing shape, through movement of its fingers, and this gave it more aerial control. Ultimately wings would have evolved from these gliding membranes and eventually flapping flight would follow.

Echolocation

As early bats became more agile, before in fact they became bats, they would have had to improve their orientation skills to be successful night fliers. Echolocation, orientation by analysis of the echoes from emitted sound pulses, probably evolved alongside flight. It is difficult to imagine how the two could have reached their present level of sophistication unless they co-evolved. It is likely that the ancestors of microbats, like some modern insectivores, emitted ultrasonic sounds and perhaps had a simple form of echolocation, which became increasingly sophisticated as bats became more agile fliers. Novacek (1985) produced evidence to suggest that the very earliest fossil microbats, *Icaronycteris index* and *Palaeochiropteryx tupaidon*, had a well developed echolocation system, better developed in fact than some modern microbats. This evidence came from a study of the

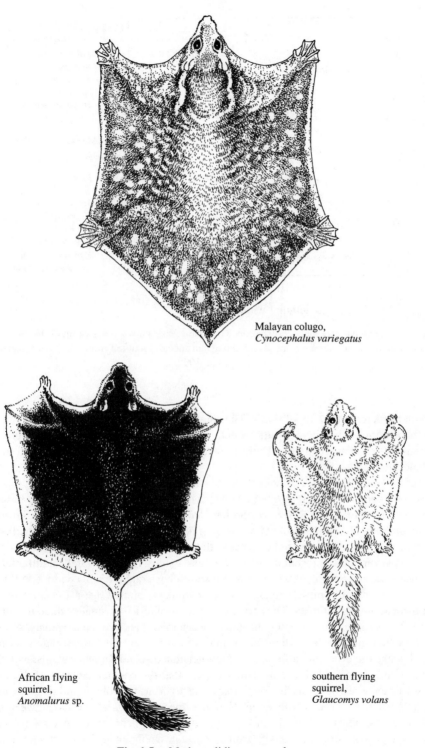

Malayan colugo,
Cynocephalus variegatus

African flying
squirrel,
Anomalurus sp.

southern flying
squirrel,
Glaucomys volans

Fig. 1.5.   Modern gliding mammals.

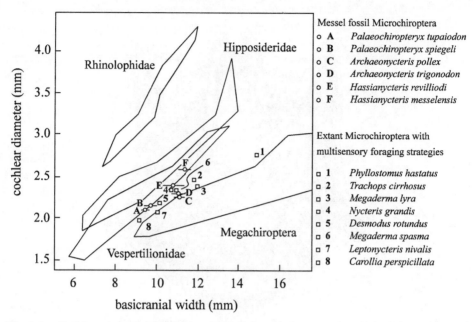

Fig. 1.6. Cochlear size and echolocation. The relationship between the width of the cochlea and skull width for a sample of 6 Eocene and 286 extant species (adapted from Fig. 4, Habersetzer and Storch, 1992).

internal structure of the fossil skulls. The single most important feature is the large size of the basal turn of the cochlea—the structure in the inner ear which sorts and processes sounds by frequency. The basal turn is receptive to the echoes of very high frequency echolocation calls.

The size of this basal turn will obviously depend upon the size of the bat, but when these two parameters were plotted against each other, so that the size of the basal turn was shown relative to the size of the bat, *Icaronycteris index* and *Palaeochiropteryx tupaidon* both fell in the middle of a cluster of data points for modern microbats. For their size, their basal turns appeared to be as well developed as those of most modern microbats. However, a more recent analysis of a more extensive data set, tells a different story (Habersetzer and Storch, 1992). Figure 1.6 shows basicranial (skull) width (skull length, as used by Novacek, may depend on feeding strategy) plotted against cochlea diameter for the Eocene Messel bats. They have cochleas similar to, or smaller than, the smallest of the Vespertilionidae, bridging the gap between microbats and the megabats. A number of the extant microbats studied fall in the same area, and all have foraging strategies which make use of vision, olfaction, or prey-generated sound. In other words, they do not depend entirely on echolocation. This suggests that the cochlear system of the Eocene bats was not as advanced as that of modern insectivorous microbats, and that they too did not rely exclusively on echolocation. Note that there is minimal overlap between megabats and microbats. Why? Because megabats do not echolocate. All microbats can echolocate, even those that feed on fruit and nectar. On the other hand, only a few megabats echolocate, all from the genus *Rousettus*. They use a very different and less capable form of echolocation. Megabats, which all feed on fruit, pollen, or nectar do not have the same need for echolocation—a banana does not present the same aerial challenge as an insect in a spiral dive. Nevertheless, if all bats have a common ancestor, as has been assumed for the last 200 years, then this observation prompts some important questions. For example, if the ancestors of megabats did echolocate, isn't it remarkable that megabats have lost not only the ability to echolocate, but all trace of the anatomical and physiological adaptations which make it possible? It is perhaps better to step back and ask another, more fundamental, question: did the microbats and megabats indeed have a common ancestor?

The origins of megabats, and their relationship to microbats

The modern colugos, or flying lemurs (Fig. 1.7), are in some respects the nearest mammals to our hypothesised ancestral bat, with an extensive gliding membrane and webbed fingers. They are not lemurs, but dermopterans, and they do not fly, but glide. The two living species are, in fact, the only dermopterans. Colugos can glide well in excess of a hundred metres, and move their limbs around to turn and change altitude. In one recorded glide of 136 m, an individual lost only 11 m in altitude. They are squirrel-sized herbivores, and their adaptations to gliding have left them very clumsy on the ground. For a long time, they were assumed to provide a useful illustration of how bats might have evolved. They are now believed by some biologists to be the closest living relatives of the megabats.

The evolutionary pressures on ancestral megabats which led to the evolution of flight, and the mechanisms by which it was achieved, were probably similar to those which gave us the microbats. I will not dwell on them, because a more fascinating debate has developed in recent years about the origins of megabats. The earliest megabat is *Archaeopteropus transiens*, which dates back 35 M years to the Oligocene (36–25 myr BP), which was found in Venetia, Italy (Dal Piaz, 1937). Until recently it was widely accepted that all bats had a common ancestor. However, it has recently been suggested

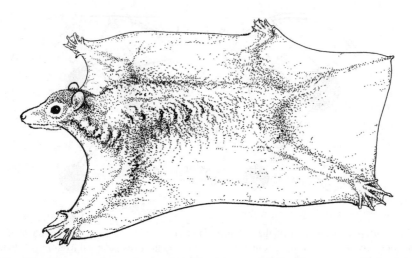

Fig. 1.7. The Malayan colugo, *Cynocephalus variegatus*, a gliding dermopteran (flying lemur).

that the megabats evolved independently, following a quite different evolutionary line to that of the insectivorous microbats. There is now a strong body of evidence in support of this idea, which has triggered a healthy controversy and new research. It is a topic worth going into in some depth, and for several reasons. First, to dispel the common idea that taxonomy plays little part in modern biology. Second, to show that answers to many important biological questions only come with input from a wide variety of fields— biology is a truly multidisciplinary subject. Finally, because of the implications of independent origins for microbats and megabats—principally that flight, the most anatomically and physiologically specialised and demanding mode of locomotion, evolved twice in the mammals, and that the striking similarities between microbats and megabats are the result of convergent evolution. We have already noted the absence of echolocation and the small cochlea in megabats. What other evidence has been put forward in support of diphyly (independent origins) in bats, and what evidence is there for monophyly (common origins)?

The modern debate has been around for some time (e.g. Jones and Genoways, 1970; Smith and Madkour, 1980) but gained momentum with the publication of a paper in *Science* (Pettigrew, 1986) which showed that the pattern of neural connections between the mid-brain and the retinal cells of the eyes were very different in microbats and megabats.

Neurones in the right superior colliculus (s.c.) of the mid-brain all project to the retinal cells of the left eye of a microbat and those of the left s.c. to the right eye (Fig. 1.8). This is a pattern which has been found in all mammals except primates, and is believed to be the ancestral mammalian pattern. In contrast, neurones from the right s.c. of a megabat project to both eyes, but only to the left half of the visual field. Neurones from the left s.c. projected to the right half of the visual field of both eyes. This pattern is unique to megabats, primates, and Dermoptera. Pettigrew argued that it is highly unlikely that either of these two patterns could have evolved from the other, suggesting that microbats and megabats are not at all closely related, and that megabats are in fact 'flying primates'. It is interesting to note at this point that Linnaeus originally classified bats as primates as far back as 1758, after studying megabats. Subsequent evidence

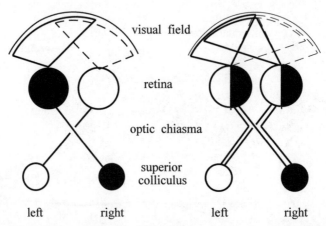

Fig. 1.8. Simplified diagram of the primitive/microbat (left) and primate-like/megabat (right) connections between the midbrain (superior colliculi) and the eyes (adapted from Fig. 1, Pettigrew *et al.*, 1989).

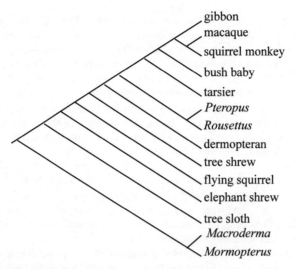

Fig. 1.9. Cladogram based on the analysis of 24 neural characters. The megabats *Pteropus* and *Rousettus*, appear to be closely related to the primates and dermopterans, and are separated from the microbats, *Macroderma* and *Mormopterus,* by several other taxa (adapted from Fig. 8, Pettigrew *et al.*, 1989).

which showed that microbats were not related to primates resulted in **all** bats being re-classified.

A cladistic analysis of some 24 different characteristics of the nervous systems of 14 mammalian species (Pettigrew *et al.*, 1989) concluded that microbats appeared very early in mammalian evolution, and that their nearest relative **among the mammals studied** was the tree-sloth *Bradypus*! Megabats appear to have evolved much later, from an early primate branch, around the same time as the Dermoptera. The cladogram is shown in Fig. 1.9. A cladogram is a form of evolutionary tree which links species according to shared, *derived* characteristics. That is, those characteristics which are not ancestral to all of the species in the group being studied, but evolved after their divergence from a common ancestor. The more characteristics shared between two species, the more closely related they are. A cladogram is constructed by computing the evolutionary tree which uses the least number of evolutionary steps to explain the different degrees of relatedness between the species. Cladograms can be very persuasive, but have their problems. For those interested, Box 1 takes a closer look at cladistic techniques, since they are now widely used in evolutionary biology by the traditional morphologist, and as we will see below, the molecular taxonomist.

Box 1—Cladistics

The philosophical framework of modern taxonomy is based on the concepts of evolutionary theory. Cladistics was developed in an attempt to introduce a set of more objective and rigidly applied rules than those used in traditional evolutionary taxonomy (Hennig, 1966). In cladistic analysis, given a group of animals to classify, the first and most crucial task is to sort out which forms of a particular character are ancestral and which are derived. There are three lines of evidence, but it is rare to be able to use all three in any particular case.

1. *Outgroup analysis*. A comparison of characters with those of another species, or group of species, which is known not to belong to those under study, but which is relatively closely related. Any shared characteristics are by definition ancestral. It sounds fine in principal, but it requires prior knowledge of the relationships between groups. This has led some people to criticise the technique as circular. I think this is an unfair simplification, and would prefer to view it as part of an iterative process—constant refinement of the model to arrive at an answer which best fits the known facts—a perfectly valid scientific technique. Another criticism is that the method assumes that there is no evolutionary convergence, or at least that it is rare. The problem is one of separating homologous structures, i.e. those with a common origin, from analogous structures, which are derived from different parts of the body, but serve a similar function. Good examples of convergent evolution, and analogous structures, are the wings by birds and insects, and the eyes by vertebrates and cephalopods. Convergence probably is rare, but when it does occur, it will lead to errors in cladistic analyses: but then it can upset traditional methods too.

2. *Palaeontological evidence*. A good fossil record will provide good evidence of which characters are ancestral and which derived. However, the fossil record of a particular group is usually full of gaps, and many characters are simply not preserved in fossils. The technique therefore has limited practical value in many cases.

3. *Embryological evidence*. It is assumed that in the embryological development of a group of species, the general, ancestral characters appear before the more specialised, derived characters. This assumption is certainly not valid all of the time. The big debate concerns the frequency with which it is valid. It is perhaps safest to say that any evidence drawn from embryology should be used with some caution.

Given the difficulties, it is clear that cladistics must use all of the techniques at its disposal and cross-reference wherever possible. The use of *unrooted* trees can help greatly. An unrooted evolutionary tree indicates the relationships between a group of animals, but does not indicate the order of their evolution. Unrooted trees can be constructed first on morphological or biochemical evidence, and *rooted* later, if key evidence can be found. Once a root has been found, the direction of the trees 'growth' is known, and the evolutionary relationships between the species can be resolved.

Finally, in constructing cladograms, the various methods and computer programmes used are generally based on the concept of parsimony. The tree which uses the least number of evolutionary steps, and the smallest number of assumptions, to explain the data is sought. This is not necessarily the way nature works, it is simply a practical scientific approach—that of Occam's razor. Other methods are being developed, and these may lead to different conclusions. Good accounts of cladistic theory and methods, and the debates surrounding them, can be found in Ridley (1986) and Patterson (1987).

The argument that primates, dermopterans, and megabats are closely related, and that microbats are unrelated to megabats, is strengthened by other evidence, in addition to that from the central nervous system and visual pathways. This evidence is very diverse, from factors as simple as a consideration of body size ranges, to the analysis of the amino-acid sequence of haemoglobin, obtained using modern molecular biology techniques. Table 1.1 lists some of the differences between megabats and microbats not discussed in the text. The most comprehensive list is given in Pettigrew *et al.* (1989). This evidence is countered by Table 1.2, which lists features common to mega- and microbats, but not

Table 1.1. Some of the differences between megabats and microbats not covered in detail in the text. Discussed by Pettigrew *et al.* (1989)

	Microbats	Megabats
distribution	worldwide	palaeotropical (Old World tropics)
orientation	primarily by echolocation, all species generate sonar pulses in the larynx	primarily visual, tongue clicking orientation sounds produced by a few species only
diet	ancestral insectivores, a small minority have evolved to feed on fruit, nectar and pollen, vertebrates and blood	fruit, nectar and pollen
teeth	W-shaped cusps, or evidence for past possession of such teeth	simple, no evidence of W-shaped cusps (i.e. of insectivorous ancestry)
eyes	simple retinal blood circulation tapetum lucidum (reflective layer behind receptor cells) rarely present ganglion cell streak below optic disk eyes open after birth	complex retinal blood circulation tapetum lucidum often present ganglion cell streak above optic disk eyes open before birth
ears	pinna (external ear) often complex, margin incomplete tragus (cartilaginous projection) often present inside pinna Paaw's cartilage in middle ear cochlea (sound reception and processing apparatus in inner ear) variable in size and often large cochlea has large, extra basal turn for high frequency sound reception cochlea acoustically isolated from skull	pinna simple, margin complete to form a tube tragus never present Paaw's cartilage absent size of cochlea closely related to size of bat extra turn absent cochlea in contact with skull
limbs	metacarpals (palm bones) long in relation to first phalanges (finger bones) thumb and forefinger have minimal independent mobility limbs move independently, many species very agile on the ground	metacarpals and phalanges similar in length opposable thumb and mobile forefinger forelimbs move together, movement is slow and clumsy
skin	hair erector muscles are striated (like skeletal muscle)	hair erector muscles are smooth (like those of internal organs)
penis	corpus spongiosum not enlarged to form glans penis	corpus spongiosum enlarged to form glans penis
torpor	widespread in two families and highly developed	poorly developed, and only found in nectar feeders
roosting posture	neck extended (head bent towards back)—neck vertebrae specially adapted	neck flexed (bent towards chest)

Table 1.1. *Continued*

	Microbats	Megabats
threat behaviour	primarily acoustic, wing spreading not seen	often involves wing spreading and other visual threats
central nervous system	inferior colliculus (auditory centre) larger than superior colliculus (visual centre)	superior colliculus larger than inferior colliculus
	primitive pathway between eye and brain	primate-like pathway between eye and brain
	forebrain usually less well developed than hindbrain	forebrain well developed as cerebral cortex
	low frequency sounds map at rear of auditory cortex	low frequencies map at front of auditory cortex
	motor cortex shows primitive arrangement of cortico-spinal areas	motor cortex shows primate-like arrangement of cortico-spinal areas
	hindlimb is represented by a small area of somatosensory cortex	hindlimb is represented by a large area of somatosensory cortex

Table 1.2. Some of the characteristics shared by microbats and megabats. For detailed coverage, see Baker *et al.* (1991)

Anatomical features common to microbats and megabats.
Occipitopollicalis muscle along the leading edge of the wing
Digits 2–5 of forelimb greatly enlarged
Claws restricted to digits 1 or 1 and 2
Hindlimbs rotated 90° outward, i.e. knee directed to the side
Calcar present on foot
Head of the femur aligned almost parallel to the shaft
Premaxilla greatly reduced
Jugal greatly reduced
Several anatomical features of the middle ear
Anatomy of preplacenta and placenta
Somatosensory map of forelimb reversed relative to other mammals

found in other mammals. It is these differences which lead to uncertainty, and introduce controversy, into the debate on bat evolution.

One feature which has been used persistently to argue for a close relationship between megabats and microbats is the similarity in the wings. The first part of Table 1.2 lists just a few of those cited by Baker *et al.* (1991) relating to the wings. The wings of mega- and microbats certainly do look very similar. This is to be expected: there is considerable similarity in mode of flight, and therefore in the evolutionary pressures moulding wing shape. Flying is not easy: there are a limited number of basic ways in which the vertebrate body plan can be adapted to meet the intolerant energetic and aerodynamic demands of flight. Pettigrew and his colleagues therefore advocate caution in using morphological features which may have a functional importance in flight. This said, they argue that wing morphology in fact yields evidence for the independent evolution of mega- and microbats, and for the close relationship between megabats, primates, and dermopterans. The hypothesis put forward is that the relative lengths of the bones of the third and fourth fingers are not going to be important in determining flight performance, and therefore not subject to the evolutionary pressures of flight. (Finger 5 is known to play an important role in altering wing camber, and should, by Pettigrew's reasoning, be excluded from the analysis.) We might expect these fingers to be similar in all bats, or at least for no clear pattern to emerge between groups, if all bats are closely related.

This is clearly not the case. In Fig. 1.10 the ratio between the length of the metacarpals and the first phalanges of fingers 3 and 4 have been calculated for a large number of mega- and microbats. These ratios have then been plotted against the forearm length of

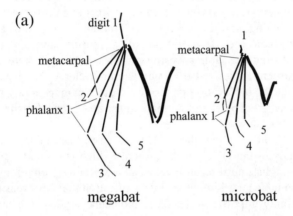

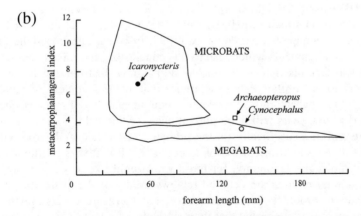

Fig. 1.10. Forelimb morphology in bats. (a) The forelimb skeletons of megabats and microbats. (b) The ratio of metacarpal length/first phalanx length (for fingers 3 and 4), plotted against forearm length for a large sample of microbat and megabat species. A fossil microbat, *Icaronycteris*, and megabat, *Archaeopteropus*, and the dermopteran *Cynocephalus* are also included (adapted from Figs 10 and 11, Pettigrew *et al.*, 1989).

each species. There is no overlap between the data for microbats and megabats: the microbats have proportionally longer metacarpals. Can it be argued that the wings of megabats and microbats are so very similar? The relationship holds true for the hindlimb too, which is under very different functional constraints. The dermopteran *Cynocephalus*, and the oldest megabat fossil, *Archaeopteropus*, fall among the megabats, as do primates. The ratio for the forelimb is very variable in microbats, but shows little variation in megabats.

By the same argument against functionally important morphological characteristics, the muscles of the wing should also be excluded from the list of supporting evidence for monophyly. The specialised occipito-pollicalis muscle complex (which controls the shape of the leading edge of the wing) has been cited as evidence for monophyly (Wible and Novacek, 1988), but it is present not only in microbats, megabats, and dermopterans, but also in the clearly unrelated flying squirrels (Johnson-Murray, 1977) and birds (Raikow, 1985). Thewisen and Babcock (1991) have presented us with an interesting twist to this story. They looked not at the muscle complex, but at its pattern of innervation. If the occipito-pollicalis muscles are truly homo-logous rather than analogous they should have similar innervation patterns, due to the close link between the development of a muscle and its nerve supply. (Homology: derived from the same ancestral muscles, analogy: convergent evolution leading to similar structures derived from unrelated muscles.) Thewisen and Babcock found that features of the innervation pattern were quite unique among mammals, and common to microbats, megabats, and dermopterans: good news for the proponents of monophyly.

So far I have said nothing about the evidence derived from molecular taxonomy— that is, from the study of the DNA, or the proteins which DNA codes for. Whilst this approach is not new, it has, until recently taken a back seat to morphology and palaeon-tology. The boom in molecular biology and its application to many areas of biology has given it an increasingly important role. Early molecular evidence in taxonomy came from immunological studies, to be followed by protein sequencing, and finally the sequencing of DNA itself. Like the morphological evidence, it is controversial. Several recent studies (e.g. Ammerman and Hillis, 1992; Bailey *et al.*, 1992) have come down firmly on the side of monophyly, but Pettigrew (1994, 1995) has questioned the validity of some of the base alignments which lead to this conclusion, and raised another com-plication. Megabat DNA is rich in the nucleotide bases A–T at the expense of G–C: microbats appear to be similar. Pettigrew argues that an A–T content of more than 70%, as is found in megabats, raises real doubts about the validity of recent sequencing evidence. The next few years will be important ones for this field. As I write, several laboratories are working specifically on the problem, and whatever I write will cer-tainly be out of date by the time this book is published. Box 2 says a little about the complexities of molecular taxonomy, for those who would like to know more, and I have included references to some detailed reviews. Many of the difficulties revolve around the cladistic problems discussed above, but there are others. In the past, some molecular biologists suggested that their methods were more objective and more quantitative than those of morphology, but I think the consensus view now is that bio-chemical and morphological evidence should be viewed with the same degree of caution.

Box 2—Molecular taxonomy

The principles:

1. To identify homologous DNA sequences (or the proteins they code for) in a group of animals. That is, identify the DNA sequence or gene responsible for producing a particular protein, which has essentially the same function in all of the organisms under study.
2. Determine the nucleotide (or amino acid) sequences of these homologues.
3. Determine which is the ancestral form, and the paths by which each derived form evolved. In other words, construct an evolutionary tree, usually by cladistic analysis.

Molecular taxonomy has a major advantage over morphological methods: the degree of difference between homologues can be quantified, in terms of the differences in their nucleotide sequences. Morphology is a complex, and poorly understood, expression of these molecular differences which cannot be readily quantified. As is usually the case in biology, there are a number of flies in the DNA soup. Perhaps the most important difficulties relate to the identification of homologous DNA sequences—the crucial first step in the process. Let's look at a few of them.

1. *Gene duplication*. Genes commonly occur in families, through the process of gene duplication. For example, in a given animal, there are numerous genes for the synthesis of the proteins which make up muscle, principally actin and myosin. There are several myosin genes whose products are found predominantly in fast contracting locomotory muscle fibres, others are expressed in slow contracting muscles, yet others in cardiac muscle. There are genes for embryonic myosins, genes for myosins which are only found in particular, specialised muscles, myosin genes which appear never to be expressed, and so on. These genes are no longer subject to natural selection in the same way, and some may be able to mutate more freely. However, they are all myosin genes, and may be mistaken for each other. Molecular taxonomists, to chart the evolution of species, must be sure that they are looking at true homologues. Otherwise, they may only be charting the evolution of the genes themselves, and not that of the organisms.

2. *Exons and introns*. Proteins are coded for by short sequences of DNA called exons. Exons are separated in genes by typically very much longer sequences called introns. These are transcribed into RNA, but are 'spliced out' before the RNA is translated into amino acids. Introns may make up 95% of a gene. A problem for the molecular taxonomist is that exons are duplicated, and are moved around by chromosomal mutations: new genes are formed, which may be only partially homologous with those in another species. Again the scientist may be looking at complex gene or gene/species evolution, instead of the intended species evolution.

3. *Pseudogenes*. Pseudogenes are dead genes, redundant copies of a functional gene which are not turned into proteins because they are defective. Pseudogenes appear to be very common: 25% of some gene families studied are pseudogenes. Since they are no longer functional they are free from selective pressure. Mutation can run riot, since it will not lead to impaired function and perhaps extinction. Apparently homologous functional genes may in fact be *different* members of a once large gene family, whose 'siblings' have become pseudogenes. They could therefore have rather different histories, reflecting the history of the gene family, not that of the species under study.

Different genes appear to undergo mutations at different, but remarkably constant rates. Functionally important DNA changes slowly: any deleterious mutations, which impair the function of its protein products, will be eliminated by natural selection. Introns mutate more rapidly, and in homologous DNA sequences, show greater differences between species than their functional exons. Pseudogenes have the highest evolutionary rates, as predicted from their non-functional nature. This may complicate things for the evolutionary biologist, but also offers one potentially enormous tool—molecular clocks to monitor evolution itself—assuming each clock can be calibrated. For excellent reviews of the snakes and ladders of molecular taxonomy, see Patterson, 1987; Patterson *et al.*, 1993; Honeycutt and Adkins, 1993 and Stewart, 1993.

So, is it monophyly or diphyly? Can we come to a decision in the face of all the conflicting evidence? The most complete debate can be found in a series of papers in Systematic Zoology, covering more ground, in more detail, than I have space for (Pettigrew, 1991a,b; Baker *et al.*, 1991; Simmons *et al.*, 1991), and the last word, as I write, is by Pettigrew (1995). Pettigrew *et al.* (1989) present four interpretations of the relationships between microbats, megabats, and primates. They exclude the possibility that microbats and primates are monophyletic on the grounds of a complete lack of supporting evidence. This leaves two possibilities: (1) microbats and megabats are monophyletic, and the primates are a sister group, (2) megabats and primates are monophyletic, and the microbats are a sister group. For each, they present two ways in which the situation might have arisen, and discuss the implications.

1.1 The fallen angel

Wings evolved first, as a shared feature of all three groups, and the primates subsequently lost them. This is clearly a non-starter. There is nothing in an extensive primate fossil record to suggest that primates or their ancestors ever had wings. In this scenario megabats must have arisen before primates, and despite a poor megabat fossil record, this seems highly improbable.

1.2 The deaf fruit bat

Megabats arose from microbats, losing the capacity for echolocation, and the associated anatomical and physiological features, and acquiring a primate-like brain in the process. This explains the presence of primate brain features in megabats, and is consistent with the recent origin of megabats, and some interpretations of immunological and musculoskeletal data. However, it is a hypothesis with real difficulties. Why should the megabats lose so completely the advantageous attribute of echolocation? What possible selective advantage could there be, and why have no fossil intermediates been found? Similarly why are there no bats, living or extinct, with intermediate metacarpal/phalanges indices, and why did this character alone undergo such change when so many wing features remained unchanged? Surely, it is difficult to accept that during the microbat to megabat transition the numerous differences listed in Table 1.1 arose, accompanied by the appearance of a brain strikingly similar to that of primates? It is generally accepted that the Dermoptera are transitional to bats, one or both groups. If so, and the megabats arose from microbats, then the primate features of the Dermoptera must have been lost by the microbats, only to reappear in the megabats, or these primate features evolved independently in dermopterans, megabats, and primates. Both alternatives seem highly unlikely.

2.1 The blind cave bat

Microbats evolved from megabats, losing the primate features inherited from the mega-bats and their primate ancestors. The evolution of microbats from megabats provides an explanation for the data in Table 1.2, but presents its own problems. Although the megabat fossil record is poor, the available evidence is not favourable. The earliest megabat is 20 million years younger that the first microbat, *Icaronycteris*, which has virtually all of the features of a modern microbat, including a well developed echolocation system. This places the evolution of the microbats well before 50 myr BP and that of the megabats even further back. A much older fossil megabat is urgently needed to support this hypothesis. The evolutionary divergence of the structure of haemoglobin is much lower in megabats than in microbats, again suggesting a much more recent origin.

2.2 The flying primate

Microbats evolve. Megabats evolve independently on an early branch of the primate line. Is it likely that flight could have evolved twice in the mammals, and that megabats and micro-bats could have undergone such striking convergent evolution? As pointed out earlier, gliding has evolved many times in the vertebrates and three times in the marsupials alone (Archer, 1984). Powered flight almost certainly evolved from gliding in all living and extinct animals (see Chapter 2), so its independent origin in microbats and megabats is a reasonable possibility. What about the similarity of form? Given a five-fingered mammalian forelimb, just how many ways could it develop into an aerodynamically functional wing? Probably not many, and there are a number of well known and striking examples of convergent evolution to lend credibility to the idea: the eyes of vertebrates and cephalopods have already been mentioned, the gills of fish and cephalopods are another, and the hydrodynamically efficient form of fast pelagic swimmers among cetacea, teleost fish, and sharks another.

Some of the assumptions underlying these interpretations have been questioned (Baker *et al.*, 1991; Simmons *et al.*, 1991), but I find them persuasive. I also find the whole debate exciting. Even if the flying primate hypothesis proves to be wrong, as Pettigrew (1991a) himself says 'it will still have been a most fruitful, wrong hypothesis". It has raised some interesting questions, prompted new research, unlikely collaborations, the application of new techniques to the study of bats, and made us question long-held beliefs. That is what keeps research buzzing.

CLASSIFICATION AND THE DISTRIBUTION AND DIVERSITY OF BATS

A brief tour of modern bat families

Bats are the most widely distributed and (by species) the second most numerous group of mammals. They are outnumbered only by the rodents (1700 species). Precisely how many species of bats there are in the world is uncertain. The uncertainty is due to the difficulties of defining a species: when does a sub-species become a new species, and so on? The arguments are rarely clear cut, leaving us with a range of possible solutions to each taxonomic problem. There are even big debates at the family level: e.g. most bat biologists include the vampires in the Phyllostomidae, a few like to give them their own family. The classification of the two largest microbat families, the Phyllostomidae and the Vespertilionidae, is particularly fluid and prone to revision. The latest list I've seen is that provided by Findley (1993), who opts for 963 species; Hill and Smith (1984) suggest 966. Bats therefore account for almost one quarter of the 4200 species of mammals. New species may be waiting to be discovered. Very recent work (Jones and van Parijs, 1993; Jones and colleagues, in preparation) suggests that one of the most studied of all species, the European pipistrelle, *Pipistrellus pipistrellus*, may in fact be two species. Initially separated on the basis of differences in echolocation call structure, the two types are morphologically different, are not found together in maternity or harem roosts, and studies of mitochondrial DNA support the idea of two species.

All bats are currently included in the order Chiroptera (meaning hand-wing), which has two sub-orders, the Megachiroptera (megabats, 175 species) and the Microchiroptera (microbats, ~790 species). If they really did evolve independently, they should both be elevated to the level of order. The Megabats all belong to the same family, the Pteropodidae—the Old World fruit bats or flying foxes. The microbats have been distributed across four superfamilies, and a total of 17 families within these.

Before taking a look at the families, let's look at the distribution of bats. Among mammals, only humans (and some of the mammals closely associated with humans) are more widely distributed than bats. Bats are found everywhere bar the highest latitudes, the most inhospitable deserts, and the most remote islands. In common with all other forms of life, the number of species declines away from the equator, although the pattern is disturbed by geographical features such as the Sahara Desert. The numbers of species in different regions of the globe are shown in Fig. 1.11. The neotropics of South and Central America is the richest area, with over 200 species, followed by the palaeotropical regions of Asia and then Africa. Temperate regions are impoverished by comparison, with about

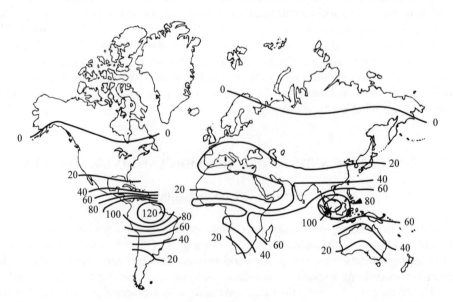

Fig. 1.11.   The number of bat species in 500 km^2 quadrats in different parts of the world (adapted from Findley, 1993).

40 species in North America (nearctic) and 85 or so in northern Eurasia (palaearctic). A number of species of the family Vespertilionidae spend the summer in high latitudes in both hemispheres, and a few are found north of the Arctic circle. The megabats have island-hopped half way across the Pacific from the western rim, and on some islands rare, endemic species have evolved. The vespertilionid hoary bat, *Lasiurus cinereus* has colonised the Galapagos and Hawaiian Islands. New Zealand's only native mammals are the single remaining species of the endemic family Mystacinidae, and another member of the well-travelled vesper bats. Bats probably evolved in the tropics, and almost 80% of all species are tropical. Most families are found only in the tropics: just two families, the Vespertilionidae and Rhinolophidae, contain truly temperate species.

Figure 1.12 summarises the chiropteran family tree down to the subfamily level, with the number of genera and species in each. What follows is a thumbnail sketch of each family. The classification used is essentially that given by Hill and Smith (1984) who provide a more thorough account of the families for those who want more information. Some small changes suggested by Findley (1993) have been incorporated. The major external features of bats used in the descriptions are shown in Fig. 1.13.

The megabats

Family: Pteropodidae The Old World fruit bats, or flying foxes, are confined to the Old World tropics and feed exclusively on fruit, flowers, nectar, and pollen. As a group, they are larger than the microbats, but show considerable variation, with forearm lengths of 40–220 mm. The length of the forearm is relatively consistent within a species, and can be easily measured to the necessary degree of accuracy in a live bat. As a general indication of overall size, the body length of a bat (without the head) is similar to its forearm length. Megabats weigh anything from 20 g to 1.5 kg, with wingspans approaching 2 m. With the exception of several species of the genus *Rousettus*, megabats do not echolocate, but rely on vision (and smell) for night orientation. They generally have large eyes, simple ears, and simple muzzles (Fig. 1.13). The second and third fingers are largely independent of each other, and the second has a claw (Fig. 1.13). Tail and tail membranes are typically small or non-existent. Although strong flyers, they lack the wide variation in wing form and flight style seen in the microbats, nor do they possess their complex shoulder anatomy. Most megabats have rather dog-like faces, hence the name flying foxes. Skull and teeth are adapted to their particular feeding habits. Skull and jaws are typically large and strong, with large muscles, to deal with tough-skinned fruit. The

Egyptian fruit bat, *Rousettus aegyptiacus*

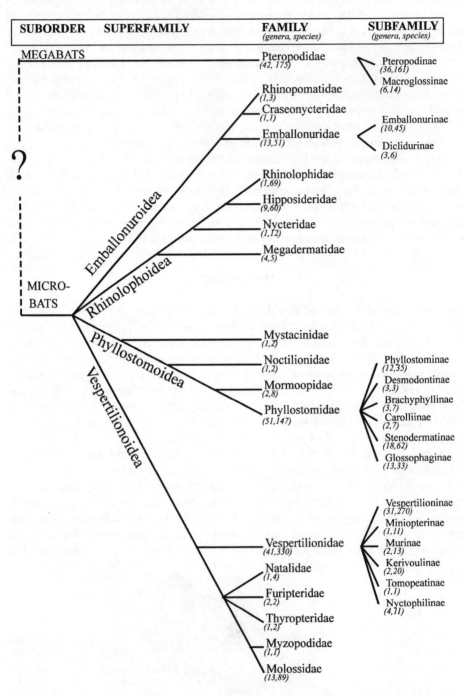

SUBORDER	SUPERFAMILY	FAMILY (genera, species)	SUBFAMILY (genera, species)

MEGABATS

Pteropodidae
(42, 175)

Pteropodinae
(36,161)

Macroglossinae
(6,14)

Rhinopomatidae
(1,3)

Craseonycteridae
(1,1)

Emballonuridae
(13,51)

Emballonurinae
(10,45)

Diclidurinae
(3,6)

Rhinolophidae
(1,69)

Hipposideridae
(9,60)

Nycteridae
(1,12)

Megadermatidae
(4,5)

MICRO-
BATS

Emballonuroidea

Rhinolophoidea

Phyllostomoidea

Vespertilionoidea

Mystacinidae
(1,2)

Noctilionidae
(1,2)

Mormoopidae
(2,8)

Phyllostomidae
(51,147)

Phyllostominae
(12,35)

Desmodontinae
(3,3)

Brachyphyllinae
(3,7)

Carolliinae
(2,7)

Stenodermatinae
(18,62)

Glossophaginae
(13,33)

Vespertilionidae
(41,330)

Natalidae
(1,4)

Furipteridae
(2,2)

Thyropteridae
(1,2)

Myzopodidae
(1,1)

Molossidae
(13,89)

Vespertilioninae
(31,270)

Miniopterinae
(1,11)

Murinae
(2,13)

Kerivoulinae
(2,20)

Tomopeatinae
(1,1)

Nyctophilinae
(4,11)

Fig. 1.12. An evolutionary tree for the bats to subfamily level. Considerable uncertainty surrounds some parts of this tree, in particular the relationship between megabats and microbats, and the detailed classification of the Phyllostomidae and the Vespertilionidae.

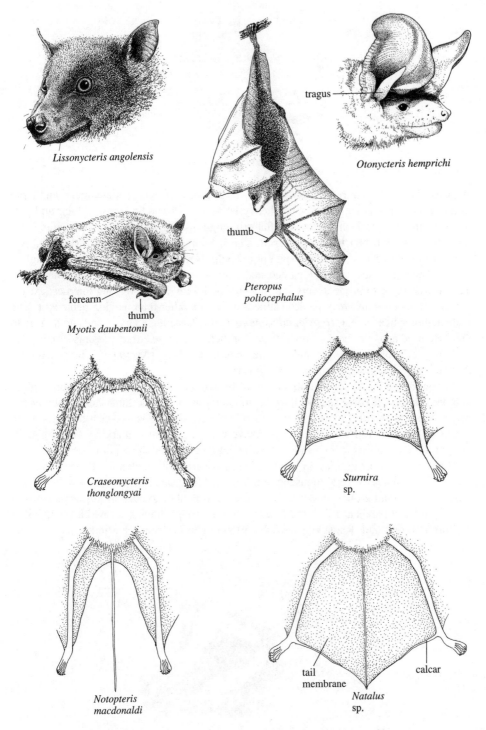

Fig. 1.13. Some important features of the external anatomy of bats.

Tube nosed bat, *Nyctimene* sp.

shape of the head often reflects the need for large areas for muscle attachment, and large biting forces: this often means short, heavy jaws, and a large braincase. Molar and pre-molar teeth have large, and relatively flat grinding/crushing surfaces, and the canines are large to grasp and penetrate tough fruit. The incisors are usually small. Many species crush fruit to extract the juice and spit out the pulp. Nectar and pollen feeders have lighter skulls. Their jaws are often elongated and narrow with correspondingly smaller teeth. This allows them to probe deeply into flowers, and with the aid of long tongues, extract nectar. Facial structure may be determined by factors other than feeding behaviour. The male hammer-headed bat, *Hypsignathus monstrosus*, has a huge larynx and snout, used to generate loud and spectacular hoots, as part of their display to attract passing females to a lek, or group of displaying males. The tube-nosed bats (*Nyctimene*) have laterally directed, tube-like nostrils, of uncertain function.

   Although generally rather drab shades of brown, some are patterned and/or brightly coloured. Males of some species have bright colouration around the head and shoulders, often found with tufts of long hair and associated scent glands—features related to courtship behaviour. The face itself may have white or coloured markings. A number of species have wing membranes mottled with white, yellow, or shades of red.

   Most species roost in trees, in large and occasionally noisy colonies. Tree colonies, or camps, may number several thousand individuals. Many species, often the smaller mega-bats, roost in small groups, or even singly. Cave roosts of echolocating *Rousettus* bats can be very large. Megabats will often forage in large groups, having located a flowering or fruiting tree or stand. Roost sites may be 50 km or more from a particular feeding site,

Masked fruit bat, *Pteropus personatus*

and the colony will take flight before dusk to travel to it. Some species undergo seasonal migrations, following the fruiting season of particular species of tree.

Until recently two subfamilies of megabat were recognised, the generalist Pteropodinae (36 genera, 161 species), and the nectar and pollen eating Macroglossinae (6 genera, 14 species), but new evidence disputes this split. Two small groups of Pteropodinae are sometimes given subfamily status: the tube-nosed bats (Nyctimeninae, 2 genera, 14 species) and the harpy fruit bats (Harpyionycterinae, 1 genus, 2 species).

The microbats

The microbats are a large and very diverse group of mammals. Forearm length ranges from 22 to 110 mm. All species have the ability to orientate by echolocation, and most make full use of it. The ears are often large and complex, and many species have nose-leaves. Both features are associated with echolocation. Microbats generally have small eyes, but their visual capacities are often found to be very good—none are known to be blind. Some species often locate their prey without echolocation, by listening for prey generated sounds, and/or by using vision. These species have very large eyes and excellent vision. The eyes are often forwardly directed, and probably give good binocular vision. Wing and tail membranes vary enormously in shape and size, and with echolocation characteristics are related to prey type, foraging strategy, and habitat, although it should be said that most species have flexible feeding habits. Microbats probably evolved from an early insectivore, and their teeth reflect this ancestry, despite their diversification into a wide range of feeding habits. The chewing teeth have W-shaped cusps, for cutting and crushing food. Skull and jaw shape is very variable, and determined primarily by the food taken, but in some cases by roosting habit. The enormous diversity of microbats can really only be dealt with in a family by family account.

Superfamily: Emballonuroidea Three families of aerial insectivores, the Emballonuridae, Craseonycteridae, and Rhinopomatidae. Robbins and Sarich (1988) suggest that the Rhinopomatidae should be included in the Vespertilionidae.

Family: Emballonuridae (13 genera, 51 species) The sheath-tailed bats in the Old and New World tropics. They are currently divided into two subfamilies, the Emballonurinae (10 genera, 45 species) and the New World Diclidurinae (3 genera, 6 species). Hill and Smith (1984) disagree, and raise an interesting problem. All of the New World species have evolved from a common ancestor, and although quite distinct from the 20 species of Old World tomb bats (*Taphozous*) they do appear to be related to other Old World genera. This is one of many intriguing, but unresolved, problems in bat taxonomy.

Emballonurids have long narrow wings, typical of fast flying, aerial insectivores. The wings are so long that, relative to other bats, at rest they have one extra fold. The tail is loosely bound to the tail membrane, and curls over the top surface when the bat is roosting. They are sometimes called sac-winged bats, because of the pheromone-producing glands present near the shoulder in some New World species. These sac-like glands are usually larger in the male. The four *Diclidurus* species are white or grey/white, with pink wings, ears, and face, and are known as ghost bats. *Saccopteryx* species have two thin white stripes running the full length of the back, but are otherwise brown, like most other

Black-bearded tomb bat, *Taphozous melanopogon*

species. Stripes are found on bats of several unrelated groups (e.g. the Phyllostomidae), and are thought to be cryptic, breaking up the outline of the bat in the roost. Some species have pale grey and yellow patterning, to camouflage them against lichen covered rocks and branches.

Emballonurids use a wide variety of roosts: caves, tree holes, and man-made structures. They are very agile, and often remain alert when roosting.

Family: *Craseonycteridae (1 genus, 1 species)* Discovered in 1973 in Thailand, the bumble-bee bat is the smallest known bat (1.5 g, forearm length 22–26 mm), and arguably the smallest known mammal (Hill, 1974). It roosts in limestone caves, high in the ceiling. It feeds by aerial hawking in open spaces, using calls of high frequency and intensity (Surlykke *et al.*, 1993). It is apparently rare, and under some threat due to deforestation of its habitat.

Family: *Rhinopomatidae (1 genus, 3 species)* The insectivorous mouse-tailed bats are found in the arid and semi-arid regions of the Old World, from North Africa east to Thailand and Sumatra. Possible adaptations to their desert life are the valved nostrils, which may prevent the entry of dust, and kidneys modified for the production of concentrated urine to limit water loss. They are colonial roosters in caves and man-made structures. In the cooler months they may remain dormant for long periods, living off accumulated fat. As the name suggests, they have very long tails, which project well beyond the end of the tail membrane.

Superfamily: Rhinolophoidea Four Old World families of insectivorous or carnivorous bats with complex noseleaves, the Megadermatidae, Nycteridae, Hipposideridae, and Rhinolophidae. They have short, broad wings for slow manoeuvrable flight, and many often forage by hovering, gleaning, or by hawking from perches. Wing loading (body mass/wing area) is low, enabling them to carry heavy prey. The long, constant frequency echolocation pulses emitted by many Rhinolophidae and Hipposideridae are used to detect fluttering prey.

Lesser mouse-tailed bat, *Rhinopoma hardwickei*

Family: Megadermatidae (4 genera, 5 species) The Old World false vampire bats (so-called because, like many bats, they were once thought to feed on blood) are large and spectacular. *Macroderma gigas,* the Australian ghost bat, has a forearm length of 105 mm, a wingspan of 0.6 m, and weighs up to 150 g. *Megaderma lyra,* the Asian greater false vampire has very attractive blue-grey fur, *Macroderma gigas* is more or less white, and *Lavia frons* from Africa, has blue-grey fur in addition to its yellow wings. *Lavia frons* frequently flies in daylight. Most are partly carnivorous, feeding on a range of small vertebrates, including fish, frogs, reptiles, birds, rodents, and other bats, as well as large invertebrates. These bats have a formidable array of senses for detecting prey,

Lesser mouse-tailed bat, *Rhinopoma hardwickei*

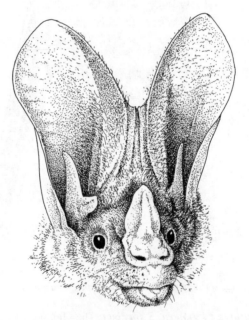

Australian ghost bat, *Macroderma gigas*

which may be responsible for their very adaptable hunting strategy. Their echolocation pulses are short, low in intensity, and broadband (sweeping a broad range of frequencies)—effective in cluttered environments, but not easily detectable by prey. The large ears are sensitive not only to the weak echoes returning from these pulses, but also to prey-generated sounds. The bats need not use echolocation under all circumstances, but can simply listen. Finally, they all have very well developed, forward-pointing eyes, and

Australian ghost bat, *Macroderma gigas*

can locate prey visually. They hunt both by hawking from perches, and by flying low over the ground. Prey is usually taken to a favourite perch, and the discarded remains beneath these perches reveal a lot about the bats' diet. *Macroderma gigas* has been known to take prey weighing more than 60% its own body weight. They roost in caves, rock crevasses, and hollow trees, in small groups.

Family: Nycteridae (1 genus, 12 species) The Old World slit-faced bats are found in the African tropics, and the arid regions of the Near-East. Oddly, one species is isolated from

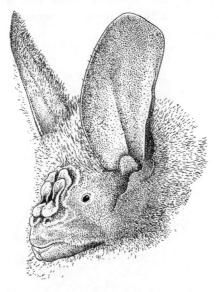

Large slit-faced bat, *Nycteris grandis*

the rest, in Indonesia. The feature which gives them their name is a prominent slit running back along the muzzle from the nostrils, bordered by fleshy protuberances, and though to be important in sound emission for echolocation. They have large ears and short, broad wings. They are primarily insectivorous, taking prey in the air and from the ground. *Nycteris grandis* (forearm length up to 66 mm) also takes scorpions and small vertebrates, including frogs, birds, and bats. Like the megadermatids, they take their prey back to favourite feeding perches. They roost in small groups or singly, in caves, hollow trees, and man-made structures. Some have been known to roost in the burrows of aardvarks and porcupines.

Family: Hipposideridae (9 genera, 60 species) The leaf-nosed bats are sometimes included in the Rhinolophidae, and there is no doubt that they are closely related. They are found throughout the Old World tropics and subtropics. They have elaborate noseleaves but generally not as complex as those of the Rhinolophidae. They are primarily colonial or solitary cave roosters.

Family: Rhinolophidae (1 genus, 69 species) Widespread, insectivorous Old World bats ranging from Britain and the whole of Africa in the west to Japan and eastern Australia in the east. Characterised by the most complex noseleaves and large, mobile ears. The noseleaf is very variable in form and complexity (species can often be identified by it), and it is believed to serve as an acoustic lens, focusing the nasally emitted echolocation pulses. Rhinolophids often rely on constant frequency, flutter detecting, echolocation pulses. They are broad winged bats commonly foraging in cluttered environments, feeding by gleaning (taking prey off foliage and the ground) aerial hawking, usually close to the ground, and 'flycatching'—making sorties from a perch after passing insects. The majority are tropical, but some can tolerate low temperatures by becoming torpid, a feature rare in tropical bats. About 15 species have colonised temperate regions of Europe and Asia and, like many vespertilionids, are truly heterothermic (i.e. they are true physiological hibernators). They are predominantly cave roosting, colonial or solitary, often in association with *Hipposideros* species.

Sundevell's leaf-nosed bat, *Hipposideros caffer*

Lesser horseshoe bat, *Rhinolophus hipposideros*

Lesser horseshoe bat, *Rhinolophus hipposideros*

Superfamily: Phyllostomoidea This is a large New World superfamily, very diverse in its biology, which originated in the neotropics, colonised subtropical regions, and has even penetrated some south temperate areas. It may be seen under the name Noctilionoidea. There are four families, the Mystacinidae, Noctilionidae, Mormoopidae, and Phyllostomidae.

Short-tailed bat, *Mystacina tuberculata*

Family: Mystacinidae (1 genus, 2 species, 1 probably extinct) A rather unique and enigmatic family. There were two species, but there have been no confirmed specimens caught or seen of the greater short-tailed bat since 1965, and it is probably extinct. New Zealand has only one other native terrestrial mammal, a vespertilionid bat. The short-tailed bats were thought to be an ancient group, related to the vesper and free-tailed bats. Recent morphological and molecular evidence suggests close affinities with the Phyllostomoidea, and the noctilionids in particular. *Mystacina tuberculata* is a small bat with remarkable adaptations to a partly terrestrial way of life. The wing membranes are very tough close to the body, and the delicate distal regions can be folded away and tucked into skin pouches on the flanks. The legs are short and stout, and the toes and thumb have talons near the base. It evidently spends much of its time on the ground, will burrow for food, and search for insects in the burrows of seabirds. It even burrows into fallen trees, particularly the kauri, to roost. They forage in the air, in trees, and on the ground, on a wide variety of food. Although primarily insectivorous, they will also eat fruit, nectar, and pollen. An equally unique, and monotypic (i.e. 1 species), family of bat fly feeds on the fungi and yeast which grow on its guano.

Family: Noctilionidae (1 genus, 2 species) The fisherman bats of the New World tropics and subtropics include two species. Both have large droopy lips, and are sometimes referred to as the bulldog bats. The larger species *Noctilio leporinus* (forearm length up to 88 mm, weight to 60 g) trawls for fish up to 100 mm in length, and the bat will adjust its flight path to intercept a moving fish. With long legs, big feet, and long claws for gaffing the fish, it is well-adapted to its foraging style. The tail membrane is kept out of the water by long calcars—cartilaginous projections from the feet towards the tail, which support the trailing edge of the tail membrane in many bats (Fig. 1.13). Fish are carried to a perch to be eaten. The diet also includes aquatic insects and small crustacea. Like its smaller, mainly insectivorous, relative *N. albiventris*, it feeds on coastal waters as well as rivers and lakes. They can swim, and take off from the water. Both species roost primarily in caves and hollow trees, as clusters of non-breeding males, or harem groups—a pattern common to many bats.

Family: Mormoopidae (2 genera, 8 species) The Mormoopidae are found in tropical and subtropical areas of the New World. They are variously known as the moustached or naked-backed bats (*Pteronotus* spp.) or ghost-faced bats (*Mormoops* spp.). The features

Small fisherman bat, *Noctilio albiventris*

Sooty moustached bat, *Pteronotus fuliginosus*

responsible for the first two names are a fringe of long hairs around the mouth, and wing membranes which arise close to the midline of the back. The hairs round the mouth, together with flaps on the lower lip, may help to focus the echolocation pulses and/or funnel insects into the mouth. At least one species (*Pteronotus parnellii*) has independently evolved a flutter-sensitive echolocation system, analogous to that used by the Old World Rhinolophidae. Moustached bats (*Mormoops* in particular) have the long, narrow wings characteristic of fast flying aerial insectivores, and they feed close to the ground like swallows. The unusual wing membrane attachment may serve to increase wing area without increasing span, but there have been no attempts to test this idea. They typically roost in hot humid caves, often in large colonies, in forest and arid areas. The Mormoopidae may have shared a common Palaeocene (54–64 myr BP) ancestor with the Phyllostomidae and Noctilionidae.

Family: Phyllostomidae (51 genera, 147 species) The 147 species of New World leaf-nosed or spear-nosed bats exhibit greater diversity than any other family, including the Pteropodidae and Vespertilionidae (families with more species, but fewer genera). They almost certainly evolved from an insectivorous ancestor, but now feed on a wide variety of food. Six subfamilies are usually described, although some authorities lay claim to as many as nine. The **Phyllostominae** eat insects and other arthropods if they are small, and include vertebrates in their diet if they are large. Some larger species eat fruit. The **Stenodermatinae** are specialised fruit eaters, and the **Glossophaginae** feed mainly on nectar, and pollen. The **Brachyphyllinae** eat fruit, nectar, and pollen. The **Carolliinae** show a marked preference for the fruit of Pepper (*Piper* species). Finally, the **Desmodontinae** are the vampires. Most Phyllostomidae (vampires are a notable exception) have a relatively simple, vertical, blade-like noseleaf, and the ears are simple but often long. In almost all other respects, the family is very variable, a reflection of their diverse foraging behaviour and diet. They are found only in the tropics and sub-tropics of the New World, but in habitats as varied as hot and humid lowland forests, cool montane forests and semi-arid deserts. They exploit virtually all possible roosts, and several species of Stenodermatinae build foliage tents.

Subfamily: Phyllostominae The earliest fossil phyllostomid, *Notonycteris magdalensis*, dates back to the Miocene (13–25 myr BP) (Savage, 1951), and has been assigned to the subfamily Phyllostominae, generally regarded as the oldest group of Phyllostomidae. There are 35 species of Phyllostominae, in 12 genera. Most species are omnivorous, taking insects and fruit. There is a trend towards carnivory in some of the larger species. *Chrotopterus auritus, Trachops cirrhosus*, and *Vampyrum spectrum* all feed extensively on small vertebrates. *Phyllostomus hastatus* also takes vertebrates, but to a lesser extent than the others. However, they all take insects and fruit. Both carnivory and frugivory appear to be an extension of insectivory in these bats. The teeth of even those Phyllostominae which feed extensively on fruit are arguably less well developed to that end than those of other members of the family: one of the reasons for suggesting that they are the most primitive (in the sense that they evolved first) of the Phyllostomidae.

Subfamily: Brachyphyllinae Relatively specialised fruit, nectar, and pollen feeders from the islands of the West Indies. Most have a long muzzle, the teeth are small and simple, and the tongue is long and extensible. They are closely related to the more specialised Glossophaginae.

Subfamily: Glossophaginae The flower bats, as they are known, have progressed further along the road to specialisation in nectar, pollen, and soft fruit. They typically have long, often very long, muzzles and greatly reduced teeth. The extensible tongue frequently ends in a brush-like collection of papillae, which increase the quantity of nectar or pollen that can be carried. Many of the smaller species can hover in front of flowers. It is possible that this feeding strategy evolved more than once in the Glossophaginae, as it may have done in their Old World equivalents, the Macroglossinae.

Subfamily: Stenodermatinae These bats have a short muzzle, broad flat molars, and often a cutting edge to some of the teeth: adaptations for dealing with courser fruit than that eaten by the Glossophaginae. Some species also take insects at certain times of the year.

Tome's long-eared bat, *Lonchorhina aurita*

Fringe-lipped bat, *Trachops cirrhosus*

The group includes some fascinating bats: the tent-making *Uroderma bilobatum*, and the all white *Ectophylla alba*, another tent-maker. The most bizarre is *Centurio senax*, the wrinkle-faced bat, with its face full of fleshy folds, the transparent chin flap which covers its face when roosting, and its partially transparent wings.

Subfamily: Carolliinae A small but very abundant group of bats specialising in the fruit of the genus *Piper*, pepper plants. Although related to the Glossophaginae, they lack their specialisations, and some certainly take insects.

Sanborn's long-nosed bat, *Leptonycteris curasoae (sanborni)*

Tent-making bat, *Uroderma bilobatum*

Honduran ghost bat, *Ectophylla alba*

Wrinkle-faced bat, *Centurio senax*

Subfamily: Desmodontinae The three members of this family all feed exclusively on blood, and have a number of specific adaptations for this. They have heat sensors in the noseleaf for locating capillary-rich areas of skin; modified canines for fur clipping; long, sharp incisors for painlessly opening a wound; anticoagulants to prevent clotting; and a grooved tongue to help move blood rapidly to the mouth. A specialised stomach and kidneys rapidly remove the blood plasma, which the bats often begin to excrete before they have finished their meal. Since a blood meal may be up to 60% of the bat's body weight, and only the red blood cells are of value, removal of the plasma is essential: the return flight to the roost may otherwise be impossible. Does the name *Desmodus rotundus* come from their after-dinner appearance? These 30–40 g bats are remarkably agile on the ground, and will often land before approaching their prey. *Desmodus* feeds primarily on domestic mammals, but will take blood from native mammals and birds. *Diaemus* also feeds on cattle in some parts of its range, and on birds in others: *Diphylla* feeds mainly on birds. Both species are much less common than *Desmodus*. All roost in caves or tree cavities.

Common vampire, *Desmodus rotundus*

ADAPTIVE RADIATION—Why are the Phyllostomidae so numerous and so diverse?

Many different factors have played a part in the evolution of the phyllostomids, some of which we can only make informed guesses about. Some influences are of general biological relevance, others are specific to the bats themselves. First of all, the phyllostomids evolved in the neotropics, which provide three important influences—age, climate, and size. The neotropical forests have been around since the end of the Cretaceous, 65 million years ago, giving lots of time for the bats to evolve. The first known phyllostomid is probably less than 25 myr old (Savage, 1951). In both animals and plants, species diversity typically decreases with distance from the equator: few people are unaware of the tremendous biodiversity of tropical rainforests relative to that of northern boreal forests, for example. More species can be supported by large areas. This is one of the few general statements that most ecologists would agree on (Schoener, 1986): the neotropical forests are by far the largest in the world.

Back in the Miocene, and probably earlier, the first insectivorous phyllostomids were evolving in the vast neotropical rain forests. Most modern bats have pretty flexible foraging strategies, and there is no reason to believe their ancestors were any different. As well as taking insects in the air, during continuous flight or by 'flycatching' from perches, early bats probably gleaned prey from a range of surfaces, including fruit and flowers. Bats must have exploited this source and frequently taken a mouthful of fruit, got a snoutful of pollen, or a taste of nectar. It is easy to see how insectivores could become omnivores, as many modern phyllostomids are, and eventually fruit or nectar/pollen specialists. The absence of competition from the Old World fruit bats may also be an important factor in the evolution of the fruit eating phyllostomids.

Insects also gather on larger animals, often around wounds, and Fenton (1992) has suggested that the vampires may have evolved from bats feeding on insects and their larvae on the wounds of large mammals and even birds. He provides persuasive arguments as to why vampires have only evolved in the New World. Only here were the conditions right: lots of large mammals and large birds with the requisite wounds and insects (mammals frequently bear scars from predators or inter-specific conflict), bats with a flexible foraging strategy, and most importantly, with large, sharp incisors to puncture skin. The large animal-eating bats of the Old World lack this last important requisite.

Whether hawking, flycatching, or gleaning, a bat will encounter vertebrates, and to a large bat, a small vertebrate, like a large arthropod, is food. Mammals (including other bats), birds, reptiles, and amphibia are all taken by some of the larger Phyllostominae, such as *Chrotopterus auritus* and *Vampyrum spectrum* (and in the Old World, the megadermatids and nycterids). None appear to be exclusively carnivorous: vertebrates are just a greater or lesser part of their varied diet, made possible by their flexible foraging strategies.

The smaller fisherman bat, *Noctilio albiventris* (a close relative of the phyllostomids) feeds by trawling for insects over water. Its larger cousin, *N. leporinus*, is large enough to take fish, and has become a fish specialist, an obvious transition. Fish are part of the diet of several trawling Vespertilionidae (e.g. *Myotis vivesi*).

Flexible foraging involves flexible prey detection. All phyllostomids echolocate, and more of that later, but many use prey-generated sounds to catch their food—as do some bats in other parts of the world. One phyllostomid, *Trachops cirrhosus*, listens to the calls of male frogs, which can make up a substantial part of its diet at some locations

(Tuttle and Ryan, 1981). *Tonatia sylvicola*, a related species, is attracted to singing katydids (Tuttle *et al.*, 1985).

Superfamily: Vespertilionoidea The largest superfamily, dominated by the Vespertilionidae, and to a lesser extent the Molossidae. All are insectivores, but several species also take fish. It includes the following families: Vespertilionidae, Natalidae, Furipteridae, Thyropteridae, Myzopodidae, and Molossidae.

Family: Vespertilionidae (41 genera, 330 species) The vesper or evening bats are the second largest mammalian family after the Muridae (Old World rats and mice), and one of the most widespread mammalian groups after man. They are absent only from the Antarctic, the most northern areas of North America and Eurasia, and some isolated oceanic islands. They thrive even in desert environments, and many species survive temperate winters by hibernating. Some species undertake substantial migrations to avoid the worst of the temperate winter, and to find suitable hibernation sites. Most species have simple faces with no noseleaf, but their ears are very variable. Although typically small with a simple tragus (a cartilaginous projection inside the external ear or pinna, Fig. 1.13), some ears are as long as the bat that wears them. These long ears are often furled around the head at rest, and pumped up with blood when the bat becomes active. Large ears are sometimes partially fused along their inner edges. The tail membrane is usually large, and with the wings, is used to catch insects. Vesper bats are almost exclusively insectivorous, feeding by aerial hawking, gleaning, and flycatching. The term insectivorous covers other arthropods. The Mexican fish-eating bat, *Myotis vivesi*, and several other species of *Myotis* (e.g. *Myotis adversus*) take small fish, and have the large feet and sharp claws of other fish-eating bats.

Most vesper bats are shades of brown, grey, and black, but there are some colourful exceptions, including the painted bats of the genus *Kerivoula*. *Kerivoula picta* has bright

Noctule bat, *Nyctalus noctula*

Brown long-eared bat, *Plecotus auritus*

red-orange fur, and the colour extends along the fingers, in stunning contrast to its black wings. Bright and cryptic colouration is most common in those species roosting in trees, often in the open.

Vesper bats exploit virtually all possible roost sites: trees, tree holes, under bark, in flowers, inside bamboo stalks, old birds' nests, caves, mines, tunnels, houses, and so on. Members of several genera have suction pads on their thumbs and feet, an adaptation for roosting inside the smooth, furled leaves of plants like banana.

Vesper bats are divided into five subfamilies, but there is considerable uncertainty about the classification of these bats, and we can expect frequent revisions. The largest

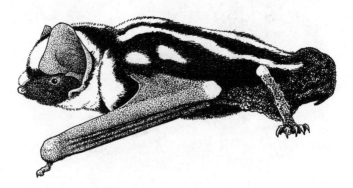

Butterfly bat, *Glauconycteris superba*

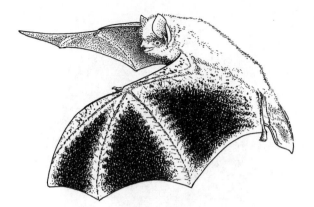

Welwitsch's hairy bat, *Myotis welwitschii*

subfamily is the Vespertilioninae, composed largely of the very widespread genera *Myotis* (94 species), *Pipistrellus* (48 species), and *Eptesicus* (33 species). The Miniopterinae are the long-fingered bats of the genus *Miniopterus*. Other subfamilies are the Murinae (tube-nosed bats), Kerivoulinae (mainly *Kerivoula* species), Nyctophilinae (which includes the pallid bats, *Antrozous*), and the Tomopeatinae (a single species, possibly related to the Molossidae).

Family: Natalidae (1 genus, 4 species) The funnel-eared bats of the New World tropics are small and delicate, with the broad wings of a slow-flying, manoeuvrable gleaner of small insects. The ears are large, forward pointing funnels. They roost in large colonies in humid caves. They are probably related to the next two families.

Family: Furipteridae (2 genera, 2 species) The smoky bats of the South American tropics resemble the Natalidae and Thyropteridae, with a high, domed skull, and funnel

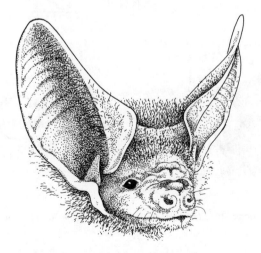

Australian big-eared bat, *Nyctophilus timoriensis*

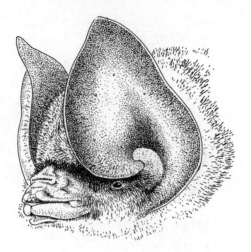

Funnel-eared bat, *Natalus micropus*

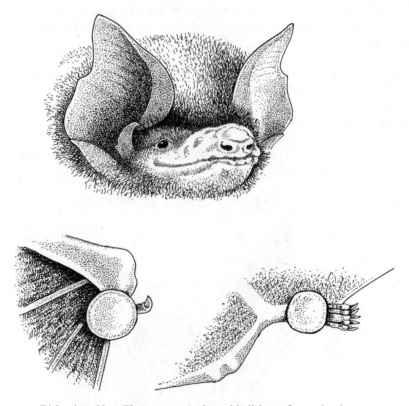

Disk-winged bat, *Thyroptera tricolor*, with disks on feet and wrists

shaped ears. A characteristic feature is the tiny thumb. The single species of *Amorphochilus* is one of the few bats known to live in the dry, low country west of the Andes.

Family: Thyropteridae (1 genus, 2 species) The disk-winged bats of the neotropics have tiny suction cups on their wrists and feet, which are used to grip the smooth walls of their roost: the furled leaves of *Heliconia* and related banana-like plants. As the roost leaves grow and unfurl, the small colonies must constantly move on to younger leaves. They have the domed skull and funnel shaped ears of the Natalidae and Furipteridae. Recently, it has been suggested that they may be related to the Phyllostomidae!

Family: Myzopodidae (1 genus, 1 species) *Myzopoda aurita*, the Old World sucker-footed bat, is confined to Madagascar. It resembles the New World *Thyroptera* in several respects: the high domed skull, large ears, small thumb, toes with only two phalanges, fused toes, and suckers on hands and feet. However, the ears are not funnel shaped, and the thumb sucker is not stalked. Nevertheless, it has been suggested that the two groups may be related.

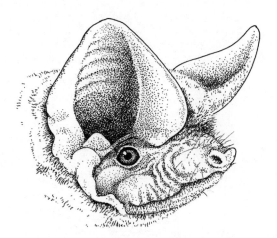

Egyptian free-tailed bat, *Tadarida aegyptiaca*

Naked bat, *Cheiromeles torquatus*

Family: Molossidae (13 genera 89 species) The free-tailed bats are found in the Old and New Worlds, including warmer temperate regions. They are adapted for rapid aerial pursuit of insects in the open, with long, narrow wings. Wing membranes are generally very tough. The tail always projects beyond the end of the tail membrane. The ears are frequently stiff, tilted well forward, and joined along part of their length. The skull is flattened in some crevice roosting species. The two *Cheiromeles* species are naked, but most molossids have a thick covering of short fur.

They use a wide variety of roosts, and some cave roosts of the Mexican free-tailed bat, *Tadarida brasiliensis,* house several million bats. Bats may fly over 50 km a night in search of food. In temperate zones *T. brasiliensis* and several other species are migratory, and it has been suggested that some may even undergo short periods of torpor.

2   Flight

Basic aerodynamics—aerofoils, flight theory, and the mechanics of flapping flight. The evolution of flight. Why flight evolves, and why it has not evolved more often— advantages conferred, anatomical/physiological adaptations, and constraints. Ecology of flight—power vs speed curves. Maximum range and minimum power speeds. Wing morphology and flight performance in relation to ecology—aspect ratio, wing loading, and wing shape. Scaling effects.

SOME BASIC AERODYNAMICS: AEROFOILS AND FLAPPING FLIGHT

Aerofoils

There are several excellent accounts of aerodynamics in relation to animal flight, and all will be mentioned somewhere in the chapter, but for a recent and very wide ranging book on all aspects of vertebrate flight, you should go to Norberg (1990). Pennycuick (1972) has written a short and very readable book on animal flight, and more recently (1989) a book and computer program for experimenting with flight morphology and performance. A real understanding of flight can only be gained if you are familiar with a little of the terminology and some of the concepts of aerodynamics, so that is what we will start with.

The shape of an idealised aerofoil, and that of a bat's wing, are shown in Fig. 2.1a. The tapered profile and convex upper surface are responsible for the forces generated by an aerofoil which keep the bat in the air and move it forward. Because of this shape, air flowing over the top of the wing must move faster than that flowing below (Fig. 2.1a). This results in an area of low pressure above the wing, and high pressure below, and therefore a net aerodynamic force (NAF) which raises the wing (Fig. 2.1b). If the bat is to go forward, then the NAF must have two components, a vertical, lift component to overcome the effect of gravity, and thrust to overcome drag. The wings and body of the bat experience drag which resists forward movement. Drag is usually minimised by having a streamlined shape, but is always significant, at around 10–20% of the lift. Since lift acts at right angles to the movement of the wings, the wings must move forwards and downwards relative to the airflow. A gliding bat (Fig. 2.1c) achieves the right angle of incidence to overcome drag by losing height. The angle of incidence (or attack) is the angle the aerofoil makes with the plane of the airflow. A flapping bat must use appropriate wing movements (kinematics) during the downstroke and the upstroke to overcome drag.

Blade-element and momentum jet theories

The wings of birds and bats have been dealt with in the same way as fixed wings in many theoretical analyses of flight. The blade-element and momentum jet theories are applied

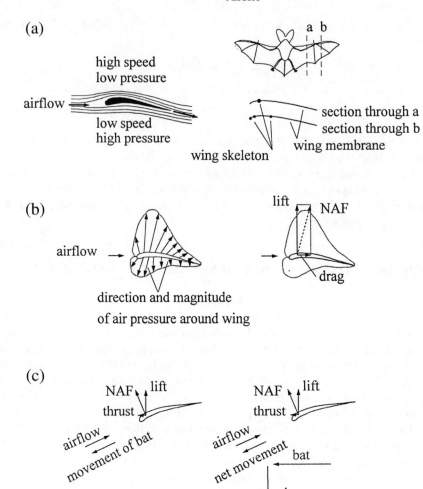

Fig. 2.1. Aerofoils and the generation of lift and thrust. (a) Transverse section through an aerofoil in an airstream. A bat's wing (right) has a similar section, and also acts as an aerofoil. (b) The pressure differences around the wing (left), and the Net Aerodynamic Force (right) which results from them. The NAF is conventionally resolved into lift and drag components. (c) How gliding and flapping bats gain lift and forward thrust (based in part on Rayner, 1986).

when it is thought that steady-state or quasi-steady-state conditions are operating. In the blade-element approach, the velocities and forces operating on different sections along the wing are calculated for each phase of the wing beat, and summed for the whole wing. The momentum jet theory calculates the air velocities in the momentum jet of air behind the wing. The aerofoil action of the wing, with its upward and forward force, induces an equal and opposite jet of air, backwards and downwards. These two approaches are often applied together.

In a steady- or quasi-steady-state analysis, the lift and drag coefficients of the wing must be calculated. Drag and lift are defined by the following equations:

$$\text{Drag, } D = 0.5\rho V^2 S C_D$$
$$\text{Lift, } L = 0.5\rho V^2 S C_L$$

where ρ = air density, V = forward velocity of the wing, S = wing area, and C_D, C_L are the coefficients of drag and lift respectively. The last two indicate the capacity of the wing, at a given angle of incidence, to generate drag and lift. As I said above, a good aerofoil has a lift:drag ratio of about 10:1. Total drag on the flying bat has three components, all of which must be calculated. *Induced drag* is due to perturbations in the airflow round the wing, *profile drag* is the friction and pressure drag on the wings, and *parasite drag* is the friction and pressure drag on the body. A discussion of how these are calculated is beyond the scope of this book, but details can be found in Norberg (1990). The relevance of these calculations will become apparent later in the chapter when we look at the power requirements of flight.

Vortex wake theory and wing kinematics

Although still widely applied, and very useful, blade-element theory underestimates the NAF generated under certain conditions, and a number of people have developed a new approach which often gives a better match between theory and experiment—this is vortex wake theory. The camber of a wing, in addition to increasing the velocity of air flow over it, also deflects the air downwards, and induces rotational flow around the wing, and behind it: these are the bound and trailing vortices shown in Fig. 2.2. If Newton's third law is to be obeyed (action and reaction are equal and opposite), then the downward momentum of the trailing vortices in the wake of the bat (action) is balanced by the upward NAF acting on the wings (reaction). A study of the vortices in the wake of a flying bat (the momentum jet of the previous section) will therefore tell us a lot about how the wings generate lift and thrust.

Detailed descriptions of wing kinematics and vortex wake theory in relation to bat flight can be found in Rayner (1986, 1987): what follows is a simplified account. To recap, in flapping flight a bat must use its wings to support its weight and overcome drag if it is to move forward. It cannot do this by simply flapping its wings with fixed wing geometry and angle of incidence with the airflow. This would keep it airborne, but would generate equal amounts of forward and backward thrust in the downstroke and upstroke respectively. This is shown in Fig. 2.3a.

A bat must therefore change its wing shape and/or the angle of incidence during a wing beat if it is to maintain forward flight. Lift acts at right angles to the direction of wing movement. It is proportional to the wingspan, the speed of movement, and to the circulation, or strength, of the bound vortex. The circulation is determined primarily by the angle of incidence, increasing with increasing angle until the airflow becomes turbulent, when the wing stalls and lift is lost. An active downstroke will give weight support and forward thrust, and will be the most important phase of the wing beat. To get a mean forward thrust over the wing beat, the upstroke must therefore be changed.

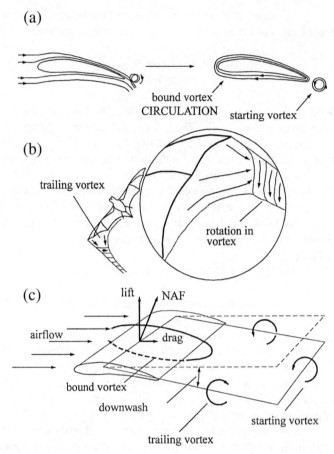

Fig. 2.2. Vortex wake theory. (a) The motion of the wing at the start of the downstroke sets up the starting vortex at the trailing edge, and induces an equal and opposite rotation of air around the wing—the bound vortex, or circulation. (b) As the wing goes through the downstroke, a trailing vortex forms at each wing tip, as air is shed and rotated. (c) A schematic of an active aerofoil showing: the downward deflection of the air (downwash), the starting and trailing vortices, and the bound circulation responsible for the NAF (based in part on Rayner, 1986).

Circulation can be reduced by decreasing the angle of incidence (Fig. 2.3a) or changing aerofoil section. Alternatively (or in addition), the wingspan can be reduced by flexing the wing, or sweeping back the tip (Fig. 2.3b). Whether or not a bat generates lift on the upstroke will depend upon the relative size of the lift and drag components. If drag is small, the bat may be in a position to generate lift on the upstroke, but when drag is large, the upstroke is likely to be passive, to avoid negative thrust. Drag is determined by flight speed and wing morphology, so we can expect these to have a major impact on wing kinematics.

This brings us back to vortices. In combination with analyses of wing kinematics they can tell us a great deal about how bats fly. By flying bats through neutrally buoyant, helium-filled soap bubbles, Rayner *et al.* (1986) were able to visualise the trailing vor-

(a)

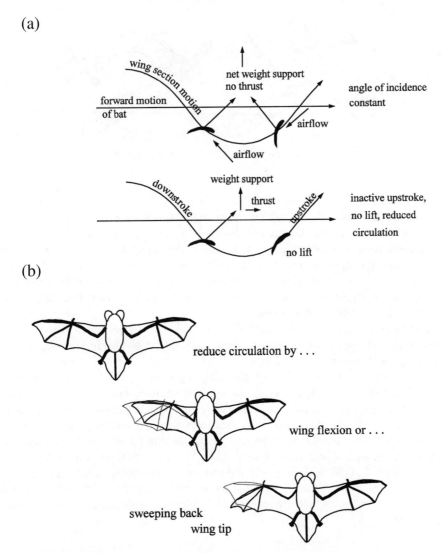

(b)

Fig. 2.3. How to generate lift and net forward thrust. (a) Top—with a constant angle of incidence to the airflow, the wing supports the weight of the bat, but there is no forward thrust. The lower diagram shows one method of overcoming the problem. The wing is 'feathered', and the upstroke is aerodynamically inactive. The upstroke can remain active by flexing the wing, or sweeping back the wing tip. (b) Circulation is reduced, but forward thrust is maintained, at the cost of reduced lift during the upstroke, relative to the downstroke (based in part on Rayner, 1986).

tices. This was done by taking stereo photographs of the bubbles at 8 ms intervals, and plotting their paths to reveal the direction and velocity of air flow.

Let's look at a noctule, *Nyctalus noctula*, first: a moderately large, fast-flying microbat, with long, narrow wings. Figure 2.4 shows idealised trailing vortices behind a noctule flying at 7.5 m/s. The bat trails a continuous vortex from the tip of each wing, indicating that the bound circulation remains constant throughout the wing beat. Both the

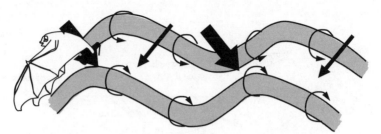

Fig. 2.4.   Fast flight. Vortices behind a fast flying noctule.

downstroke and the upstroke are active and generate lift. This is achieved because the wing remains flat, and the wing has a positive angle of incidence, over most of the wing beat. The armwing (that part between the body and wrist) is merely flexed a little during the upstroke, reducing the wingspan (and hence lift) and ensuring that there is net forward thrust. The upstroke is active, supporting the bat's weight over the whole wing beat, at the cost of some negative thrust during the upstroke. The negative thrust is not very important because drag is low at these speeds. As we will see below, drag is high only at very low and very high speeds.

At low speeds, wing kinematics and trailing vortices are very different. The wake of a noctule flying at 3 m/s is made up of a series of discrete, roughly circular ring vortices, shed during the downstroke (Fig. 2.5).

Trailing vortices are only shed when the wing is generating lift, i.e. during the downstroke. The absence of vortices during the upstroke indicate that it is aerodynamically inactive. When the circulation of the bound vortex changes, a transverse vortex, equal in magnitude to the change in circulation, is shed from the wing's trailing edge. In this case it occurs when the circulation is created at the beginning of the downstroke, and destroyed at the end. These transverse vortices break the trailing vortices into rings, which are opened at the beginning of the downstroke, and closed at the end. The wing beat frequency is faster than at 7 m/s, and the upstroke is made inactive by flexing the wings to reduce the span, and by rotation to reduce the angle of incidence to zero or negative values.

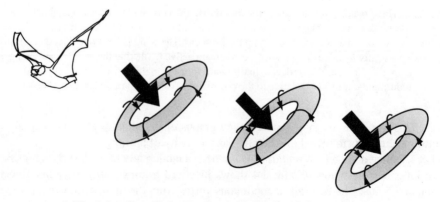

Fig. 2.5.   Slow flight. Vortices behind a slow flying noctule.

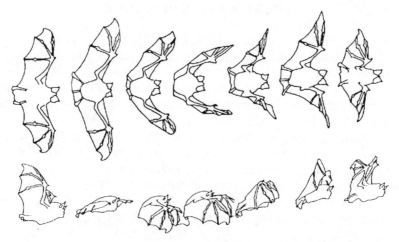

Fig. 2.6.   Wing movements during slow flight of a greater horseshoe bat (from Aldridge, 1986).

Figure. 2.6 shows the wing kinematics of a greater horseshoe bat during slow flight, with an inactive upstroke. At the top of the wing beat, the wing is, so to speak, palm down, and the back of the wing tilted slightly forward. The aerodynamic forces acting on the wing as it is swept down in this position will move the bat forwards and upwards. As the wing reaches the bottom of its stroke, it is quickly flipped over, so that the palm faces forward, and may tilt slightly backwards. It then sweeps up in this position, and folds as it goes.

The noctule therefore has two gaits: at high flying speeds the wings are aerodynamically active throughout the wing beat, and at lower speeds, when drag is higher, the upstroke becomes inactive. The noctule has high aspect ratio wings (i.e. long and narrow, see below), with pointed tips. Wings of this shape have low induced drag (drag due to the movement of the wings themselves), which may explain why this species can use a gait at high flight speeds which has a negative thrust component in the upstroke. The brown long-eared bat (*Plecotus auritus*) has only been seen to use the passive upstroke gait. The high drag of their low aspect ratio, rounded wings may prevent them from using an active upstroke. I will come back to wing shape and the different components of drag later in the chapter.

I noted earlier that increasing the angle of attack of the wing increases lift. As a bat slows down, it needs to do this to keep airborne. Many bats need to fly slowly when foraging—to hover or turn rapidly. If the angle of attack is too great, the vortex bound to the wing breaks away, and there is turbulence and loss of lift. Bats can flex their fingers, and the wing membrane itself has thin sheets of muscle in it to keep it taut. The wing also attaches to the hind limb, and bats can move this too. They therefore have considerable control over their wing shape and position; more control than birds. Flexing the wing increases camber (increased curvature, convex up), just like lowering the flaps on an aeroplane, and this reduces the stalling speed, by allowing a higher angle of attack before breakaway. This makes bats particularly good at slow speed, highly manoeuvrable flight. This is just what is needed to chase flying insects, which are also often highly manoeuvrable.

THE EVOLUTION OF FLIGHT

Vertebrates took to the air a long time ago. The first to do so were the reptilian weigelti-saurs of the Permian period, which died out at the time of the great end-Permian mass extinction, about 240 myr BP. The weigeltisaurs, like the later Keuhneosaurs of the Triassic (245–208 myr BP), had gliding membranes supported by extended ribs. *Longisquama*, another Triassic glider, had a spectacular double row of long scales on its back, which probably dropped into a horizontal position for gliding. At around the same time as *Longisquama* was gliding, the first vertebrates to use powered flight were evolv-ing—the pterosaurs. Among the first to appear, 230 myr BP, were *Eudimorphodon* and *Dimorphodon*, and the last to die, 165 myr later in the end-Cretaceous extinction, included *Pteranodon* and *Quetzalcoatlus*. In the midst of all these gliding and flying pterosaurs, the first known bird, *Archaeopteryx*, emerged 135 myr BP, and the unknown first bat was probably flying towards the end of the pterosaurs' reign.

Gliding or jumping?

Two theories have been put forward to explain the evolution of flight (flight refers to powered, flapping flight, as distinct from gliding), the arboreal and the cursorial. The arboreal theory for the evolution of bat flight was probably put forward first by Darwin (1859), and has been elaborated many times since. Put simply, tree or cliff dwelling ancestors evolved flight through an intermediate gliding stage. The cursorial theory is more recent, and has not had a wide following, but Caple *et al.* (1983) formalised it, and raised numerous objections to the arboreal theory. These objections have been effectively countered by a number of authors (e.g. Norberg, 1985; Rayner, 1992), and the arboreal or gliding theory is widely favoured. In birds, there are reasons for considering the cursorial theory (Rayner, 1986), but it can be discounted when considering bats. The cursorial theory demands that the animal runs and leaps, gaining sufficient speed to get lift from its outstretched wings to glide, and then fly. There is little doubt that our protobat was unable to run at any speed! In the absence of evidence from the fossil record, work on the evolution of flight in bats (and birds) has concentrated on a study of living animals, often from a biomechanical viewpoint. Let's take a look at the idea that bats evolved from a gliding ancestor, and see why it is the preferred option. A very concise and readable account has been given by Rayner (1992).

First of all, if the ancestral bat is going to glide, it has to be able to climb, to gain height for its jump. When an animal climbs a tree, its muscles do work, and use energy. Some of this muscular energy is converted into *potential* energy (potential energy = the mass of the animal × its height above the ground × acceleration due to gravity). The higher it climbs, the more energy it expends, but the more potential energy it gains. This potential energy is used by the animal to glide. When the protobat jumps (Fig. 2.7), gravity pulls it to the ground, and it loses potential energy.

Gliding is powered by potential energy: when the protobat opens its wings as it falls, they generate a force which counteracts the force of gravity acting on the animals body, holding the protobat up. In other words the wings act as an aerofoil. However, as the aerofoil moves through the air, there is a backwardly directed force (drag) as well as the upward force (Fig. 2.7 and see previous section). Drag resists the forward motion of

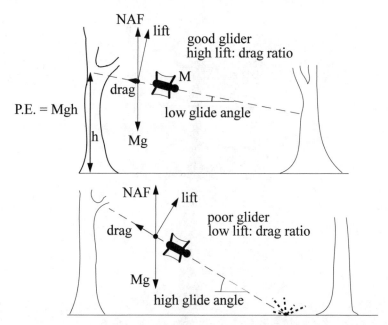

Fig. 2.7. Gliding. A gliding mammal climbs a tree to gain potential energy, P.E. (P.E. = Mgh; M = body mass, g = acceleration due to gravity, h = height above ground). Its gliding membrane generates lift to keep it airborne, and the loss of height (and therefore loss of P.E.) provides the energy to overcome drag and maintain glide speed. The higher the lift to drag ratio, the shallower the glide.

the animal, and slows it down. A gliding animal maintains speed because it is falling. The energy needed to overcome drag and maintain gliding speed comes from the loss of potential energy as the animal approaches the ground. Good gliders have good aerofoils, with little drag. They can glide a long way because only a little potential energy (height loss) is needed to overcome drag, so less height is lost over a given horizontal distance: their glide angle is small (Fig. 2.7).

So, we have established that a glider and future flier needs to be able to climb. We do not need to look very far to find evidence which suggests that our protobat, a small mammal, could climb: the world is full of very agile mammalian climbers, of all sizes. What does it need to be able to glide? A gliding surface or aerofoil, and the strength to hold the aerofoil open. Rayner (1992) has calculated that the muscular strength required to hold the aerofoil open is much less than that needed for climbing, so a climber can glide if it has an aerofoil. Aerofoils and gliding have evolved at least once in every verte-brate group, and several times in most. There are gliding fish, frogs, lizards, snakes, and mammals, and some of their aerofoils (pectoral fins, webbed feet, extended ribs, flattened bodies, flaps of skin between the fore- and hindlimbs) differ little from the standard anatomical plan of their non-gliding cousins. The protobat would have little difficulty in becoming a bad glider as the skin flap between fore- and hindlimbs developed, and from there, would become a better one.

How was the aerofoil's performance improved? First of all, the amount of lift gener-ated increases as the area of the aerofoil increases. More lift means slower, safer speeds,

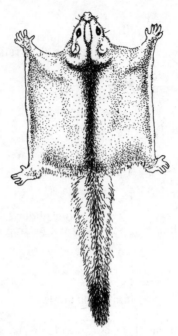

Fig. 2.8.   The low aspect ratio gliding membranes of the sugar glider, *Petaurus breviceps*.

and longer glides, so an evolutionary selective pressure for increased wing area is under-
standable. Another factor is wing shape. Modern mammalian gliders such as flying squirrels and marsupial sugar gliders have aerofoils of low aspect ratio (Fig. 2.8).

Aspect ratio is a measure of wing shape, calculated as the length from tip to tip (span),
divided by the width, front to back (chord). For the oddly shaped wings of animals, a
better measurement is wing span squared divided by area. Low aspect ratio wings generate lots of drag, the lift to drag ratio is low, the glide angle is steep, and the glide therefore short (Norberg, 1985). The length of the glide can be increased by lengthening the
wing, thus increasing aspect ratio, which increases the lift to drag ratio. Although the
area of the gliding membrane can be increased, there is little scope for increasing aspect
ratio without significant modification of the limb skeleton. If the gliding membrane
extended to between the fingers, then simple elongation of the fingers could increase
aspect ratio. In principle, adjustments to the flight path could also be made by movement
of the fingers to change the shape of the aerofoil. Modern day flying lemurs (dermopterans) have webbed hands with short fingers—a step away from a long-fingered flying bat.

So, there's no reason why a gliding protobat should not have evolved, and there are
several good reasons why it should. A single tree would have been unlikely to provide our
protobat with all of its food, or cater for other needs, such as a safe shelter and mates, and
like many modern mammals it would have moved from tree to tree. It had two choices,
jump from one tree to the next, or climb all of the way down, cross the ground, and climb
back up again. The latter is an expensive option: climbing down can use as much energy
as climbing up. Gliding on the other hand is cheap. A good glider, like a colugo, can travel
over 100 m, lose only 10 m height, and expend almost no energy. Gliding is also fast: five

or more times faster than running on the ground (Rayner, 1986; Scholey, 1986). Although the cost of climbing is high, the high gliding speeds mean that the overall cost of transport (cost per unit distance travelled, or unit time travelling) is low. A small animal on the ground could pay the ultimate cost—its life—if caught by a ground predator. A jump, or better still a glide from tree to tree, is a good way to avoid a more agile predator. Lots of animals have learnt to move through trees by jumping, and many spread their limbs for stability and for landing. It is a small step from there to gliding.

The next step is to active, flapping flight. Rayner (1986) has calculated that flapping the wings over an amplitude of 25° or more, with flexing on the upstroke, is sufficient to generate useful thrust to assist gliding, and that a climbing animal could supply the appropriate energy: the way to flapping flight is therefore open. A detailed aerodynamic model for this transition has been developed by Norberg (1985, 1990).

THE ADVANTAGES OF FLIGHT, AND THE DEMANDS ON THE FLYER: PHYSIOLOGICAL AND BIOMECHANICAL ASPECTS OF FLIGHT

What are the advantages conferred on our protobat by the evolution of flight, and the obstacles, physiological and anatomical, which stand in its way?

The advantages: why fly?

I have already noted one major advantage, the cost of transport. Flight may demand twice the energy per second as running, but a flying animal travels very much faster, and the cost of transport may therefore be five times lower than that of a flightless counterpart of similar size. In terms of energy expended per unit distance moved, flying is cheap. Bats can therefore forage over wide areas, exploiting food supplies which are ephemeral or show seasonal fluctuations. They are able to commute over considerable distances, between roost site and foraging area, and in so doing, exploit otherwise unavailable resources. Flight gives them access to new food sources, such as airborne insects, the fruit and flowers of many trees, and vertebrates such as fish and birds. A wide range of roost sites can be used, many safe from all, or almost all, predators. Flight itself also reduces predation risk (Pomeroy, 1990). Migration is an option open to flying animals, allowing different, distant environments to be exploited at various times of the year. Flight enables bats to cross major barriers such as deserts, seas, and mountains. The advantages conferred by flight may have substantial consequences. One feature common to the three living groups of flying animals–bats, birds, and insects—is the relatively large number of species in each group. The mobility given to them by flight has probably been at least partly responsible for their diversification.

The obstacles: why is flying difficult?

If flight can give an animal enormous advantages in life, why hasn't it evolved more often? One answer is that flying is difficult. If you are going to fly well, you have to be built for the job, and built to a high specification plan. The mechanical, physiological, and

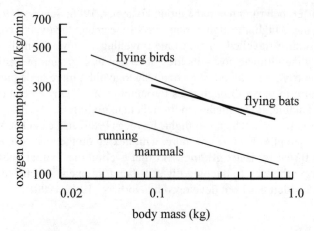

Fig. 2.9. The cost of locomotion in relation to body size. As animals get bigger, the amount of energy consumed per kg of body weight (in this case oxygen consumption) declines—locomotion becomes more efficient. Flight in both birds and bats is about twice as expensive as running in mammals (adapted from Thomas, 1987).

aerodynamic conditions which must be fulfilled make it unlikely that flight will evolve very often. I have already said that flight is expensive in terms of the rate at which energy must be supplied to the flight muscles. This is shown in Fig. 2.9: the metabolic cost of transport decreases with increasing body size, but it is greater in bats than non-flying mammals, and comparable with that of birds.

To meet the sustained high energy demands of flight, oxygen must be taken in by a capable respiratory system, an effective heart and circulatory system must deliver it to the flight muscles, and the flight muscles must work for long periods without fatigue. If a bat needs to supply twice as much energy to its muscles as a mammal on the ground, it must have some special physiological adaptations.

When a bat takes off, its breathing rate rapidly increases 4–6 fold, to match its wing beat frequency (around 10 Hz for an average-sized microbat). Not only is there one breath to one wing beat, but the two processes are closely coupled in the bat species studied (e.g. Carpenter, 1986). Bats breathe out late in the upstroke when the forces pulling the wing down are greatest, and these forces also compress the thorax (Rayner, 1991). The movements of the thorax during flight may assist ventilation and thus save energy, as has been suggested for some terrestrial mammals (Alexander and Young, 1992; Young *et al.*, 1992). Not surprisingly, microbats often emit their echolocation pulses late in the upstroke too, and echolocation, expensive in a stationary bat, comes at little or no extra cost to a flying bat (Speakman and Racey, 1991). When a terrestrial mammal starts running, the changes in respiration rate are smaller than in bats, but not always that much smaller. The extra oxygen supplied to the flight muscles of a bat cannot be attributed to differences in the breathing rate. Nor can it be explained by the volume of air moved per breath, between bats and other mammals, although it must be said that data are available for few bat species. What about the circulatory system? Heart rates of resting bats are comparable with those of other mammals of similar size (e.g. Studier and Howell, 1969; Thomas and Suthers, 1970; Carpenter, 1985), but are higher in flight than those of running mammals, and comparable with those of flying birds (2–6 times the resting rate) (Berger and Hart, 1974; Carpenter, 1986). A bat's heart, like a bird's, is as much as three times the size of that of a terrestrial mammal of the same body size. This means that in a single heartbeat, it may be able to pump around twice as much blood to the flight muscles—data are still a little sparse (Thomas and Suthers, 1972). Oxygen from the lungs is carried in the blood bound to haemoglobin in the red blood cells. Some bats have more red blood cells than birds and terrestrial mammals, and can therefore carry more oxygen. To sum up, there are no startling physiological adaptations as seen in birds: the high energy demand of bat flight muscle is apparently met by cumulative, small changes in several physiological parameters, but the picture is far from clear in many of the species studied, and much more work needs to be done. More detailed accounts of these physiological aspects can be found in Thomas (1987) and Norberg (1990).

The flight muscles of bats are typically mammalian. They must be capable of sustained activity, and are therefore highly aerobic. They have a rich capillary blood supply, the fibres themselves are rich in myoglobin to facilitate oxygen transfer from the blood to the muscle, and they have numerous mitochondria to synthesise ATP aerobically.

Measurements of oxygen consumption during flight (Thomas, 1975; Carpenter, 1986; Speakman and Racey, 1991) show that there is a tight relationship between flight cost and body size which can be used to predict oxygen consumption for bats of known weight. Norberg calculated that a 9 g brown long-eared bat, *Plecotus auritus*, should need 1.83 W to fly. Using her blade-element theory, the calculated mechanical power input was 0.36 W (Norberg, 1990). Assuming an efficiency of 0.25 for the conversion of chemical energy to mechanical work, the metabolic input = 0.36/0.25 = 1.44 W, add 0.11 W for resting metabolism, and this results in a total metabolic input of 1.55 W, in good agreement with the physiological estimate. Metabolic rate during flight would therefore be 14 times that of resting metabolism. In bats, the flight muscles are typically 10% of the body weight; this will be 0.9 g in a brown long-eared bat, and predominantly fast contracting, oxidative fibres (Altenbach and Hermanson, 1987). They will produce their maximum power output at the wing beat frequency of 10–14 Hz (see Altringham and Young, 1991). Recent measurements of mammalian skeletal muscle power output under conditions simulating those operating during locomotion (e.g. James *et al.*, 1995) suggest that these fast contracting muscles should be capable of generating up to 150 W/kg. The total mechanical power available to *Plecotus* is thus 0.14 W: lower than the 0.36 W calculated by Norberg for *Plecotus*. However, it is identical to the 0.14 W recently calculated by Norberg *et al.* (1993) for a 12 g *Glossophaga soricina* in forward flight. Total power required was 1.63 W, or 12 times resting metabolic rate.

The flight musculature of bats is complex relative to that of birds, since the muscles have a role to play in both flight and terrestrial locomotion. There are five major downstroke muscles, and two major upstroke muscles: in birds there is one major downstroke muscle, assisted by one other (reviewed in Hill and Smith, 1984; Norberg, 1990). Altenbach and Hermanson (1987) have carried out the most detailed experiments on bats, which show that the downstroke muscles begin to contract late in the upstroke, and similarly the upstroke muscles are active before the downstroke is complete. This early onset of activity presumably acts to brake the wings at the top and bottom of the strokes, and initiate changes in wing shape. Few muscles are active in the middle of the strokes.

The discussion so far has concentrated on physiological adaptations for flight: there are also biomechanical constraints. Flying animals are best made light, so that less energy is

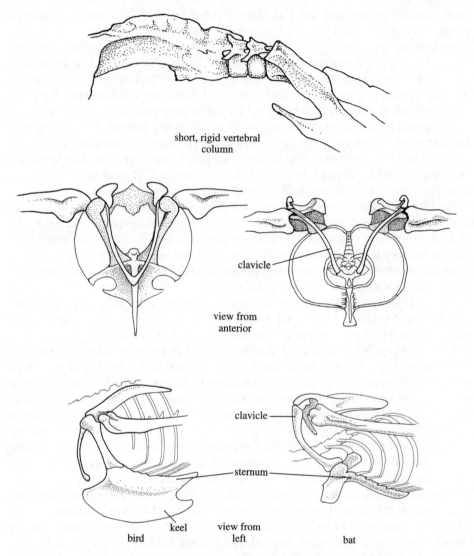

short, rigid vertebral
column

clavicle

view from
anterior

clavicle

sternum

keel   view from
bird   left   bat

Fig. 2.10. Adaptations of the skeleton for flight. See text for details.

needed in flying, and the forces on the body are smaller, placing smaller demands on the
musculo-skeletal system. Bats show a number of adaptations which reduce weight,
notably in the bones and membranes of the wings (Norberg, 1970). However, these structures must also be strong, to stand up to the large forces which act on them during flight.
The wing bones of bats are unusually rigid, with the greatest diameters oriented in the
planes of maximum bending force (Norberg, 1970). We will look at the wing in more
detail in the next section: first, a brief look at other skeletal adaptations, summarised in
Fig. 2.10.

In common with birds and pterosaurs, bats have short, streamlined bodies, and the vertebral column has regions of restricted movement, and even rigidity due to the fusion of
bones. The large ridge (keel) on the sternum seen in birds, for the attachment of the major

flight muscle (pectoralis), is often absent in bats. However, it may be replaced by a ligamentous sheet which serves the same function. The shoulder girdle is attached to the sternum by the clavicles, to form the strong support needed for the wings.

THE WING AND WHAT IT DOES IN FLIGHT

All the major features of a typical microbat's wing can be seen in Fig. 2.11. The wing membrane, or patagium, is supported primarily by the elongated forelimb. This is made up of the humerus, the long radius (the ulna has regressed), and the elongated metacarpals and phalanges of fingers 2–5. Fingers 2 and 3 are usually joined at the distal section of the wing's leading edge by a short ligament. The increased rigidity resulting from this resists the large strains present at the leading edge during flight. The metacarpals are much longer than the phalanges. The thumb has a free claw, used in climbing and grooming. The humerus interlocks with the scapula at the top of the upstroke, so that during the downstroke, the fulcrum of the wing is at the joint between the clavicle and the scapula. This increases the mechanical efficiency of the downstroke (Altenbach and Hermanson, 1987). Aerodynamic forces bulge the wing during flight, and shape is maintained by thin muscles in the membrane, in addition to a network of elastin and collagen fibres. The hindlimb is also long, and supports the posterior part of the flight membrane, which ends somewhere along the tibia/fibula or the proximal part of the foot. The leg has rotated during the evolution of bats, and the foot and claw point backwards. Bats are generally less agile on the ground than other mammals (but not universally so!), but they can use their legs to alter wing shape, and hang in very awkward sites. A special locking mechanism in the tendons of the foot enables bats to hang upside down without effort (Schaffer, 1905; Bennett, 1992). (A thought relevant to the controversy over the origins of bats: do megabats and microbats use the same locking mechanism?) A cartilaginous projection from the ankle, the calcar, extends towards the tail, and supports the trailing edge of the flight membrane.

A small flap of skin, the post-calcarial lobe, may project beyond the calcar. Finally, the long tail is typically incorporated in the flight membrane. but at the other extreme, may be completely free in some species. A number of small muscles extend from the limbs into the flight membrane, and some are found entirely within the membrane. They are used to tension parts of the wing during flight manoeuvres, and aid wing folding at rest.

The wing membrane can be divided into several functional parts. A section of the membrane, the propatagium, lies anterior to the humerus and radius. With the small membrane between digits 2 and 3 (dactylopatagium minus), it acts as a leading edge wing flap, which can be lowered by the thumb and digit 2. These flaps can delay stalling at high angles of attack by maintaining laminar flow over the wings, preserving lift at low flight speeds. The propatagium is largest in slow flying, manoeuvrable bats. The lowering of these flaps increases the camber of the wing (the degree of upward curvature of the wing in cross section), which can also be achieved by flexing digit 5. Increased camber increases lift, at the expense of increased drag. This compromise is worthwhile in slow flying bats, when drag is low. Bats with the broadest wings, e.g. the megabats, in addition to a large propatagium, have short metacarpals, enhancing their ability to camber the wing. Pettigrew and colleagues (see Chapter 1) have suggested that the short metacarpals of megabats are non-adaptive, and attribute their presence to the separate origins of

Fig. 2.11. Skeleton of a greater horseshoe bat, *Rhinolophus ferrumequinum*, to show wing structure.

microbats and megabats. Although their role in changing camber may be adaptive, the observation that the metatarsals of the foot are also short still lends credibility to the argument.

Bats have one other mechanism for preventing stalling at high angles of attack—the wing bones may act as turbulence generators. Stalling occurs when the laminar airstream over the wing separates from the upper surface, creating major turbulence and loss of lift.

Frictional forces slow the air down close to the wing surface, and so there is a gradient of increasing air velocity from the surface out. If this gradient is too steep, separation occurs. Separation can be prevented by introducing controlled microturbulence into the boundary layer, which reduces the velocity gradient. The wing bones project above the upper surface of the wing and, together with hairs on the leading edge of the membrane, may introduce this microturbulence into the boundary layer (Pennycuick, 1971; Norberg, 1972). Fast flying bats have wing bones which are flattened in the plane of the wing to give a smooth profile. Slow flyers, which would benefit from turbulence generation, have rounded bones, which project above the wing surface (Vaughan and Bateman, 1980).

The wing section between the body and the fifth digit is the plagiopatagium (armwing), which provides most of the lift or weight support during flight. The dactylopatagium (handwing), between fingers 2 and 5, generates most of the forward thrust. The uropatagium (tail membrane) provides some lift, and in fact moves up and down synchronously with the wings. It may be used as a brake, and (with the wings) can be used to catch insects in flight. Of course bats are constantly changing direction and this is achieved by subtle movements of the wings and tail membrane. The wings can be moved independently, and by folding one wing rapid tight turns can be made (Fig. 2.12). Analyses of how bats perform some of these manoeuvres have been made by Norberg (1976, 1990).

Because of their hindlimb structure, take-off is a tricky business for many bats, and although most are capable of taking off from level ground, many are not very good at it. They get round the problem by launching themselves from their roost site: after a short free-fall, they are going fast enough to open their wings and gain sufficient lift to stay in the air. Some of the fastest flying bats with long narrow wings fall 5–6 m before unfurling them.

ECOLOGICAL ASPECTS OF FLIGHT

The power required for flight and its relation to flight speed

Figure 2.13 shows the various components which contribute to the aerodynamic power required for flight in relation to airspeed, determined using blade-element theory. Let's see how this graph was arrived at, and what it means in ecological terms. The total power

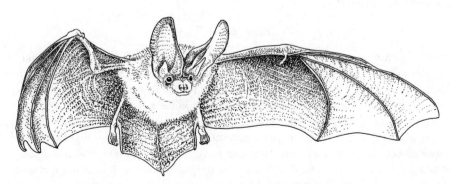

Fig. 2.12.   A turning brown long-eared bat, *Plecotus auritus*.

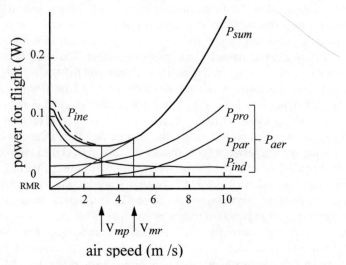

Fig. 2.13. The power required for flight, and its dependence on flight speed for a small (9 g) bat. P_{sum} = total aerodynamic power required in watts (W). P_{pro}, P_{par} and P_{ind} = profile, parasite and induced power respectively. P_{ine} = inertial power. V_{mp} = minimum power speed, the speed at which power consumed per unit time is lowest. Maximum range speed (V_{mr}) is the speed which will take the bat furthest on a given amount of fuel. The mechanical equivalent of resting metabolic rate (RMR) is also indicated, with RMR set at zero (from Norberg, 1987, 1990).

required for flight is the sum of the aerodynamic power and the inertial power. The aerodynamic power (P_{aer}) is needed to generate the lift and thrust which keep the bat in the air, and move it forward. The inertial power (P_{ine}) is needed to move the wings up and down, and is thought to be negligible at all but the slowest speeds, since wing inertia is turned into useful aerodynamic work at the end of the downstroke (Norberg, 1987). It may be significant during slow flight and hovering, but is unlikely to be more than a minor component of total flight power (P_{sum}).

$$P_{sum} = P_{aer} + P_{ine}$$

The aerodynamic power has three components: parasite power (P_{par}), profile power (P_{pro}), and induced power (P_{ind}).

$$P_{aer} = P_{par} + P_{pro} + P_{ind}$$

Parasite power is needed to overcome the drag on the body. It is proportional to the frontal area of the body, and increases dramatically with flight speed (α speed^3). Streamlining is therefore important, particularly to fast flying bats, if parasite power is to be minimised. Profile power overcomes the drag on the wings, and increases with speed in a similar fashion to parasite power. It also increases with wing area. The induced power is that needed for lift and thrust generation and decreases with flight speed. It is the major power component of slow flight and hovering. Induced power also increases with increasing body weight, and decreases as wingspan increases. Power requirements will therefore be minimal in a streamlined bat (low P_{par}), with low body weight (low P_{ind}), long wings (low P_{ind}) and high aspect ratio (low area, low P_{pro}).

Box 1—power for flight

It is worth putting down a few equations which describe the factors determining flight power. They will help you understand the discussion of wing morphology in relation to lifestyle which follows this section.

(1) $P_{ind} \propto Mg^{3/2}/b$ in hovering flight
(2) $P_{ind} \propto Mg^2/b^2V$ in forward flight
(3) $P_{pro} \propto b^3S/T^3$ in hovering flight (T is approx. $\propto b$, thus $P_{pro} \propto S$)
(4) $P_{pro} \propto SV^3$ in forward flight
(5) $P_{par} \propto AV^3$ in forward flight

M = mass of bat, g = acceleration due to gravity, b = wingspan, V = forward velocity of bat, S = wing area, T = duration of a wing beat, A = frontal area of bat's body.

The sum of all the power components, P_{sum}, has a distinct minimum at a speed characteristic of each species. What does all this mean to bat behaviour? Let's look at some examples. If a bat is on migration, with no real opportunity to feed, it wants to go as far as possible for the minimum cost. In other words, it must maximise airspeed and minimise power requirements. This is its maximum range speed (V_{mr}) and can be found by drawing a tangent from the origin of the graph to the P_{sum} line (Fig. 2.13). If food is plentiful, and the bat is in the

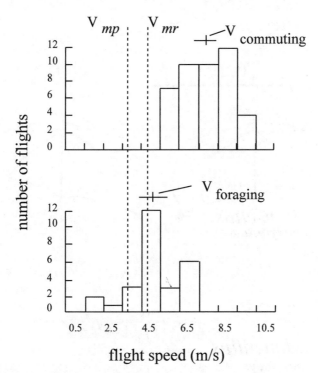

Fig. 2.14. Observed commuting and foraging flight speeds of the pipistrelle bat in relation to calculated minimum power (V_{mp}) and maximum range (V_{mr}) speeds (from Jones and Rayner, 1989).

air for a long time, but not in a hurry, then it may want to fly at a speed which keeps the cost per unit time as low as possible: i.e. maintain the minimum cost of transport. This is the lowest point on the P_{sum} line, the minimum power speed, V_{mp}. A foraging bat wants to keep transport costs down, but it may need to fly faster than V_{mp} to cover sufficient ground to catch sufficient food. This will be a delicate equation for the bat to balance, but it should fly somewhere between V_{mp} and V_{mr}. When a bat leaves the roost to fly to its foraging site, it may be important to get there fast—to maximise foraging time when the insect populations peak at dusk, and also to avoid predators. It might then exceed V_{mr}. Is there any evidence that bats actually follow these rules? The answer is yes. Work on pipistrelle bats,

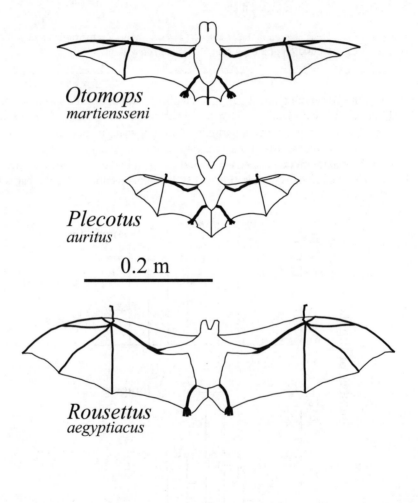

Otomops
martiensseni

Plecotus
auritus

0.2 m

Rousettus
aegyptiacus

Mimetillus
moloneyi

Fig. 2.15. Variation in the wing shapes of bats.

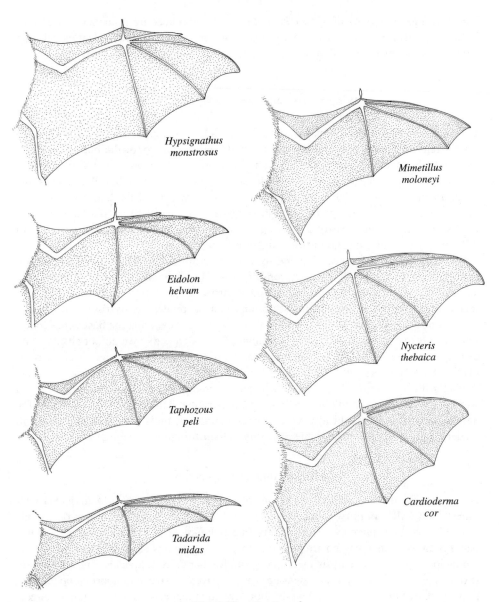

Hypsignathus monstrosus

Mimetillus moloneyi

Eidolon helvum

Nycteris thebaica

Taphozous peli

Tadarida midas

Cardioderma cor

Fig. 2.15. *Continued.*

Pipistrellus pipistrellus, (Fig. 2.14) by Jones and Rayner (1989b) shows that individuals commuting to and from the roost fly significantly faster than V_{mr}, and foraging bats fly close to V_{mr}, as predicted. Daubenton's bat (*Myotis daubentonii*) flies between V_{mp} and V_{mr} when foraging (Jones and Rayner, 1988), but the similar *M. adversus* foraged at speeds slightly above V_{mr} (Jones and Rayner, 1991). The nectarivore *Leptonycteris curasoae* commutes at speeds between V_{mp} and V_{mr} (Sahley *et al.*, 1993). There are complications however: e.g. the speeds of *M. daubentonii* and *M. adversus* are influenced by aerodynamic 'ground effects', because they fly close to water. Furthermore, different models (e.g. Norberg and Rayner, 1987; Pennycuick, 1989) may give slightly different results.

Wing morphology and foraging strategy

Bats have wings of different shapes and sizes and a few examples are shown in Fig. 2.15. The differences are largely a reflection of the foraging strategy of the bat—where they feed, how they feed, and what they feed on. There are two main ways in which wings can vary. First, wing area can be large or small relative to the size of the bat. We describe this using a measurement called wing loading. This is the weight of the bat, divided by the total area of its flight membrane. A high wing loading means we have a large bat with relatively small wings. Secondly, wings can be short and broad (low aspect ratio, AR = span^2/area) or long and narrow (high AR).

Other structural differences in wing form are also important. The relative lengths and areas of the arm-and handwing vary considerably. The shape of the wing tip is also variable—it may be broad and gently rounded, or narrow and pointed. All of these measurements tell us about a bat's flight style, and can be related to its foraging strategy. Evolution is working on bats to ensure that each species is evolving the best wings for the job. The biggest problem we have explaining wing design is that we do not always know exactly what that job is. There may also be considerations beyond the purely aerodynamic: the best wings for a particular flight style may not be suited to another aspect of the bat's lifestyle. However, a general picture is emerging, which we'll look at after a word of caution. For the sake of analysis and illustration, bats are put into particular foraging categories. It should always be remembered that most bat species are flexible feeders, and can show considerable plasticity in their foraging strategies.

Wing loading and aspect ratio

Let's start with the two major components of wing morphology, wing loading (WL) and aspect ratio (AR). With two variables, we can have four possible combinations, represented by the four quadrants of Fig. 2.16. In this figure, species whose flight/behaviour patterns are well documented are placed in their appropriate positions on a scatter plot of a principal component analysis by Norberg and Rayner (1987). Species referred to in the text are named. The analysis compensates for the effects of size, an important point, since mass increases in proportion to length^3, but wing area increases in proportion to length^2, so that bigger bats tend to have higher wing loadings, if they remain geometrically similar (that is, all parts of the body increase in the same proportions). We will come back to matters of size a little later. The equations in Box 1 in the last section should help you in the discussion which follows.

The higher the WL the faster the bat must fly, if its small wings are to generate the lift needed to stay airborne. However, profile drag on the small wings is low (eqn. 4), so less energy is wasted, and flight efficiency is high. High WL is often found in combination with a high AR: the narrow wings are more aerodynamically efficient than broad ones of the same total area, since induced power is low (eqn. 2). So, if a bat regularly flies long

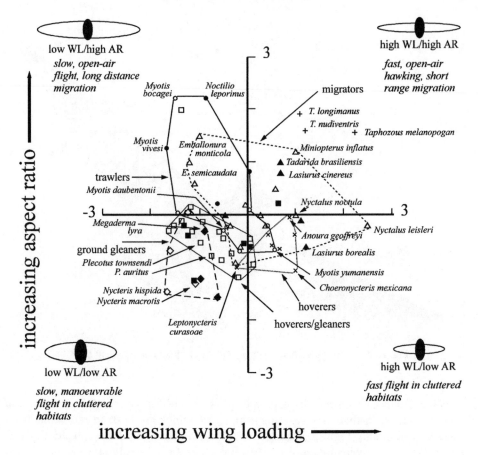

low WL/high AR
*slow, open-air
flight, long distance
migration*

high WL/high AR
*fast, open-air
hawking, short
range migration*

increasing aspect ratio →

Myotis
bocagei

Noctilio
leporinus

migrators

+ *T. longimanus*
T. nudiventris
+
+ *Taphozous melanopogan*

Myotis
vivesi

*Emballonura
monticola*

△ *Miniopterus inflatus*

▲ *Tadarida brasiliensis*
▲ *Lasiurus cinereus*

E. semicaudata

△

trawlers →
Myotis daubentonii

■ *Nyctalus noctula*

-3

3

Megaderma
lyra

× *Anoura geoffreyi*

△ *Nyctalus leisleri*

ground gleaners

Lasiurus borealis

Plecotus townsendi
P. auritus

Myotis yumanensis

Nycteris hispida
Nycteris macrotis

Choeronycteris mexicana

hoverers

Leptonycteris
curasoae

hoverers/gleaners

low WL/low AR

*slow, manoeuvrable
flight in cluttered
habitats*

high WL/low AR

*fast flight in cluttered
habitats*

increasing wing loading →

open symbols = insectivores *or* short range migrators
closed symbols = also take vertebrates *or* long range migrators

Fig. 2.16. Wing loading and aspect ratio combination in bats. A principal component analysis (adapted from Figs 11–15, Norberg and Rayner, 1987).

distances to feed, it needs to be fast to get to the feeding site quickly (high WL), and it needs to waste as little energy as possible getting there (high AR and WL). These bats are also streamlined to keep down parasite power (eqn. 5). Bats which fall into this category include *Nyctalus, Lasiurus,* and *Miniopterus* species among the vespertilionids and *Tadarida* species from the molossids. The best examples are perhaps some *Taphozous* species from the emballonurids and other molossids (Figs 2.16 and 2.17). They feed in the open, catching insects on the wing. Their fast flight means that they cannot turn tight circles. They would not be good at hunting among trees, or at hovering to pick insects off foliage.

These, and other bats may fly long distances during migration. Energy efficient, high AR wings are therefore useful, and so too is a high WL if high speed and a short migration time are important (e.g. noctules, Fig. 2.16). If the bat is not in a hurry, or

Fig. 2.17.   Free-tailed bat, *Otomops martiensseni*, a fast, efficient flyer.

migration distances are short, its wing area does not need to be so small in relation to its body weight. In this case very long, high AR wings are best, to reduce induced power to a minimum (eqn. 2), and WL may be quite low (e.g. the emballonurids *E. monticolla* and *E. semicaudata*, Fig. 2.16). Long-distance, fast flying migrants should have the longest, high AR wings, with a high WL (e.g. *Tadarida brasiliensis*, Fig. 2.16). These species all need to fly in the open, since their long wings would be a hindrance in vegetation.

High AR and low WL are also found in fish-eating bats such as *Noctilio leporinus* and *Myotis vivesi* (Figs 2.16 and 2.18). Flying in the open over water, with no need to make tight turns, they can have long, efficient wings. WL is low so that they can carry heavy pay loads—the fish they feed on. The insectivorous trawlers tend to have average AR and WL (e.g. *Myotis daubentonii* and *M. yumanensis*), although *Myotis bocagei* is an interesting and extreme exception (Fig. 2.16).

Low WL, in combination with low AR is found in many bats which feed among vegetation. This combination allows them to fly slowly without stalling, make tight turns, and even hover: at low speed profile power is low even with a large wing area (eqn. 4). All of the bats on this part of the plot are gleaners and hoverers. The low wing loading also enables them to carry heavy prey, and take off easily, even if they are carrying prey. Short wings are also useful when taking off from the ground, and moving in cluttered environments, in addition to conferring high manoeuvrability. The slit-faced bats (Nycteridae) are typically ground gleaners, and have the lowest AR/WL combination (Fig. 2.16). Next to them on Fig. 2.16 are the long-eared bats (*Plecotus* species,

Fig. 2.18. *Noctilio leporinus*, the fisherman bat.

Fig. 2.19), representatives of a group of gleaners which take food from the ground and from foliage, and which may hover.

The specialist hoverers fall into the low AR/high WL quadrant. Long wings would be aerodynamically more efficient for hovering, since induced power decreases with increasing wingspan (eqn. 1), but they are a hindrance in a cluttered environment, and limit manoeuvrability. These bats are principally nectar and pollen feeders and are found among the phyllostomids (e.g. *Glossophaga, Anoura, Leptonycteris, Choeronycteris,* (Figs 2.16 and 2.20)) and the smaller megabats (e.g. *Macroglossus* species). The high WL gives them high flight speeds, an important factor when food supply is patchy and commuting time between patches must be minimised—some of these bats dart from flower to flower like hummingbirds. The long wings ideal for hovering have been compromised by the need for speed and possibly access to flowers.

Carnivorous species, which are essentially big-time gleaners, have low AR and low WL, for the same reasons as their insectivorous cousins. A good example is *Megaderma lyra* (Figs 2.16 and 2.21). Many of these bats have large ears for detecting prey without echolocation. Big ears would produce a lot of drag, so they are generally only found on slow flying bats.

Arm- and handwings, wingtip shape, and camber

There are more variables to consider than WL and AR, as I said at the beginning of this section: e.g. relative lengths and areas of the arm- and handwings, wing camber, and wingtip shape. Baagøe (1987) and Norberg and Rayner (1987) have carried out the most extensive analyses of these characteristics. Norberg and Rayner (1987) have shown that short, rounded wingtips are found on slow flying, manoeuvrable bats, in association with low AR and low WL. To be *manoeuvrable*, that is to have a small turning circle, a bat must fly slowly. The size of the turning circle increases with flight speed, hence the association with low WL. Bats which need to be manoeuvrable are usually those which

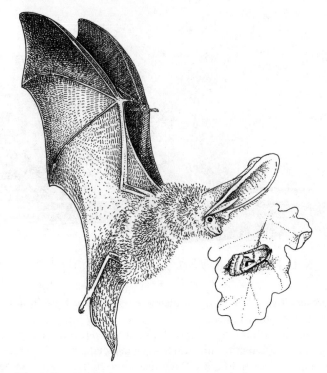

Fig. 2.19.   Brown long-eared bat, *Plecotus auritus*, a gleaner.

Fig. 2.20.   A hovering nectar feeder, the long-tongued bat, *Glossophaga soricina*.

forage in a cluttered environment, hence the low AR. These bats also tend to have high camber wings, and have the ability to control camber by flexing digit 5 and/or lowering the hind-limbs. The long-eared bats of the genus *Plecotus* fit into this category.

The fast, efficient flyers hawking on insects in the open, the high WL, high AR species, are not very manoeuvrable. However they often have pointed wingtips, which increases their

Fig. 2.21.   The Indian false vampire bat, *Megaderma lyra*, a carnivorous ground gleaner.

agility. Agile bats have the ability to rapidly initiate a roll, altering their flight path. The relationship between wing morphology and agility is complex, but some important factors can be identified. The maximum angular acceleration, α_{max}, (i.e. the fastest roll) is given by:

$$\alpha_{max} = \tau/J$$

where τ = rolling torque, J = total roll moment of inertia (the inertia resisting the roll).

$$\tau = Mgb\lambda$$

where M = mass of bat, g = acceleration due to gravity, b = wingspan, and λ = moment of distribution of lift across the wingspan. Thus,

$$\alpha_{max} = Mgb\ \lambda/J$$

To initiate a roll λ should be large, and J should be small. The wings perhaps play a more dominant role in determining J than the body (Norberg and Rayner, 1987). Wing inertia can be minimised by having pointed wings, that is by having the 'heavy' carpel joint shifted towards the body. This seems to be the important factor in fast flying bats such as the noctule, *Nyctalus noctula*. The pointed wingtip also increases aerodynamic efficiency (by reducing wingtip vortices), reducing flight costs, so it is a feature seen in migrating species.

It is also possible to have good low speed agility. Horseshoe bats, *Rhinolophus* species. have high roll rates, yet they have small, rounded wingtips, which increase inertia. This is compensated for by the high camber and low WL, which gives them extra lift on the handwing, and therefore gives them a high λ. This ability to roll rapidly at low speeds is used by horseshoe bats, and those of similar morphology, such as *Myotis nattereri*, *Barbastella barbastellus*, and *Cardioderma cor* to roll into their roosting positions with remarkable agility.

Baagøe (1987) categorised the 14 species of bat found in Scandinavia on the basis of five morphological measurements, roughly speaking: wing camberability, size and move-ment of propatagium, mass, AR, and wingtip shape. The bats included fast aerial hawkers like the noctule (*Nyctalus noctula*), the gleaning long-eared bat (*Plecotus auritus*), the trawling Daubenton's bat (*Myotis daubentonii*), and small, slow hawkers, such as the whiskered bat (*Myotis mystacinus*) and the pipistrelle (*Pipistrellus pipistrellus*). Predictions about their flight performance and foraging habits were made on the basis of these measurements and compared with field observations of each species in 'search phase' flight. Correlations between observed and predicted behaviour were generally good. Studies of this nature are of value in attempts to look at the structure of bat communities.

Body mass

There is one morphological feature we have yet to cover, the size of the bat. So far we been concerned with largely size-independent variables, such as WL, AR, and wingtip shape. Although bats range in size from 1.5 g to 1.5 kg, the range is much greater in birds: 1.5 g to 15 kg. Why are there no really big bats? The answer lies in the effects of size on flight performance (Norberg and Rayner, 1987). On the positive side, bigger bats fly faster, and the cost of transport decreases with increasing size. However, the mechan-ical power required for flight increases more rapidly with size than the power available from the muscle, so there has to be a size beyond which flight is impossible. This is around 15 kg, and explains the upper limit for flying birds, but not for bats. Wing inertia increases with size, so large bats are not very agile. Manoeuvrability also declines with increasing size—one good reason why bats which have to chase insects are small. Since prey are detected at short-range by echolocation, high manoeuvrability enables bats to turn and capture prey detected at the short ranges over which echolocation operates (Barclay and Brigham, 1991). Since most bats link breathing and echolocation pulse emission with the wingbeat, very large bats, with low wingbeat frequencies, would have low pulse emission rates: perhaps too low for effective prey capture and orientation (Jones, 1994). Increased manoeuvrability also accounts for the small size of nectarivores such as the glossophagine phyllostomids which hover in front of flowers. The macroglos-sine megabats are larger, and often perch to feed from flowers. Large bats tend to take large food items, bigger fruit eaters take bigger fruits, and the larger microbats take large invertebrate or vertebrate prey.

Aerodynamic factors do not appear to set a lower limit on bat size, but there may be mechanical constraints in skeletal strength. One important factor is the surface area to volume ratio, which increases as size decreases. The large surface area of a small endotherm loses heat quickly, and the small volume cannot generate sufficient heat to maintain a high body temperature. Small mammals have to eat constantly to meet the high metabolic demand, and below a certain size, they simply do not have sufficient foraging time (McNab, 1982).

3 Echolocation

What is echolocation? Sound generation and perception by microbats—anatomy and physiology. Sound for the non-physicist. Echolocation pulse characteristics: FM pulses—basic properties. Autocorrelation function and range acuity. Spectral changes in echoes and target fine structure. Movement detection using FM spectral changes. Target location in 3-D space. Can bats intercept prey? CF pulses—basic properties. Doppler shift and velocity determination in CF bats. Prey detection and identification using CF pulses. How do bats avoid being confused by other bats' sonar? Auditory adaptations, and the neural basis of echolocation. Field studies—evidence for prey selection. Echolocation and navigation. The cost of echolocation—the linkage between the wing beat, respiration, and pulse emission. Hunting by other methods. The ecology of echolocation: interactions between flight, food, and foraging habits.

WHAT IS ECHOLOCATION?

Echolocation is a complex and highly evolved process which has given bats the ability to exploit an ecological niche closed to all but a few animal groups—the night sky. Echolocation is not unique to bats, but it has arguably reached its evolutionary peak in these mammals. What is echolocation? A simple definition is that it is the analysis by an animal of the echoes of its own emitted sound waves, by which it builds a sound-picture of its immediate environment. A number of animals use sound in this way, and many use high frequency sounds or ultrasounds, beyond the range of human hearing. These include, as well as the bats, the Cetacea (whales and dolphins: see Au, 1993) and the insectivores (shrews and tenrecs). It is not clear how sophisticated ultrasonic echolocation is in the insectivores but there is no doubt about its value in cetaceans. Ultrasonic sounds are also emitted by some rodents and a number of marsupials, but we do not know if they are used for echolocation, or just for communication (Sales and Pye, 1974).

High frequency sound is not essential for echolocation, although as we will see shortly, it does confer some major advantages. A number of animals echolocate with lower frequency sounds. The best known examples are the cave dwelling birds (Fig. 3.1): the South American oilbird or guacharo (*Steatornis caripensis*) and the South-East Asian, Indo-Australian cave swiftlets (*Collocalia* species, Fig. 3.1), which use 2–10 kHz sounds of 1 ms duration, at repetition rates of up to 20 Hz. The birds use these loud, audible sounds to locate their nests or roosting sites in dark caves, but switch off when there is enough light to see by (Sales and Pye, 1974; Pettigrew, 1985; Fullard *et al.*, 1993).

Megabats of the genus *Rousettus* (Fig. 3.1) echolocate within their cave roosts, generating sound by clicking the tongue. The pulses are short (1–2 ms), of high frequency 10–60 kHz, at a pulse repetition rate of around 7 Hz. Their navigational ability has been studied in the lab, and although it does not match that of the microbats, it is well developed. I am not going to say any more about megabats—microbats are much more

Fig. 3.1. *Rousettus aegyptiacus*, an echolocating megabat, and two echolocating birds, *Steatornis caripensis* and *Collocalia fuciphaga*.

interesting. For those who are interested, the best general account can be found in Sales and Pye (1974). Throughout history, people have wondered just how bats navigate in the dark, but real scientific enquiry started in the 1790s, when Spallanzani performed some meticulous experiments which clearly indicated that hearing was crucial to orientation, and sight largely unimportant. No-one knew about ultrasound, so a plausible explanation wasn't found until this century. In the late 1930's Griffin cracked the code with the first generation of ultrasonic detectors, which he borrowed from a physicist colleague. Griffin went on to do much of the early pioneering work on echolocation, and a fascinating account can be read in his book *Listening in the Dark* (Griffin, 1958, reprinted 1986).

SOUND GENERATION AND PERCEPTION IN MICROBATS

First of all, we need to look at how bats generate their sonar calls, and how they detect the echoes. In common with other mammals, sounds are generated in the larynx. The larynx in microbats is proportionally larger than in megabats and most other mammals, but the mechanism of action is the same: air passing over the vocal chords makes them vibrate, and the muscles of the larynx are used to adjust the tension in the vocal chords, and change the frequency of the sound. Bats emit their calls through the mouth or the nostrils. Those using the nostrils often have complex noseleaves: folds of skin and carti-lage of varying complexity, which may extend over a large part of their face (see Fig. 3.2). In many species, the noseleaf appears to act as an acoustic lens, focusing the sound into a narrow beam in front of the bat.

Microbats have to hear well, so they generally have large external ears or pinnae. They may also have a tragus (Fig. 3.2), a cartilaginous projection from the base of the ear, which sits inside the pinna. The ear/tragus combination may be designed to limit the major receptive field to an area 30–40° either side of the midline, and improve the direc-tionality or sensitivity to incoming echoes.

Figure 3.3 shows a cross section of the ear structures of a microbat, but the basic layout is common to all mammals. Sound passes along the canal from the external ear, and vibrates the eardrum or tympanic membrane. This is only 2–11 μm thick in microbats. The vibrations are passed along the malleus, incus, and stapes, the 3 ear ossicles, to the oval window. The higher the frequency of the echolocation pulses used by a bat, the smaller the area of the eardrum, and the smaller and lighter the ossicles—because they need to be able to vibrate more rapidly. The external and middle ear cavities are air filled, the inner ear is fluid filled.

Vibrations of the oval window are transmitted along the spiral canal of the cochlea. The cochlea does the work of sifting and categorising the sound by frequency before the brain interprets it. It consists of three canals which spiral in parallel, and between them is the organ of Corti. From the base of the spiral to its apex, cells in the organ of Corti respond to sounds of decreasing frequency. Microbats have 2.5–3.5 complete turns, rela-tive to the 1.75 of megabats and primates, and the basal turns are particularly large. Sound waves vibrate the tectorial membrane, which triggers the tiny cilia on the sensory cells. Electrical impulses from these cells pass along the auditory nerve to the midbrain for initial signal processing, before final processing in the auditory cortex.

Recorded from <1 m, a pipistrelle's echolocation pulses may be up to 120 dB: loud enough to be uncomfortable if we could hear it. High frequency sounds rapidly decrease in amplitude or loudness as they travel through the air, or to use the technical term, they are rapidly attenuated. This presents the bat with a challenge. They need very sensitive hearing to detect the very weak echoes returning from their insect prey, and their hearing is in fact very acute. But, how do they avoid deafening themselves by the very loud

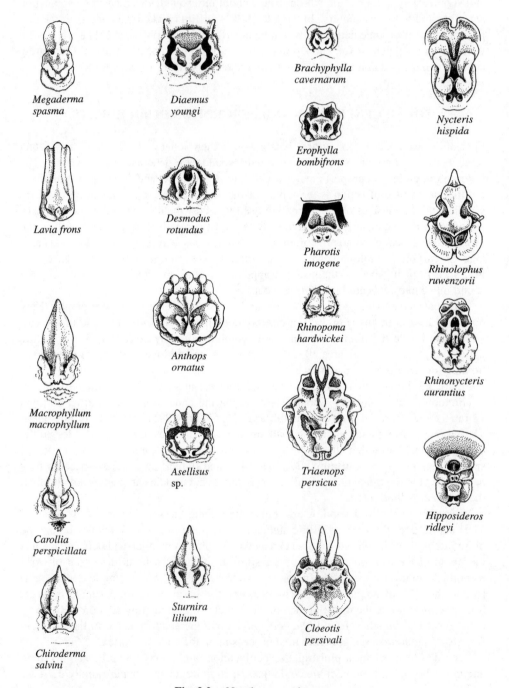

Megaderma spasma

Lavia frons

Macrophyllum macrophyllum

Carollia perspicillata

Chiroderma salvini

Diaemus youngi

Desmodus rotundus

Anthops ornatus

Asellisus sp.

Sturnira lilium

Brachyphylla cavernarum

Erophylla bombifrons

Pharotis imogene

Rhinopoma hardwickei

Triaenops persicus

Cloeotis persivali

Nycteris hispida

Rhinolophus ruwenzorii

Rhinonycteris aurantius

Hipposideros ridleyi

Fig. 3.2. Noseleaves and ears.

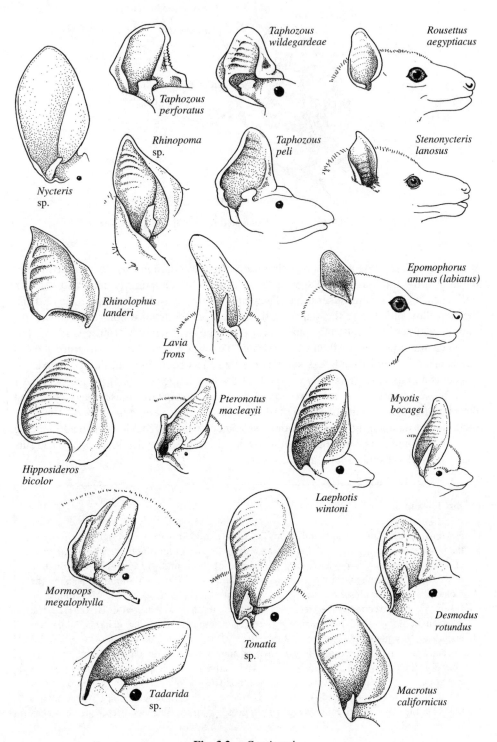

Fig. 3.2. *Continued.*

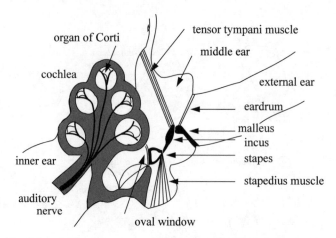

Fig. 3.3. Auditory apparatus (adapted from Hill and Smith, 1984).

sounds they emit? Bats do not emit echolocation sounds continuously: they come in short bursts. During the burst, some species make themselves temporarily deaf, and between bursts hearing is at its most sensitive. There are two tiny muscles in the ear. One of them, the stapedius, attaches to the stapes. Just before a bat emits an echolocation pulse, this muscle contracts and pulls the stapes away from the oval window (Henson, 1965). The sound cannot now be passed on to the cochlea, which is a very delicate structure and can be damaged by loud sounds. As soon as the pulse has been emitted, the bat relaxes its stapedius and its hearing is fully restored. In the final stages of taking an insect, a bat's sonar pulse repetition rate may exceed 200 Hz, and its stapedius muscle may operate at the same frequency—one of the highest rates recorded in vertebrate muscle. There are other sound dampening specialisations associated with the cochlea—instead of being fused to the skull as is common in mammals, it is loosely suspended in its cavity, and surrounded by blood sinuses and fatty deposits.

Box 1—sound

For those lacking any background in physics, this is a good place for a brief description of the physics of sound, and for defining some of the important terminology. Sound is a wave of vibration passing through the air. The source of the sound, for example the vibrating larynx of a bat, sends out a wave of compression of the air at each vibration, packing the molecules of the air closer together (Fig. 3.4a). The number of times a wave of compression is sent out every second is the frequency of the sound, and is measured in Hertz (Hz). The wavelength of the sound, the distance between each compression, is the reciprocal of the frequency or 1/frequency.

Sound is normally represented by a wave, as shown in Fig. 3.4b. You can think of it as a vibration travelling over a water surface. The frequency is simply the number of waves which pass a given point in space in one second. The wave is passing through the air at a speed of 340 ms^{-1}, the speed of sound. As frequency increases, and since sound always travels at the same speed, more waves pass a given point in one second. This means that as

(a)

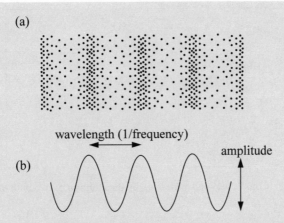

wavelength (1/frequency)

amplitude

(b)

Fig. 3.4. Sound compression of molecules in the air in sound generation, and its graphical representation as a sine wave, having a frequency and amplitude.

frequency goes up, wavelength goes down. The wavelength is the distance between two corresponding points on a wave, say from one peak to the next. Low frequency sounds are low pitched, similar to the sound of a double bass. High frequency sounds are high pitched like a violin. Human hearing ranges from around 40 Hz up to 20 kHz. Echolocation calls of most bats fall somewhere in the range 20 kHz to 120 kHz. The other main feature of a sound wave is its height or amplitude, that's the distance between peak and trough. The amplitude is determined by the amount of energy put into the sound. High energy sounds have high amplitudes, and are loud. Sound intensity is measure in decibels (dB).

The waveform shown in Fig. 3.4b is the most simple, a sine wave. It is a pure tone, the sound you get from a tuning fork. Most sounds are more complicated, as shown in Fig. 3.5.

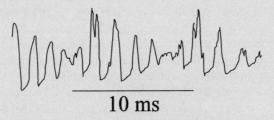

10 ms

Fig. 3.5. A natural sound—human voice.

Why are they so complicated? Each is made up of sounds of more than one wavelength and more than one amplitude. Pure tones are very rare in nature; most biological sounds are more complex, and are determined by the structures which make them, the human larynx, or a grasshopper rubbing its legs together, for example. Each sound will have a fundamental frequency, that is the lowest frequency. Let's say it is 1000 Hz. All the other components of this complex sound are multiples of this fundamental frequency, 2000, 3000, 4000 Hz, and so on. These are called the harmonics. 2000 Hz is the second harmonic, 3000 the third etc. Each can have a different amplitude or loudness, and this can complicate the final waveform

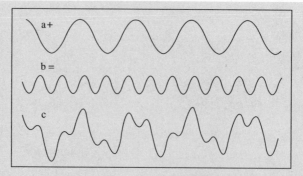

Fig. 3.6.   Complex sounds generated by the addition of two pure tones.

further, when they are all added together to give waveforms like that shown in Fig. 3.5. A simple case, the addition of two pure tones of different amplitude and frequency, is illustrated in Fig. 3.6.

ECHOLOCATION CALLS

Bats are clearly very good at echolocation. They have had a long time to perfect it, and we can probably assume that evolution has ensured that the characteristics of a bat's echolocation signals are close to the optimum for the job. A good review of the general principles of echolocation has been written by Simmons *et al.* (1975). What follows is a basic description of the properties of echolocation signals and their functions.

Let's start with frequency and wavelength. Why are high frequency calls used? There are several answers: let's quickly cover the minor ones first. To begin with, relatively few other natural sounds are so high, so interference from other natural sources is minimal. Furthermore, high frequency sounds do not travel very far in air before becoming very quiet. Energy absorption increases exponentially with frequency, and a bat echolocating at 30 kHz is unlikely to have a range exceeding 30 m, decreasing to 10 m at 100 kHz and 4 m at 200 kHz (Lawrence and Simmons, 1982a). The use of high frequencies may be one way in which bats avoid interfering with each other's echolocation. They may also enable bats to get very close to prey which can hear. High frequency sound is also less likely to alert some predators. However, by far the most important answer lies in target discrimination. This is technical jargon for how small an insect the bat can detect. As we saw earlier, high frequency sounds have very short wavelengths. Sounds of 100, 50, and 10 kHz have wavelengths of 3.4, 6.8, and 34 mm respectively. The best sound for detecting an object is one with a wavelength similar in length to that of the object. Bats catch small insects, and therefore need short wavelength, high frequency sounds. Behavioural experiments show that little brown bats, *Myotis lucifugus*, respond to 3 mm diameter wires by changing their sonar pulses when over 2 m away, and 0.18 mm wires from 0.9 m (Grinnell and Griffin, 1958). Individual fruit flies elicit a response when up to 1 m away (Griffin *et al.*, 1960). The bat may detect the target earlier, but not respond with an altered sonar signal, so these are minimum estimates of detection distances. In more subtle tests, Kick (1982) showed that the big brown bat, *Eptesicus fuscus*, detected 19 mm diameter spheres at 5.1 m, and

4.8 mm spheres at 2.9 m. Detection of the echoes occurred close to the threshold of hearing, and possibly involved integration of information from several pulses. Ambient noise and clutter in the field almost certainly leads to poorer performance, but as we will see, there are compensatory factors.

Bats emit echolocation sounds in pulses. These pulses are usually described as being frequency modulated (FM) or constant frequency (CF), but many, perhaps most, species of microbat use combinations of the two. Few bats use pure CF calls, and the terms broadband (for FM) and narrowband (for most CF) are often more appropriate. Various authors have categorised pulse patterns in various ways, and some of these classifications do have some functional value, but it should be remembered that simple labels are often used for complex calls. I will start with generalised descriptions of basic FM and CF echolocation: other patterns will come up as specific, real examples throughout the chapter. A sample of echolocation pulses is shown in Fig. 3.7.

Frequency modulated calls

Basic properties

In its simplest form, a broadband FM pulse is characterised by a short, steep sweep down the frequencies, from about 60 to 30 kHz over 5 ms in many temperate vespertilionids for example. Frequency modulation or FM simply means that the frequency of the pulse is not constant, but altered or modulated. The frequency versus time curves, or sonograms, of several species are shown in Fig. 3.7.

Broadband FM pulses are short: typically 2–5 ms long, and often less than 0.2 ms. Why are short pulses used? Bats detect objects in their surroundings by listening to the echo of each emitted pulse. Since sound travels at 340 m s, the echo from an object 1 m away returns 5.9 ms after the emitted pulse. If the pulse was more than 5.9 ms long, then the bat would be listening to the echo before it had finished emitting the pulse. In most bats which use FM sonar, neural mechanisms of echo interpretation demand that pulse/echo overlap is avoided. Having detected its prey from the echo a bat wants to know how far away it is. Since sound waves always travel at the same speed through air, by measuring the pulse-echo delay the bat can calculate the distance to the insect (Simmons, 1971). So, a bat emits a short pulse, waits for the echo, calculates the distance to the insect, emits another short pulse to update its information, and so on.

The sequence of events leading to a successful catch is shown in Fig. 3.8. Both the duration and the bandwidth, or range of frequencies swept in the pulse, change. During the search phase, as a bat hunts for its prey, but before it detects it, it emits pulses at a frequency of about 10 Hz (the frequency of the wing beat and respiration, which are coupled). When it detects its prey the bat enters the approach phase: as it gets closer, there is a shorter distance between bat and prey, and therefore less time between pulse and echo, so the pulses have to get shorter to avoid overlap. The bat also updates its information about the whereabouts of the insect more frequently, so its pulse emission rate gets progressively faster. In the terminal phase, pulses may be emitted at frequencies of more than 200 Hz, and each pulse may be only a fraction of a millisecond long. This explains the need for short duration pulses, but what about the frequency modulation? The explanation for that goes hand in hand with another feature.

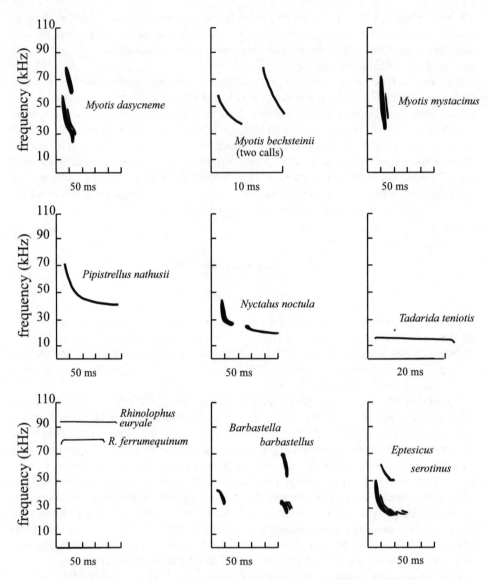

Fig. 3.7. Bat sonograms. Time versus frequency plots of echolocation calls.

The pattern I have shown in Fig. 3.8a is very simple—a sweep involving a single fundamental frequency. This type of pulse is sometimes used by bats, but in many cases, it is more complex. Fig. 3.8b shows one example of these more complex patterns. FM signals provide much more detailed 3-D pictures of cluttered environments than constant frequency signals—they are better at discerning target distance, and details of target structure. Bats therefore increase the bandwidth of their pulses when they detect and attack an insect. They do this in two ways: by increasing the range of frequencies swept over by the fundamental, and by introducing harmonics. The lower lines in Fig. 3.8b are the FM sweeps of the fundamental frequency. The lines above them are components of the second and third harmonics (not all frequencies are of the same intensity, so parts of

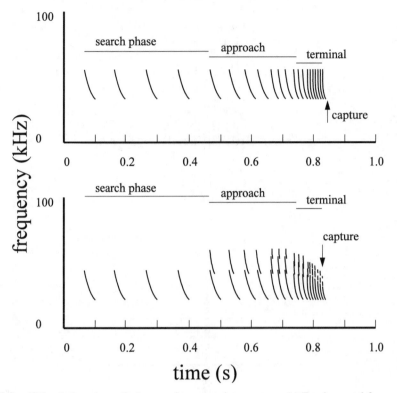

Fig. 3.8. FM echolocation call changes from search to capture. (a) Fundamental frequency only. (b) With harmonics.

the harmonics may not be detected). Other changes in pulse pattern may be seen during approach and capture. Since low frequency sounds attenuate less in air than higher frequencies, some species will put more energy into the lower harmonics during the search phase, but enhance the higher harmonics as they approach their prey for finer detail and target ranging (Simmons, 1971; 1979). Why are large bandwidth FM calls with multiple harmonics so well suited to fine discrimination?

The autocorrelation function

A bat's ability to resolve small differences in the distances to two objects is related to the properties of its echolocation call, in particular, the bandwidth and the average wavelength (or period) of the component frequencies. These two properties can be described by the autocorrelation function (ACR) of the echolocation pulse (Simmons, 1971). I am not going to try to explain this function in detail; for those interested, Simmons (1971) and Simmons and Stein (1980) give excellent accounts. The bottom line is as follows. The bat behaves, to a first approximation, as if it stores the emitted pulse (in the inferior colliculus of the midbrain), and cross-correlates it with the returning echo. Figure 3.9 shows ACRs for two pulse types, a 1 ms duration 5 kHz (25–20 kHz) bandwidth pulse in (a), and a 1 ms, 30 kHz (50–20 kHz) bandwidth pulse with its second harmonic (100–40 kHz) in (b).

The ACR describes the average period T of the signal (the reciprocal of the average fundamental frequency), which decreases with increasing frequency. The ACR also

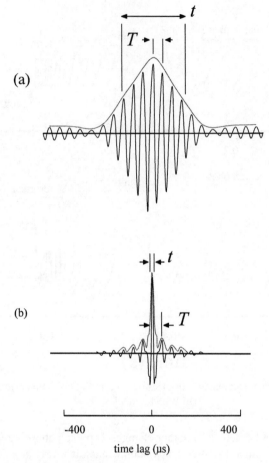

Fig. 3.9. Autocorrelation functions. (a) Narrowband, pure tone. (b) Broadband with harmonics. T = average period, $t \approx 1$/bandwidth (see text for further details) (from Fig. 4, Simmons and Stein, 1980).

defines t, the width of the envelope at half its maximum height. This is approximately the reciprocal of the signal's bandwidth. The introduction of FM higher harmonics decreases the height of the side peaks, reducing t. We can think of the bat's perceptual acuity as its ability to determine unambiguously the timing (i.e. position) of the peak of the ACR. The narrower the central peak, and the lower the side peaks, the more acute the bat's target ranging. From what has been said, it is clear that this will be achieved if the band-width is large (i.e. t is small), the average fundamental frequency is high (T is also small), and FM harmonics are present (the side peaks are of low amplitude). This is only part of the story—that for a stationary target. Simmons and Stein (1980) show how this call structure also minimises errors due to moving targets.

In Fig. 3.10a, the relationship between call bandwidth and the target ranging acuity is shown for 4 species of bat. The horseshoe bat has a 'constant frequency' call with only a short, narrow bandwidth FM tail, and can only distinguish between two objects if one is more than 12 mm closer (or further away) from the bat than the other (Fig. 3.10b). The

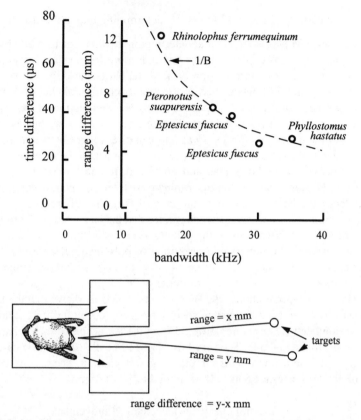

Fig. 3.10. Relationship between call bandwidth and target ranging acuity. Target ranging resolution should theoretically be equal to the reciprocal of the bandwidth, the dotted line in the figure. The 4 species studied by Simmons (1973) have target ranging abilities very close to those expected. Lower diagram shows what is meant by resolved difference distance.

phyllostomid, *Phyllostomus hastatus*, has a broad bandwidth call, and can resolve distances down to almost 4 mm. This means being able to differentiate between echoes arriving as little as 20 μs apart.

Early experiments involved training bats on a platform to fly to the nearest target for a reward (e.g. Simmons and Vernon, 1971), or by simulating echoes with variable time delays (Simmons, 1973). Whilst it is doing these tests, the bat is moving its head to investigate the targets, and this will reduce its sensitivity, since target distance changes as its head moves. To find out just what can be achieved in ideal conditions, Simmons (1979) trained bats to discriminate between a simulated echo at a constant delay of 3 ms, and one made to jitter, or oscillate back and forth by a tiny distance, at a mean delay of 3 ms. Under these conditions the big brown bat, *Eptesicus fuscus*, could identify a target jittering by just 1.3 μs. This means that the bat had to measure a delay of several milliseconds with an accuracy of 1 μs, and then store that information until it could compare it with the next pulse. In the more complex conditions encountered in the field the bat could not perform as well as this, but it gives you an idea of the sophistication of the system, and this remarkable sensitivity almost certainly has an important role in other aspects of echolocation, such as determining target fine structure.

Spectral changes in FM pulses—determining target fine structure

As I said earlier, FM pulses are good at determining the fine structure of a bat's surroundings—a communications expert will tell you that more frequencies carry more information. FM signals carry this information back to the bat because the echo is substantially changed by the target. FM bats gather information from spectral changes—modulation of the frequency components, and amplitude changes—modulation of the strength of the echo. As yet, we have a poor understanding of how this is done, but we do know that vesper bats of the genera *Myotis* and *Eptesicus* can discriminate between objects of different size, shape, and even texture. Differences in size appear to be determined from amplitude differences in the echo, shape, and textural differences must involve more subtle mechanisms. *Eptesicus fuscus* can discriminate between flat plates which have holes of different depths on their surface (Simmons *et al.*, 1974). The differences may be as little as 0.6 mm, and Simmons *et al.* originally suggested that the bats were performing this task on the basis of spectral differences in the echoes—you could think of it as a change in the colour composition. The remarkable resolution of pulse-echo delay timing suggested by the jitter experiments, later led Simmons (1979) to suggest that discrimination may be based on temporal cues. The results of some of these jitter experiments are now hotly debated (Pollak, 1993; Simmons, 1993). Schmidt (1988) has shown that the false vampire, *Megaderma lyra*, can learn frequency spectra from objects with different textures. When given two simulated echoes which differed from the learnt spectrum, the bats selected the pattern closest to the real one. The very broadband FM call (100–20 kHz) used by *M. lyra* enables it to analyse textural depths in the range 0.9–4.2 mm. The narrowband FM tail to the call of greater horseshoe bats will be limited to 1.1–1.5 mm.

Spectral change as a detector of movement

It may be that spectral changes in FM pulses are used to detect movement in cluttered environments. The complex spectrum returning from a leafy branch will carry no specific cues about potential prey. However, even the slightest movement by an insect, either flying past, or moving on a leaf, will change the echo spectrum 'colour' in a characteristic way, different to the changes due to movement of the branch by the wind. In theory, a bat echolocating at around 20 kHz will detect textural changes (movement) of around 200 μm, and at 150 kHz resolution would be a remarkable 5 μm, for a frequency shift of just 1% (Neuweiler, 1990). The movement of the bat itself introduces spectral changes which could complicate analysis. Is this why bats such as *M. lyra* and the long-eared bat, *Plecotus auritus*, often hover motionless when gleaning? Bats which feed over water may also detect prey by changes in echo spectra from the textured water surface, since all use brief broadband FM signals (e.g. *Myotis daubentonii* and *M. adversus*, Jones and Rayner, 1988, 1991; *Noctilio leporinus*, Wenstrup and Suthers, 1984; *Myotis vivesi*, Suthers, 1967). Interestingly, *Megaderma lyra*, which as we've noted, uses very broadband calls, also fishes (Suthers, 1967).

Neuweiler (1990) points out that there has been very little work on the auditory analysis of changing spectral patterns, and suggests that rich rewards await those entering this field.

Target location in 3-dimensional space

So far the FM bat has determined the distance to the object, its size and shape, and something about its texture. It needs several more very important bits of information: an object's location in the horizontal and vertical planes, and its relative velocity and direction of movement. Behavioural experiments, described below, in which bats were trained to discriminate between horizontal or vertical arrays of rods which subtended different angles at the eye, have been carried out by Lawrence and Simmons (1982b) and Simmons *et al.* (1983) (Fig. 3.11).

The big brown bat, *Eptesicus fuscus*, was capable of resolving vertical angles down to 3.5°, and horizontal angles of 1.5° When the tragus was temporarily glued down to the fur in front of the ear, vertical acuity was significantly reduced. *Eptesicus* may resolve vertical angles by analysing the timing of secondary echoes which follow different paths through the inner ear and around the tragus, depending upon their direction of origin. The tragus is known to be responsible for generating multiple reflections in the external ear as echoes travel to the eardrum, and these may play a crucial role in the process. Horizontal position may be determined by differences in the time of arrival and/or the intensity of echoes between the two ears (Fig. 3.12). Analysis by differences in the time of arrival would have to work on delays of 1–2 ms between the ears. The exact mechanism is still hotly debated, and the arguments are discussed in detail by Suthers and Wenstrup (1987).

Can bats intercept their prey?

An FM bat appears to determine prey velocity primarily by measuring the change in distance between it and its prey from one echo to the next. This facility is clearly important

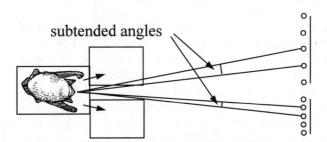

Fig. 3.11. Locating objects in 3-D space. Experimental setup for determining bats' ability to resolve horizontal (or vertical) angles. Bats are trained to identify the larger (or smaller) angles subtended by vertical (or horizontal) arrays of rods, and signal their choice by moving onto one of the forward platforms.

Fig. 3.12. How bats resolve horizontal components of position in space. Horizontal displacement is probably determined by differences in the intensity and/or time of arrival of echoes at the two ears, due to differences in echo path length (dotted lines) between object and ears.

in the approach and capture phases of the chase, and could be used by bats to plot the prey's trajectory, and hence fly on an interception course. For many years there was conflicting evidence as to whether bats can and do fly on interception paths. A study of pursuit flight sequences by Webster (1967) suggested that they do, but the patterns of head movements of bats during pursuit, although not conclusive, suggested that they do not (Masters *et al.*, 1985). Very recent work (E.K.V. Kalko, unpublished) shows that bats can, and do, fly on interception paths. Just how well do bats track their prey, and what other tricks, beyond those discussed, do they employ? Webster (1967), and Masters *et al.* (1985) have shown that both big and little brown bats aim their heads at targets with an accuracy of 5° either way, and may be able to judge target position to within 5 mm at interception. As a bat approaches its prey and the echoes get louder, its hearing becomes less sensitive (Kick and Simmons, 1984), due to the action of the middle ear muscles (Suga and Jen, 1975). In combination with accurate aiming of the head, and adjustments to the intensity of the emitted pulses (Kobler *et al.*, 1985) this acts as an automatic gain control, keeping the neural stimulation due to the echoes at a constant level.

Constant frequency calls

Basic properties

At the other end of the range from short, broadband FM sweeps, are the long, constant frequency (CF) calls used by many bats. They are typically 10–50 ms in duration, and are rarely entirely CF, since they often have brief, narrowband FM components at one or both ends (Fig. 3.7). CF pulses show a lot of interspecific variation and are more accurately referred to as CF/FM or even FM/CF/FM pulses.

CF/FM pulses commonly undergo similar changes to FM pulses as the bat homes in on its target. The pulse gets shorter, by a reduction in the central CF component, and the FM component increases in bandwidth (Fig. 3.13). Additional harmonics may also be introduced.

The pulses get shorter to prevent pulse-echo overlap, and the changes in the FM component, as described above, are to give the bat more information about the position and

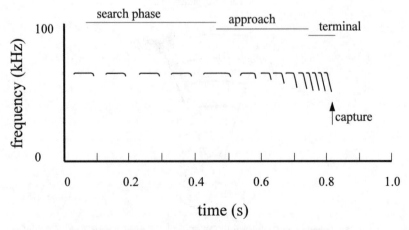

Fig. 3.13.   Call structure during prey capture in a CF bat.

nature of the target. Why is the CF component there at all? CF echolocation did not evolve without reason, so how do bats utilise these pulses? There are several possible functions for CF calls, and over the last decade evidence has been gathered in support of some subtle and remarkable uses. (Note, however—overlap appears of be an integral part of echo processing in some bats!)

I have already noted that high frequency sounds are attenuated rapidly in the air. Two ways to make the pulse carry further, are to concentrate all, or most, of the energy into one frequency, rather than spread it over a broad FM pulse, and to make this component relatively low frequency. Many bats have a prominent CF or shallow FM component to their search phase call, even species we think of as FM bats (e.g. *Pipistrellus* species). When a CF or shallow FM pulse is present, it is often as a low frequency tail to the FM sweep. Some alternate CF with FM pulses (e.g. *Nyctalus* and *Eptesicus* species). Examples of these calls are shown in Fig. 3.7. In general this trick is used by bats which hunt in relatively open environments, and the low frequency CF call may help them to detect prey simply by maintaining the intensity of the pulse, and hence that of the echo, over greater distances. This is not the whole answer, since many bats using long CF pulses (e.g. *Rhinopoma hardwickei*) include several energy draining higher harmonics in the call. Another suggestion, discussed below, is that the CF pulses are designed to detect fluttering insects. This may be plausible for some species, but in many the percentage of total time occupied by calls is so small, that the detection of fluttering wings is unlikely (Neuweiler, 1990).

Doppler shift

A phenomenon called Doppler shift appears to be exploited by some bats which use CF pulses. Everyone is familiar with the way in which the sound of a siren changes as a police car or ambulance passes in the street. As it approaches it is high pitched, and the sound suddenly becomes low pitched as it passes and recedes. This is due to Doppler shift (Fig. 3.14).

As the vehicle approaches, the sound waves from the siren are pushed against your ears due to the motion of the vehicle. The waves are compressed like a spring, decreasing the wavelength, increasing the frequency, and therefore increasing the pitch. As the vehicle passes, the sound waves are suddenly stretched by the source of the sound as it goes away from you, the wavelength increases, the frequency decreases, and the pitch goes down. The change in pitch is directly related to the speed at which the source approaches or recedes. If an echolocating bat is approaching an insect, the frequency of the echoes will be determined by the combined speeds of the bat and insect. Echoes received by a bat approaching a stationary insect will be increased in frequency, and increased further if the insect is approaching the bat. There is evidence that some bats can use Doppler shift to calculate their speed relative to objects around them.

Fig. 3.14. How Doppler shift works.

A greater horseshoe bat emits its CF pulses at a frequency of about 82 kHz. Lets say a CF pulse hits a target towards which the bat is moving at 5 m s^{-1}. The pulse will be compressed, and the returning echo will be logged at 84 kHz by the bat. It will shift its emitted pulse down to 80 kHz, so that the returning echo is logged at 82 kHz again. Figure 3.15 shows an example of a bat responding to a simulated target which suddenly moves towards it at 2 m s^{-1} for 2 s, and then stops again (Simmons, 1974; Simmons *et al.*, 1975).

The bat alters its emission frequency to keep the echo at 82 kHz. It does this because its ears are tuned to be particularly sensitive to sounds of 82–83 kHz (Neuweiler, 1970). A large part of the cochlea is given over to this frequency range (Bruns, 1976). The shift in emitted frequency required to keep the echo at 82 kHz tells the bat how fast it is moving, and in what direction, relative to the object. A similar mechanism operates in the moustached bat, *Pteronotus parnellii*, and probably in many other CF bats (see Neuweiler, 1990, for a detailed review). This should be an ideal mechanism to compute the speed of insect prey, but Doppler shift compensation is used by horseshoe bats to relate their own motion to the environment (Trappe and Schnitzler, 1982): the movement of prey is probably determined by pulse-echo delay measurements.

Noctilio leporinus uses CF/FM pulses to locate fish at the surface of the water. It is tempting to suggest that Doppler shift of the CF pulse is used for prey movement detection. Wenstrup and Suthers (1984) trained bats to approach moving targets in an indoor pool. The bats could discriminate between two targets with a velocity difference of 35–45 cm s^{-1}. Were they using Doppler shift, or simply the rate at which target distance changed from pulse to pulse, to detect prey movement? When bats were trained to respond to a simulated Doppler shift in the echoes, the best they could do was to detect an apparent velocity difference of 170 cm s^{-1}. They therefore appear to calculate velocity by using updated distance information from the FM component of their pulses. The Doppler shift mechanism is clearly important in determining prey movement, and even velocity in some species, but care must be taken not to overstate its importance.

Prey detection and identification using CF pulses

Doppler shift may have another important role to play in prey detection and identification. You can think of an insect as an acoustic mirror, reflecting sound back

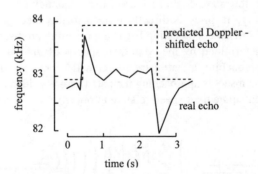

Fig 3.15. Doppler shift compensation in the greater horseshoe bat. The dotted line shows the predicted shift in the echoes returning to the bat due to the movement of a simulated target. The solid line shows the actual echoes. As the target moves and the echo frequency changes, the bat shifts its emitted frequency to keep the echo frequency constant (adapted from Simmons, 1974).

towards the bat. When it presents the flat face of its wings to the bat it acts as a better mirror than when it presents its wings edge on, in other words the echo will be more intense. This means that the strength of the echo will change as the insect beats its wings up and down, and if the CF pulse is long relative to the insect's wing beat period, the bat may be able to detect these periodic amplitude modulations. In addition to amplitude modulation, the moving wings will also lead to frequency modulation of the echo, through Doppler shift. Do bats take advantage of these effects? It is certainly the case that bats respond better to moving targets, in particular, fluttering insects. Several CF bats show a strong preference for fluttering targets (Bell and Fenton, 1984; Link *et al.*, 1986). The echolocation system of such bats is extremely sensitive to minute frequency modulations, suggesting that they are of functional importance (Vater, 1982). Recent work also shows that bats may learn rather more from the echoes than simply that an insect is present. Some of the most elegant studies have been done on the greater horseshoe bat, *Rhinolophus ferrumequinum*. With a 50 ms CF call, it could monitor a complete wing beat cycle of any insect beating its wings at greater than 20 Hz.

Figure 3.16b shows the changes in echo intensity, or amplitude modulation, of the CF pulse during two wing beat cycles of a moth flying towards, and at right angles to, the bat (Schnitzler *et al.*, 1983; Schnitzler, 1987). The bat could get quite a lot from this information. First of all, it could determine the wing beat frequency from the period of the repeating pattern. It could also work out the orientation of the insect from the rather different patterns produced. You can see that at 90° to the bat, the large wing area of the moth produces high intensity echoes or glints, when the wings are presented face on to the bat. To these can be added the FM modulation due to wing movement. This FM and AM modulation of the echo relative to the emitted pulse is species-specific, as well as being determined by prey orientation.

We can see this more clearly in the time-averaged spectra shown in Fig. 3.17 (Schnitzler *et al.*, 1983). These show the relative intensities of the different frequency components in the echoes. There is a strong component around 80 kHz, close to the

(a)

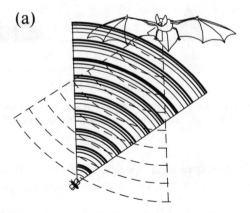

Fig. 3.16. Amplitude and frequency modulation of a CF echolocation call by fluttering insects. (a) The movement of the insect's wings lead to frequency modulation of the echo by Doppler shift (represented by changes in line spacing on the echo). Changes in wing profile, and hence the intensity of the echo lead to amplitude modulation (represented by changes in line thickness).

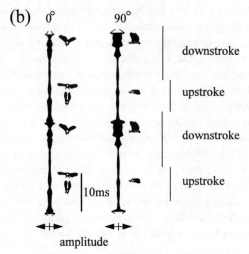

Fig. 3.16. (b) Amplitude modulation in the echo of a CF call of a greater horseshoe bat over two wing beat cycles of a moth, flying towards and at right angles to the bat (adapted from Fig. 2, Schnitzler *et al.*, 1983).

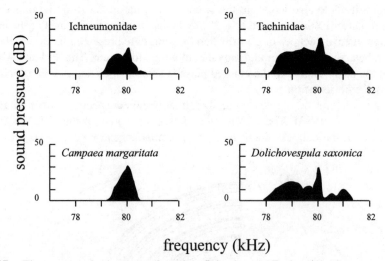

Fig. 3.17. Time-averaged echospectra from four flying insects. Each species has a spectrum with a characteristic frequency range of different intensities (adapted from Schnitzler *et al.*, 1983).

emitted frequency, in the echoes of all species, but many differences related to the size and shape of the insect and its wings, the wing beat frequency, and the patterns of wing movement.

Bats could in theory make use of all this information—do they? The answer appears to be yes: trained bats in the laboratory are capable of some astoundingly subtle discriminatory feats. Greater horseshoe bats have been trained to make a choice between pairs of real, simulated, or modified echoes from insects (von der Emde and Schnitzler, 1990).

The echoes were manipulated so that the 'phantom' targets were all fluttering at exactly 50 Hz, so that the bats could not use frequency as a guide to identification. The echoes of 4 different insects were used, a sphingid moth, a noctuid moth, a scarabid beetle and a cranefly, from 3 different orientations: head on, side view, and back view. In the first experiment, the bats were given a reward if they picked out a 90° cranefly echo in prefer-ence to any other echo from the other insects. This they did consistently after a short period of training. Without any further training, they were given a choice between echoes from the other species, and a cranefly echo at 0° or 180°—echoes they had not so far experienced. Despite this they still went for the cranefly. Whatever they had learnt about 90° cranefly echoes, they could see the same characteristics in apparently very different echoes from craneflies oriented to other angles. The experimenters themselves could identify no common characteristics between echoes from a study of the sonograms and oscillograms. Interestingly, 2 of the 4 bats were rather better at this test than the other 2. When the echoes were manipulated, to remove either the large amplitude glints, or the lower amplitude events between glints, bats behaved differently. One bat could identify the cranefly only on the basis of the information between glints, with glints only it per-formed the test badly. However, another bat could use either: different bats must *learn* different techniques. If the echoes were manipulated to remove either FM or AM compo-nents the bats could not identify the cranefly echoes.

HOW DO BATS AVOID BEING CONFUSED BY OTHER BATS' SONAR?

In real life, there are all sorts of extraneous sounds, including the sonar of other bats, to interfere with a bat's own sonar processing. There is no doubt that such factors do influence a bat's performance level, but laboratory studies have shown that echolocation has evolved to overcome many of the problems. This is a large and complex field, but I'll give you an example or two of work in this area.

The moustached bat (*Pteronotus parnellii*) overcomes the interference caused by other bats' calls by suppressing the first harmonic in its sonar pulse to around 1% of the total energy of the call. It is then so weak that other bats may not even be able to hear it. However, the bat hears its own first harmonic directly through the tissue between vocal chords and cochlea. The first harmonic is used to open a neural gate which enables the bat's auditory system to receive and process the echo from that call. The bat does not respond to the weak first harmonics of other bats, they do not therefore open the neural gate which initiates processing, and it is not therefore confused by their presence.

A similar mechanism is used by the small fisherman bat, *Noctilio albiventris*. Roverud and Grinnell (1985) trained bats to discriminate a target range difference of 5 cm, and then attempted to confuse the bats with recorded sounds. These bats emit paired pulses at 7–10 Hz: an 8 ms CF pulse followed by a CF/FM (6 ms/2 ms) pulse. The bats were found to be insensitive to a wide range of potential jamming sounds, including simulations of CF or FM components of their own CF/FM pulses. However, if simulations of the entire CF/FM pulse were used, the bats performed the discrimination tests badly. The researchers went on to perform experiments which suggested that *N. albiventris* could only receive and process the FM component, to determine target range, if it was pre-ceded by the CF component with the appropriate temporal spacing. The CF component of the CF/FM pulse is presumed to open a neural gate of short duration, enabling the bat to

Leisler's bat, *Nyctalus leisleri*, feeding around street lamps.

process the echoes from its own pulses. The CF/FM pulses or echoes of other bats are not likely to be heard during this brief window, and are therefore ignored. Finally, it is also becoming clear that in many species, each bat has its own personal call frequency.

AUDITORY ADAPTATIONS, AND THE NEURAL BASIS OF ECHOLOCATION

We saw earlier that the auditory system of bats has a number of adaptations for picking up high frequency sounds, notably the large basal turn of the cochlea. Few features of the cochlea are unique, since many small mammals have good high frequency hearing. Many of the important adaptations which enable bats to use ultrasound for echolocation are in the auditory centres of the brain. Some of the more important adaptations will be covered in this section. Neuweiler (1990) suggests that the key to understanding neural processing in echolocation may lie in the hypothesis that the **emission** of the echolocating pulses triggers specific mechanisms in the brain which enable bats to perform their remarkable sonar feats. In the previous paragraph I described two mechanisms by which bats minimise interference due to the sounds of other bats. Both mechanisms depend upon the bats' own echolocating pulses triggering neural gates, which briefly open windows enabling the bats' auditory system to receive and interpret echoes. There is evidence to suggest that mechanisms similar to those used against interference are important in target ranging, and researchers are looking to see if time windows are important in other echolocation tasks. Considerable effort is also being put in to uncovering other auditory adaptations. This research has recently been reviewed by O'Neill (1987), Roverud (1987), Pollak and Casseday (1989), Neuweiler (1990) and Suga (1990): I can only give you a flavour of what it is telling us about the way a bat's brain has evolved to meet the stringent requirements of echolocation. The brain of a bat is fundamentally like that of other mammals. Adaptations for echolocation are frequently exaggerations or refinements of existing mammalian structures and processes which make them more accessible to the scientist. The lessons being learnt from bats therefore often have much wider relevance, increasing our understanding of how the mammalian brain is organised and functions.

Paired sounds—enhanced neural response to the second sound

In most mammals, the neural response to a sound (e.g. the firing of specific cells in the brain, which trigger target ranging computation) is usually suppressed by a simultaneous or slightly earlier sound. This is also true for bats, with the exception of horseshoe bats, when the sounds are around their best frequencies—that is, the frequencies of their CF calls and echoes (Möller, 1978). A tone around 81.5 kHz dramatically increases the response to a second tone of 82 kHz. The first can be thought of as the emitted pulse, the second the weak echo, of slightly higher frequency due to Doppler shift (see *CF calls* earlier in this chapter). This mechanism is almost certainly one which has evolved to selectively enhance the brain's response to the weak echoes of the bat's CF calls. The enhanced response would work for echoes returning from up to 9 m away.

Time windows and target ranging

The neural gate used by *Noctilio albiventris* (Roverud, 1987) not only acts to filter out extraneous sounds, it also acts as a distance filter for the bat's own sounds. The window is open for 21 ms after the emission of bat's own FM component (27 ms after the CF gate opener), i.e. to echoes coming from targets up to 3.6 m away, with maximum sensitivity between 0.7 and 2.4 m. The bat can therefore attend selectively to its near environment, and ignore echoes from more distant objects. Roverud reports that a similar mechanism operates in the horseshoe bat *Rhinolophus rouxi*, which uses long FM–CF–FM pulses, and the big brown bat, *Eptesicus fuscus*, which emits short FM pulses only. The time window in all three species was open for around 30 ms, allowing the bats to target range over distances up to 5 m, more than sufficient distance for detecting and catching prey on the wing.

Target ranging by pulse-echo delay

The ability of bats to measure the distance to an object from the pulse-echo delay has been described above. Two types of mechanism appear to exist in the brain of a bat to process target range information. In the auditory centre of the midbrain of FM bats (in a region called the inferior colliculus), up to 50% of the cells sampled are of a type called

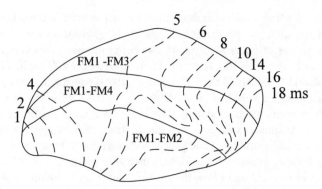

Fig. 3.18. A neural map of range-tuned neurons in the auditory cortex of the moustached bat (adapted from O'Neill and Suga, 1982).

'phasic constant latency responders' (pCLRs). This simply means that they respond to impulses from the ear (irrespective of their intensity) by firing rapidly and briefly (Suga, 1970; Pollak *et al.*, 1977a,b). They can encode very precisely the timing of pulse-echo pairs, for processing higher in the brain. These *temporal pattern-encoding neurones* are uncommon in CF bats, but another type is found in the midbrain and auditory cortex of both CF bats (Suga *et al.*, 1978) and FM bats (Feng *et al.*, 1978): the *range-tuned neurones* (see O'Neill, 1987, for references and review). These cells only fire if they receive a pair of impulses (from the sonar pulse and its echo) with a specific delay between them. Every cell is programmed to respond to a certain delay, and the higher centres of the brain will determine what the pulse-echo delay is by *which* cell fires.

In the moustached bat, *Pteronotus parnelli*, these cells make up a two-dimensional map on the surface of the auditory cortex (Suga and O'Neill, 1979; O'Neill and Suga, 1982), and are divided into three types, each sensitive to the delay between the fundamental frequency and one of the three higher harmonics present in the FM component of the call of the bat (Fig. 3.18). Delays of 2–8 ms take up most of the map, corresponding to target ranges of 0.35–1.4 m. These cells are not too sensitive to the FM frequency of the echo, so are not upset by Doppler shifts, and they are either on or off. In other words, they are *frequency* and *level tolerant*, but not *delay tolerant*. This is just what is required of cells whose function is to encode target ranging, pulse-echo delays. Although level tolerant, most neurones respond to echoes within a particular range of amplitudes—i.e. from a target of a particular size. Why the delay between fundamental and harmonics is so important is not fully understood, but the same phenomenon is seen in *Rhinolophus rouxi* (O'Neill *et al.*, 1985). One function is in the anti-interference strategy of the moustached bat described in the last section. The FM little brown bat, *Myotis lucifugus*, has range-tuned neurones responsive to FM pulses with identical spectra (Sullivan, 1982).

Going one step further into the system, researchers are asking what processes lie behind range-tuned neurones. One much studied mechanism involves delay lines in neural networks (Olsen and Suga, 1986; Suga 1990). The network delays the response of a cell in the midbrain to the pulse, so that it arrives at the range-tuned neurone in the cortex at the same time as the response to the echo, which gets there unimpeded. The delay can be introduced by a series of interneurones, each with an axon and a synapse with finite transmission times. The echo response is carried more or less directly to the range-tuned neurone. By altering the length of the delay line, or by direct neural inhibition, range-tuned neurones sensitive to different delays can be created.

Dealing with sound intensity variation

A bat must be able to process its own pulses, at 80–120 dB, followed by the echo, typically up to only 40 dB. We have already seen how the stapedius muscle comes into play here (p. 84), but there are other mechanisms. The pulse itself may increase the response of the auditory system to the echo (Grinnell, 1963; Möller, 1978). The grey bat, *Myotis grisescens,* attenuates its response to its own calls by 25 dB relative to recordings of its call (Suga and Schlegel, 1972). The intensity of the echo itself will increase as the target is approached. Bats can smooth out variation in the response to the echo by reducing the intensity of the call as they approach the target (Kobler *et al.*, 1985), or by increasing the threshold for echo detection (Kick and Simmons, 1984). Many neural responses (at all levels of the system) have upper thresholds, and do not respond differently to sounds over a wide range of intensities (e.g. Suga, 1977; Vater, 1982), a very simple way of dealing with changing intensity signals.

BEHAVIOURAL STUDIES IN THE FIELD—DO BATS SELECT THEIR PREY?

Is there any evidence that bats in the field can take advantage of the subtle discriminatory powers they show in the laboratory which I described earlier? To put the question in an ecological context: do bats take insects at random, in proportion to their abundance in the environment? Alternatively, do they select on crude criteria like size, or are they more sophisticated in their prey selection? Do they select insects which represent the best energetic returns for the effort put in to catch them? In other words, are they foraging optimally? This is an ambitious question of fundamental ecological importance, and one I'll come back to in Chapter 6. For the moment, all we need to ask is can bats select prey in the field?

Figure 3.19 shows data on feeding preferences of the little brown bat, *Myotis lucifugus,* in early August, collected by Anthony and Kunz (1977) in New Hampshire. The upper histogram shows the percentage of insects available to the bats, divided into classes of different sizes (i.e. the insects caught in suction traps). The lower shows those eaten by the bats (i.e. the insects found in droppings). There are many more small insects available to the bats than those in larger size classes, but they eat mainly those falling into the middle size classes. Although there are very few large insects available, they make up a significant part of the diet, so the bats must be selectively feeding on them. One factor limiting the upper size limit may be the physical difficulty involved in catching and eating large prey. Even if the bat can do it, it may be less economical in energetic terms than handling smaller prey. Small prey may also be uneconomical, and detected but avoided. The very smallest prey may not even be detected, so the question of selection doesn't come in to it! So, some bats appear to select by size. Can they also select by any other criteria?

The answer in the case of Scottish pipistrelles is yes, some of the time, for some insects. Figure 3.20 shows the percentage by number of insects in droppings plotted

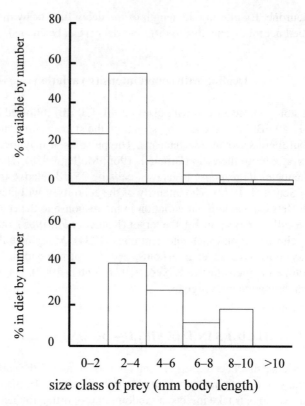

Fig. 3.19. Prey selection by size. Insect size classes available to, and eaten by, the little brown bat, *Myotis lucifugus* (adapted from Anthony and Kunz, 1977).

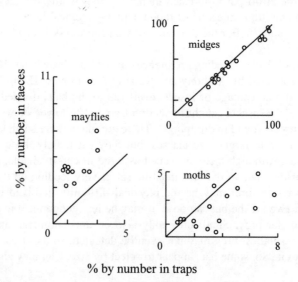

Fig. 3.20. The diet of the pipistrelle, *P. pipistrellus*. Each graph shows the number of insects available (i.e. caught in suction trap), as a percentage of the total, plotted against the number eaten (determined from faecal analysis) (adapted from Swift *et al.*, 1985).

against those found in suction traps for three different insect groups, (Swift *et al.*, 1985). Each dot represents one night's data. If the dot falls above the line, then that group of insects are over-represented in the diet, assuming the traps themselves are not selective (—incidentally, a point of continued debate, whatever the trapping method used). Mayflies appear to be actively selected, but moths are under-represented. Midges are taken in proportion to their availability. As we will discover later, some moths can hear bats and take evasive action, and some will simply be too large for the small pipistrelle to handle.

Selection is also made by the hoary bat, *Lasiurus cinereus*. The insects eaten are shown in Fig. 3.21 as a percentage of the total diet, together with the insects available, assessed by sticky and Malaise traps (Barclay, 1985; 1986). Moths made up only 10% of the insects caught in traps, but constituted 40% of the bats' diet, and a similar pattern was seen for dragonflies and beetles. Dragonflies don't fly at night—how was the bat taking these? The bats appear almost to ignore mosquitoes, flies, and caddis flies.

Insect availability of course changes throughout the summer, and this is reflected in the diet of some species. Figure 3.22 shows the composition of the diet of the greater horseshoe bat, *Rhinolophus ferrumequinum*, determined by Jones (1990): it includes some of the largest flying insects found in the UK. In early April, 50% of the diet was dor beetles, *Geotrupes*, and over 30% ichneumon flies. Later in the month, craneflies, *Tipula* species dominated, constituting up to 60% of the diet. Cockchafers, *Melolontha*, are eaten in May, but from mid-May to early July moths are the big thing, being slowly replaced by the dung beetles, *Aphodius*. A casual study might suggest opportunistic feeding: the bats simply eat what is most abundant. However, when the data were analysed it was shown

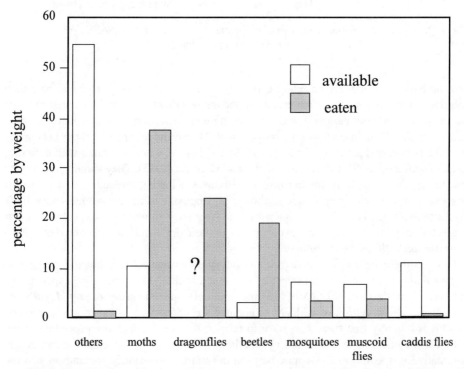

Fig. 3.21.   The diet of the hoary bat, *Lasiurus cinereus* (adapted from Barclay, 1986).

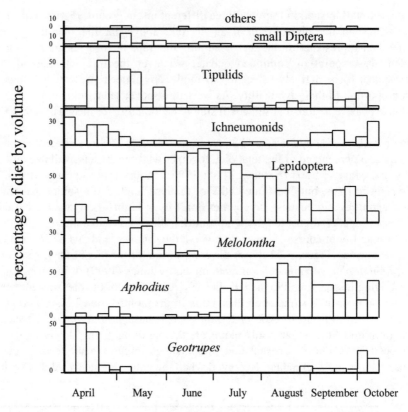

Fig. 3.22. Seasonal variation in the diet of the greater horseshoe bat, *Rhinolophus ferrumequinum* (adapted from Jones, 1990).

that the bats were actively selecting certain prey, taking them in greater numbers than predicted on the basis of their abundance in the environment. The long CF sonar pulse of the horseshoe bat could allow it to determine the wing beat frequencies of its major prey items, which fall mainly within the range 50–80 Hz. In the laboratory, these bats sit up and take notice, by increasing the length of their CF pulse, when presented with fluttering targets oscillating at 30–100 Hz (Schnitzler and Ostwald, 1983). They should certainly be able to separate these from smaller insects with faster wing beat frequencies. There must be more to it than wing beat frequency however, since one of the greater horseshoe bat's favourite items, the cockchafer, has a wing beat frequency similar to several abundant but neglected species: perhaps the experiments of von der Emde and Schnitzler (1990) described on p. 98 are relevant here?

How do these field results relate to laboratory experiments? It is not too difficult to believe that bats in the field can select by size much as they do in controlled experiments, but what about the complex task of learning frequency spectra carried out by *Megaderma lyra*, or the interpretation of AM/FM modulated CF carrier waves by greater horseshoe bats? It is unlikely that these bats have to rely on this sort of learning procedure in the wild, but they may have a head full of inherited spectra which tell them what to feed on. Alternatively, spectral analysis may be used only rarely to identify specific prey in the wild—most studies suggest feeding is opportunistic (but not random) in most bats (Fenton, 1990). This does not diminish the relevance of all this work—it is a study of the exceptions, and of the controversial, which leads to some of biology's greatest insights.

ECHOLOCATION AND NAVIGATION

Do bats use echolocation when commuting from roost to foraging site, or when migrating? It is generally stated that insectivorous bats have poor eyesight. However, it also seems to be widely believed that since echolocation works over short ranges, then sight must be more important in navigation. Homing studies have shown that blindfolded bats, released at some distance from their roost, can find their way back. They are not as good at the task as sighted bats, but nevertheless, echolocation may have a role to play, unless there is an as yet undiscovered, and very well developed, magnetic sense. Studies of commuting bats in the field support the idea that echolocation is involved in navigation. In northern Europe, many species make extensive use of linear features in the landscape when commuting. These may be walls, hedges, tracks, and even far more subtle features (Limpens and Kapteyn, 1991). When bats encounter a break in these features, their echolocation pulse characteristics change. For example Natterer's bat, *Myotis nattereri*, will briefly switch from FM to low frequency CF pulses, metaphorically switching on its head lamps to see beyond the break (Limpens, pers. comm.).

THE COST OF ECHOLOCATION

Vision is a low-cost sense, the light used to perceive objects comes from the sun at no cost to the animal. Echolocation on the other hand can be expensive—the emission of high intensity sounds at a frequency of 10 Hz costs a resting pipistrelle 10× its resting metabolic rate at 25 °C. By comparison, flight costs a pipistrelle around 15–20× its resting metabolic rate. However, a flying bat gets echolocation for free (Speakman and Racey, 1991). In flight, a bat breathes at the same frequency as it flaps its wings, breathing out on the upstroke, and in on the downstroke. The movement of the wings is driven by the flight muscles on the thorax, and these also drive the movements of the thorax which are responsible for breathing. Since the bat is expelling air from the lungs during the upstroke, it costs next to nothing to also emit its echolocation pulse at the end of the upstroke/expiration.

SOME MICROBATS DO NOT ECHOLOCATE—HUNTING BY OTHER METHODS

Virtually all bats have good auditory sensitivity in the frequency range 12–25 kHz (Neuweiler, 1990), as well as over the particular range used in echolocation, and could in principle listen to the sounds made by moving prey. This may be a legacy from their insectivorous ancestors, or a later adaptation for prey detection in the dark, and many bats do indeed locate and track their prey by this means.

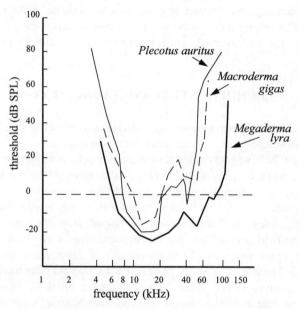

Fig. 3.23. Audiograms of 3 species of gleaning bat. These bats take advantage of prey-generated sounds when hunting, and their ears are most sensitive to sounds of around 10–20 kHz—those of animals rustling in the undergrowth (adapted from Neuweiler, 1990).

The big brown bat, *Eptesicus fuscus*, can detect katydids from over 100 m (Buchler and Childs, 1981), and *Trachops cirrhosus* identifies edible frogs from their calls (Ryan and Tuttle, 1983). Many insectivorous gleaners in particular may rely largely or even exclusively on prey-generated sounds, e.g. the pallid bat, *Antrozous pallidus* (Bell, 1982; Fuzessery *et al.*, 1993), and the long-eared bat, *Plecotus auritus* (Coles *et al.*, 1989; Anderson and Racey, 1991). Large carnivores such as the Australian ghost bat, *Macroderma gigas* (Guppy and Coles, 1988), the false vampire, *Megaderma lyra* (Marimuthu and Neuweiler, 1987) and *Cardioderma cor* (Ryan and Tuttle, 1987) also make full use of prey-generated sounds. Audiograms for three of these species have been published: all have extremely sensitive hearing in the range 10–20 kHz, and are the most sensitive mammalian ears yet documented (Fig. 3.23). This is partly due to their large external ears, which give directionality and increase sound pressure at the eardrum by up to 20–30 dB. Recent work (Obrist *et al.*, 1993) has shown that the acoustic properties of the external ear are very well matched to the particular hunting strategy of the species.

A number of bats appear to rely to a large extent on vision. The California leaf-nosed bat, *Macrotus californicus*, is another gleaner which hunts using prey-generated sound as well as low-intensity echolocation. Under laboratory conditions, when illumination is equivalent to that of a brightly moonlit night, it locates prey by echolocation only one third of the time, relying on vision for the remainder in the absence of prey movement and sound (Bell, 1985). Vision is also utilised at much lower light levels. The eyesight of many bats appears to be as good as that of *Macrotus* and other small, nocturnal mammals, and vision may play a greater role than we imagine in the foraging of other bat species too.

Daubenton's bat, *Myotis daubentonii*, trawling for emergent insects

THE ECOLOGY OF ECHOLOCATION: INTERACTIONS BETWEEN FLIGHT, FOOD, AND FORAGING HABITS

In the last chapter we looked at relationships between wing morphology/flight perform-ance and habitat/food/foraging strategy. In this chapter, I want to add echolocation char-acteristics to the story. You will have gained some appreciation of these interactions already: I want to pull the strands together and complete the picture. A very detailed review of the subject has been written by Norberg and Rayner (1987), and you can read it in a more condensed form in Norberg's recent book (1990). Other excellent reviews include Fenton (1990) and Neuweiler (1990).

Fenton (1990) has rightly emphasised the flexible nature of foraging styles in bats, and the danger of too rigidly placing species into particular ecological niches. However, a number of feeding strategies can be clearly defined, and they are usually associated with particular forms of echolocation. Among animal-eating bats, six strategies are readily identifiable. Let's go through them in turn.

Open-space hawking above vegetation

Fast-flying hawkers, with high aspect ratio wings and high wing loading (see Chapter 2), typically use low frequency, narrowband FM or CF search calls up to 60 ms in duration. With no harmonics, all of the energy is concentrated in these 15–30 kHz pulses, which can detect prey (aided by flutter detection) over long distances. Early detection is needed if these bats, which fly rapidly and have large turning circles, are to catch their prey. In such an uncluttered environment, spectral analysis using FM pulses is not needed. When prey are detected, many species will switch to short (about 5 ms) broadband FM pulses. These will enhance target ranging, and provide spectral cues which give detail of target structure. Calls can be of very high intensity. Many emballonurids, molossids, and vespertilionids fall into this category. Some species, e.g. the noctule, *Nyctalus noctula*, alternate narrow- and broadband FM pulses in their search phase flight.

Open-space hawking between vegetation

Bats feeding in this habitat are similar to those of the last section, and there is considerable overlap in flight and echolocation characteristics. There is a tendency towards higher frequency calls, both the CF search and the FM capture components. This perhaps reflects the slower flight, and the shorter distances over which prey are detected. Vespertilionids such as *Lasiurus* and *Pipistrellus* species forage in this way.

Foraging in and around vegetation

Bats which feed by slow hawking in vegetation have broad wings and low wing loading, giving them excellent low speed manoeuvrability. They detect and take insects at close range. In this cluttered environment, the bat has to deal with complex echoes from the vegetation. Two strategies are open to bats, both designed to reveal moving insects against background clutter, and both usually make use of high frequency calls (>50 kHz). Rhinolophids, hipposiderids, and some emballonurids use CF calls to detect fluttering insects. Most other bats in this group, including noctilionids and some vespertilionids, use broadband FM echolocation, often with several harmonics. Spectral analysis of the FM pulses may be used as a movement detector, and the FM pulse gives accurate range finding.

Flycatching or perch-hunting

These bats feed by hanging from a perch, intercepting passing prey. They use echolocation techniques similar to those bats feeding in vegetation, but have variable aspect ratio and wing loading since flight performance may be dictated by factors other than foraging.

Gleaning and hovering

Gleaning bats, which often hover over prey, generally have low aspect ratio, low wing loading, and rounded wingtips for slow manoeuvrable flight, and to facilitate take-off from the ground, possibly with heavy prey. They use short (<2 ms) FM echolocation pulses, of low intensity, designed to discriminate fine texture, and possibly detect target movement by spectral analysis, over short distances. Many gleaners (insectivores and carnivores) rely more on prey-generated sounds, and even vision, than echolocation. Examples of this category are plecotines, nycterids, megadermatids, and phyllostomids.

Trawling

Trawling bats (noctilionids and some vespertilionids) can have long wings, since they feed over clutter-free open water, and low wing loadings to carry heavy prey. Their

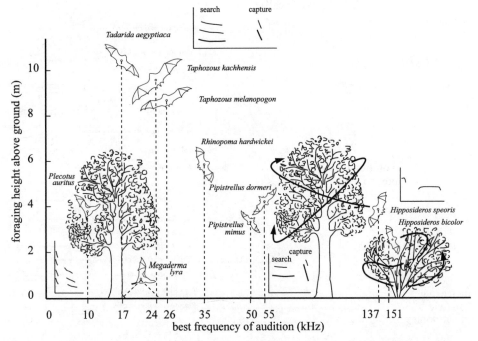

Fig. 3.24. Foraging strategy in relation to echolocation calls and auditory characteristics. Foraging height is plotted against the best frequency of audition. Bats are loosely divided into gleaners (ground and foliage), above canopy hawkers, low level open-air hawkers, and hawkers in cluttered habitats, and the characteristic sonograms of each group shown (adapted from Neuweiler, 1990).

echolocation calls are broadband FM, possibly for spectral analysis of water texture and to detect moving prey. Some have a CF component to their call. Since many also hawk for insects, this may be used for flutter detection.

Another important adaptation, to be expected from the above discussion, is shown in Fig. 3.24. The frequency range to which a species' ears are best tuned is either close to that it uses in echolocation, or in the case of gleaners, in the range of the sounds generated by their prey.

EVOLUTION OF ECHOLOCATION

Echolocation, like flight, is of such fundamental importance to the way of life of bats that it must have played a vital role in their evolution. Flight and echolocation almost certainly increased in sophistication together, as the protobats took to the night sky. Surprisingly, we still know very little about the evolution of echolocation. Perhaps the most interesting discussion of the evolutionary diversification of sonar calls is by Simmons and Stein (1980). The Rhinopomatidae are thought to be primitive on anatomical grounds, and they use short CF sonar calls with four or more harmonics. The Nycteridae also use short, multi-harmonic calls, and Simmons and Stein argue that these

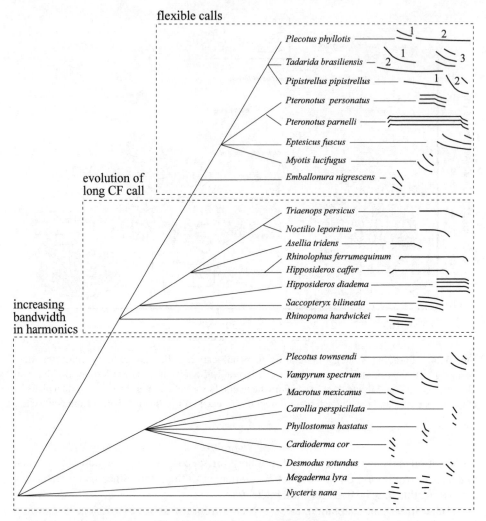

≡ presumed primitive sonar pulse from which others evolved

Fig. 3.25. Cladogram of echolocation call structure. Simmons and Stein (1980) argue that echolocation calls evolved from a short, multiharmonic, CF call. The most 'advanced' (recently evolved) species are thought to be those with calls which are flexible, with variable duration, bandwidth and harmonic component. These three features appear to have been exploited to different extents by different groups of bats (adapted from Fig. 1, Simmons and Stein, 1980).

are perhaps the least evolved. The bats have little or no adaptive control over the duration and bandwidth of their calls. The pulses may be a single-solution compromise between target detection (the CF component) and resolution (the harmonic component). These primitive calls appear to have evolved in three major directions, which can be seen in the cladogram shown in Fig. 3.25, despite some overlap. The cladogram is based on the relationships between 7 features of the echolocation calls, in 25 representative microbats.

A major advance was the increase in bandwidth of the harmonic components. The calls of megadermatids and phyllostomids, at the base of the cladogram, are still short, with multiple harmonics, and the bats vary them very little. However, all show some degree of frequency modulation, for foraging in cluttered habitats.

An alternative strategy, found in rhinolophids, hipposiderids, and noctilionids (in the centre of the cladogram) has been the evolution of long CF calls, with or without higher harmonics, and often with a terminal FM component. Again, these bats forage in cluttered environments. The CF component is probably used for prey detection (and possibly identification), the FM for target ranging, and target detail. Behavioural, physiological, and anatomical evidence indicates greater functional separation of the CF and FM components in those bats with longer CF components (refs. in Simmons and Stein, 1980). There is a trend in the cladogram for increased duration of the CF component, at the expense of the FM. At the top of this group in the cladogram are bats which use convex-downward FM calls. A CF 'tail' is often present at the end of the call.

Bats in the final group have very flexible calls, e.g. *Pipistrellus* and *Tadarida*, and are able to change the harmonics present, the duration and bandwidth of the 'CF'component (or delete it altogether), and the bandwidth of the FM signal, as required. The notch-eared bat, *Myotis emarginatus*, has recently been studied in some detail (Schumm *et al.*, 1991), and has been shown to have a very flexible repertoire. Significantly different calls are used when commuting, when gleaning in foliage, when gleaning in a barn and when hawking in the open. The feeding buzz is similar under all conditions. Changes in FM duration and bandwidth are substantial, and a CF tail can be added.

Exceptions to the 'flexible FM' patterns in this part of the cladogram are seen in the New World *Pteronotus* species, which have evolved a long-CF/FM call completely independently of the Old World rhinolophids and hipposiderids. However, although behaviourally similar, the anatomical and physiological specialisations associated with its use are rather different in these two groups. If we think of this cladogram, constructed entirely on echolocation call structure, as an evolutionary tree of the bats, then it is not so very different from one drawn up by more conventional methods. The only glaring anomaly is *Plecotus* (now *Corynorhinus*) *townsendi*, situated at the base, rather than with its relatives at the top: the call used in the analysis may be an unusual call of uncertain function recorded in other *Plecotus* species. Finally although the construction of such cladograms is informative and interesting, it has its dangers: e.g. convergent evolution can give unrelated bats similar calls e.g. the tiny *Craseonycteris thonglongyai* and *Myotis siligorensis* have very similar calls which appear to reflect the constraints of small size and foraging strategy, not phylogeny (Surlykke *et al.*, 1993).

4 Torpor and hibernation

Energy balance. Ectothermy, endothermy, and heterothermy. Torpor and hibernation. The cost of staying warm—the importance of body size. The physiology of torpor. The ecology of torpor and hibernation. Hibernacula. Biological clocks. Evolution of hibernation and torpor.

ENERGY BALANCE

All animals have a daily cycle of activity, carrying out the tasks essential to their individual survival, and those required to pass on their genes to the next generation. All of these tasks consume energy, which comes from metabolising the food they eat. Life is a continuous attempt to balance the input:output equation: energy in—food, must equal energy out—the physiological and behavioural costs of life. To be successful, that is to survive and pass on its genes, an animal must operate efficiently, and evolution drives the animal towards optimal solutions for all its tasks. If one animal feeds more efficiently than another, it can spend more time looking for a mate or a safe roost, and might therefore have a competitive edge in the fight for survival. Optimal solutions may never be achieved in a changing world, but this drive towards optimality is strong, and the solutions we see today are often marvellously close to the optimal. So, life is governed by the energy balance equation—what does it mean to bats? Bats are most active between dawn and dusk, and spend much of the day asleep, or indulging in various social activities. On average, each night a bat much catch enough food to provide the energy needed to get it through to the next night. The greatest energy demand on a bat is collecting this food in the first place. The importance of an optimal foraging strategy is therefore obvious. Each species is best adapted to a particular way of life, and the most critical factor is often the energetic cost of flight. Grooming, care of young, territorial defence, mate attraction, mating, and a range of other social needs all demand energy at different times. One factor is always a major variable in the energy balance equation: thermal homoeostasis, the maintenance of a stable body temperature above that of the environment. It is particularly important in temperate, insectivorous bats, which face the challenge of an ephemeral food supply in an often harsh climate, but is also relevant to many others too. In this chapter we will look at how bats manipulate their body temperature as part of their energy budgeting process.

CONCEPTS: ECTOTHERMY, ENDOTHERMY, AND HETEROTHERMY

First of all a definition or two. Bats, like all mammals are **endotherms**. That is they maintain high body temperatures by metabolising their food to generate heat internally. To do this they must have high metabolic rates, and high food intakes. Many reptiles can maintain high body temperatures during the day, but they achieve this by basking in the sun, and they cool rapidly at night. Reptiles are **ectotherms**: they have low metabolic rates, and cannot generate sufficient metabolic heat to compensate for heat loss across the body surface. Endothermy, as practised by mammals and birds, has big advantages—the animal can go about the business of survival independently of the vagaries of the climate. If the sun goes in, a lizard cools down and all activity slows or even stops, since all the chemical reactions which keep its body on the move slow down as temperature falls. However, endothermy also has potential drawbacks. The high metabolic rates needed for effective endothermy demand high food intake. This can create problems in two ways.

1. The food supply may be seasonal—if so, the animal needs to hibernate, switch to an alternative and more plentiful food supply, store food in times of plenty, or migrate to a place where there is food.

2. If the animal is very small, it needs to eat a lot of food relative to its body size. This is due to a simple physical law: as the size of an animal decreases it loses proportionally more of its body heat to the surrounding air, because it has a proportionately greater surface area to lose it from, relative to the volume generating it. This is why small mammals like shrews have such a prodigious appetite: they have to keep eating to provide the energy which keeps them warm. In other words, their mass-specific metabolic rate (energy produced per kg of tissue) is high (discussed in full below), although their absolute rate is low. At the other end of the scale, many dinosaurs were probably inertial homoeotherms: their large size gave them very low surface area:volume ratios, minimising heat loss, and enabling them to maintain elevated body temperatures with low metabolic rates.

Many animals cope with both small size and a seasonal food supply. Some brave it out, and remain **homoeothermic**—that is they maintain a high body temperature all the time. They can migrate (many birds), lay in food stores (many small rodents), or change diet (small birds and rodents). Others hibernate, or become **heterothermic**: they actively regulate their body temperature so as to minimise their energy requirements. The body temperature maintained is related to ambient temperature, and the energetic and behavioural demands of a bat.

Figure 4.1 shows how the western pipistrelle (*Pipistrellus hesperus*), responds to temperature change (Hill and and Smith, 1984). It is a small (3–5 g) species from the southwestern deserts of the United States, where the annual temperature range is –10 to 45 °C. The upper and lower thermal lethal limits for this species are –1 and 44 °C: in other words they die if the ambient temperature remains outside these limits for long. The thermal neutral zone (in which energy expenditure on thermoregulation by an active bat is minimal) is around 30–36 °C—a typical warm summer night over much of this bat's range. As temperature increases beyond the thermal neutral zone, energy must be expended to keep cool—through wing-fanning for example. Below the thermal neutral zone, more and more metabolic energy must be diverted into heat production. In heterotherms such as temperate bats, the body temperature thermostat can be set to a new low temperature when the ambient temperature falls below a critical level, making enormous energy savings. This critical temperature may vary, depending upon species, physiological state, the status of stored energy reserves, and the behavioural/ecological demands on an individual bat—more on this later. When the thermostat is reset, the bat enters torpor, but

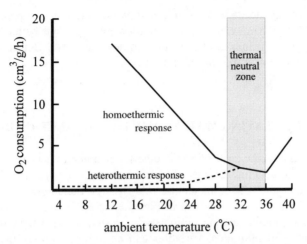

Fig. 4.1.   Energy expenditure during homoeothermy and heterothermy in the western pipistrelle, *P. hesperus* (from Hill and Smith, 1984).

even in this state energy must be expended to prevent death, if the temperature falls below a new critical level. The bat may increase its metabolic rate to prevent excessive cooling, or come out of torpor to move to a warmer hibernation site.

Heterothermy is a specialised form of homoeothermy, not a primitive one. It is found mainly in small mammals in temperate regions, and in hummingbirds, which evolved in the high, and often cool, forests of the Americas. The changes in body temperature are under the control of the animal, and they can arouse from torpor using their own energy, without an increase in air temperature. Heterothermy is therefore a facultative, not an obligate, process in bats (e.g. Audet and Fenton, 1988). This is perhaps a good place to point out that most bats are homoeothermic: with one or two controversial exceptions, only temperate members of the Vespertilionidae and Rhinolophidae are considered to be true facultative heterotherms.

CONCEPTS: TORPOR AND HIBERNATION

What exactly do we mean by hibernation and torpor? Definitions of hibernation are often vague, but we can be more specific about the term torpor. In **torpor** an animal allows its body temperature to fall below its active, homeothermic level. The fall in body temperature is slow and controlled: it does not fluctuate freely with air temperature, and is *maintained within narrow limits* at this lower level. If the air gets too cold, the torpid bat will burn off some of its stored fuel to provide the energy needed to keep itself from becoming too cold. If that is torpor, what is hibernation? Simply put, **hibernation** is an extended form of torpor, lasting for days, weeks, or months, which occurs on a seasonal basis, in response to a prolonged fall in ambient temperature or reduction in food supply. Bats do not usually spend their time in continuous hibernation, and in a maritime climate, bats may be more or less active right through a mild winter. Ransome (1990) has suggested that the difference between 'summer' and hibernation torpor hinges on the arousal process which starts at dusk in response to the peak in the bats' daily temperature cycle.

In summer, this always leads to arousal, but in winter arousal is suppressed for many days at a time. Rather than wrangle over definitions, it is perhaps better to pose a question: how does torpor fit into the life history strategy of a bat? Before answering this question, we need to look at the cost of endothermy.

THE COST OF STAYING WARM—THE IMPORTANCE OF BODY SIZE

Let's start by looking at the costs of homoeothermy and heterothermy. The most important single factor influencing the cost of homoeothermy is body size. The relationship between body mass and resting metabolic rate (RMR—metabolic rate in an alert but resting animal) for mammals is shown in Fig. 4.2, as a log–log plot. The use of such graphs is common practise among biologists interested in the effects of size, since a remarkable number of biological variables can be related to body mass (M) by the simple equation:

$$y = aM^b$$

By plotting the log of the variable y against log M, the exponent b, can be calculated from the slope of the line (a is the intercept of the line with the y-axis). If y increases in direct proportion to M, then the slope, b, = 1. If y increases more slowly than M, $b<1$, and $b>1$ if y increases faster than M. If y decreases as M increases, then b is negative. Body size has an enormous influence on all aspects of biology, and for a fascinating and readable introduction to the subject see Schmidt-Nielsen's book (1984). In the case in question, resting metabolic rate increases with increasing body mass, but it increases more slowly than if it was directly proportional to M: $b = 0.75$: larger animals have relatively low metabolic rates (Kleiber, 1932, was the first to describe this important relation).

This is seen best if we plot the metabolic rate per kg of tissue (mass-specific RMR) against body mass on a similar log–log plot, as shown in Fig. 4.3: $b = -0.25$: small

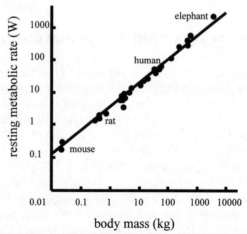

Fig. 4.2. The relationship between resting metabolic rate and body mass in birds and mammals (adapted from Schmidt-Nielsen, 1984).

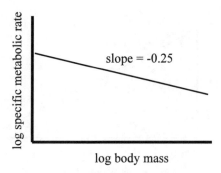

Fig. 4.3.   The relationship between mass-specific resting metabolic rate and body mass in birds and mammals (from Schmidt-Nielsen, 1984).

mammals have disproportionately high mass specific metabolic rates. This is not surprising: look at the even steeper relationship between minimal thermal conductance, the rate at which energy is lost from the body, and body mass in Fig. 4.4a. (McNab, 1969; 1982). This is a very predictable consequence of the increased surface area : volume ratio with decreasing size.

Figure 4.4b shows that, with the exception of the biggest megabats, the bats studied tended to have higher thermal conductances than other mammals. McNab (1969) carried out his experiments on tropical bats, and the higher conductances may be due to the fact that tropical mammals have poor insulation relative to temperate mammals of the same size (Scholander *et al.*, 1950). Alternatively, or in addition, they may be due to the heat lost from the wings. Thus, if a bat needs to remain homoeothermic, the smaller the bat, the higher the mass-specific metabolic rate, and the more food it needs per gram of body tissue to maintain its temperature. The 8 g little brown bat, *Myotis lucifugus,* needs food to generate 3.7 kJ/g/day, a 180 g false vampire, *Vampyrum spectrum*, only 1.1 kJ/g/day. As a bat, or any other homoeotherm, gets smaller its energy stores decrease faster (αM^1) than the rate at which it uses energy ($\alpha M^{0.75}$), so it has to feed more often (McNab, 1982). Starvation is never far away for a small mammal, particularly in a cold environment. The problem is too extreme to be solved by extra insulation: the little brown bat would need to be at the centre of a furry football. It therefore makes sense that if a small mammal has no reason to remain homoeothermic all the time, then a heterothermic option should evolve. The two extreme courses of action shown in Fig. 4.1 are not the only options. The thermostat could be set to any temperature between ambient and full homoeothermy, and the temperature chosen depends upon the ambient temperature, the energy reserves of the bat, and its physiological and ecological requirements at the time. As a general rule, however, the set temperature is usually ambient or a little above it, at temperatures above 1 °C.

A 9 g fringed myotis (*Myotis thysanodes*) has a thermal neutral zone of 30–38 °C. Flight and night roost maintenance use up 1.55 kJ/g/day. Day roost maintenance at 20 °C ambient temperature for a regulating bat costs an additional 0.67 kJ/g/day. However, if the bat becomes heterothermic, only an additional 0.34 kJ/g/day, are required (O'Farrell and Studier, 1970). This is a 15% daily energy saving. On a minute by minute basis the homoeothermic 3–5 g western pipistrelle discussed earlier uses 4–5 times as much oxygen at an ambient temperature of 20 °C, than when it is in its thermal neutral zone,

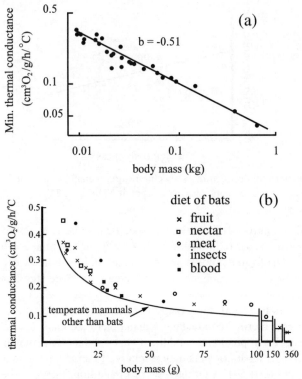

Fig. 4.4. The relationship between minimal thermal conductance and body mass in bats. (a) Log–log and (b) linear plots (adapted from Fig. 24, McNab, 1969).

and 8–9 times that of a heterothermic bat at 20 °C. Any opportunity to down-regulate body temperature can mean big energy savings. The very smallest species of bat may be obligatory heterotherms some of the time—that is they may have no option. However, it is clear that the rest are facultative heterotherms—they can choose when to be heterothermic, and how much to down-regulate.

As with many things in biology, the situation is not quite that simple. Above (Fig. 4.2), I described the relationship between body mass and resting metabolic rate (RMR) for homoeothermic mammals, saying that resting metabolic rate increased in proportion to $M^{0.75}$. Two questions have arisen about this relation. Is the slope really 0.75, and is this the slope for all homoeotherms? It is important to clear up these questions, since they are relevant to bats. First, if RMR was simply proportional to body surface area, then the slope should be 0.67. Despite much debate, discussed by Schmidt-Nielsen (1984), the slope **is** 0.75, not 0.67, and as yet we cannot explain the difference. One of the arguments against the 0.75 value hinges on the deviation from the line of some mammalian groups, in particular the shrews: depending upon which animals are included in the calculation, the slope varies. Shrews undoubtedly have higher RMRs than those predicted from the allometric equation, as do seals and whales, but desert rodents have lower rates. If **all** homoeotherms are included, however, the slope is 0.75. These deviations from the expected curve often convey an important message. Marine

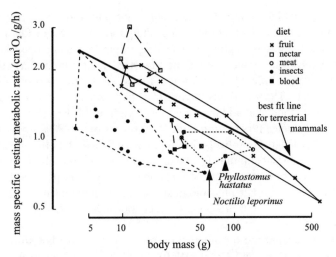

Fig. 4.5. The relationship between mass-specific resting metabolic rate and body mass in bats with different diets (from McNab, 1982).

mammals have the problem of maintaining high body temperatures in cold water, which conducts heat away from the body rapidly—hence the high metabolic rate. Desert mammals, from rats to camels, often have to contend with a poor food supply: a low RMR is therefore an adaptive advantage. It turns out that bats also deviate from the curve, and this deserves a closer look (Fig. 4.5).

As a general rule, insectivorous bats have RMRs below the predicted line, but all other bats (carnivorous and fruit/nectar eating bats) fall on, or even a little above, the line. Species with mixed diets, such as *Phyllostomus hastatus and Noctilio leporinus*, have intermediate RMRs (McNab, 1982). These differences appear to be truly related to diet rather than to phylogenetic origin (i.e taxonomic relations are unimportant). The low RMR of insectivores may reflect the low energy content and relatively unreliable nature of their food supply. The debate about the relative importance of ecology and phylogeny in biological scaling is long standing and wide ranging. For those interested, McNab (1992) has written the latest instalment in relation to metabolic rates.

THE PHYSIOLOGY OF TORPOR

Can we define torpor in physiological terms? We can certainly list some features characteristic of torpor:

1. A controlled reduction of body temperature typically to within 1–2 °C of ambient temperature.
2. A fall in O_2 consumption, breathing rate, heart rate, and metabolic rate.
3. Peripheral vasoconstriction, and in extreme cases restricted blood flow to only a few vital organs for long periods.
4. An ability to arouse spontaneously, and independently, of ambient temperature.

Let's follow a bat into hibernation and look at the physiological changes which occur. Our bat will prepare for hibernation by depositing large reserves of fat. To do this many bats appear to rely more on regular post-feeding torpor than an increase in feeding activity. Some are known to forage close to the sites used at least in the early stages of hibernation, and are thus able to enter torpor immediately after feeding (Twente, 1955; Krzanowski, 1961). The 9 g fringed myotis (*Myotis thysanodes*) can store almost 0.2 g fat per day by this method, and add over 2 g to its weight in 11 days (Ewing *et al.*, 1970). A bat will typically enter hibernation with fat reserves of 20–30% body weight (Ewing *et al.*, 1970). Day length is probably the cue for laying down fat prior to entering hibernation. The most important stimulus for the onset of hibernation itself appears to be ambient temperature, in contrast to rodents, where food shortage and photoperiod are the main factors. Hormonal and other physiological factors are undoubtedly important, but they have been little studied and are poorly understood. Once hibernation does begin, the changes are profound.

Heart rates measured during hibernation range from 10–16 beats/min in the red bat, *Lasiurus borealis* (Reite and Davis, 1966), to 42–62 beats/min in the big brown bat, *Eptesicus fuscus* (Kallen, 1977). Contrast this with 250–450 beats/min at rest, and 800 beats/min during flight (Studier and Howell, 1969; Studier and O'Farrell, 1976). The blood supply to the limbs is shut down, and the excess red blood cells are stored in the spleen. Only the vital organs such as the brain and heart retain a normal, regular blood supply. The bat breathes slowly and erratically. It may go for 60–90 minutes without a breath. The oxygen consumption rate of a hibernating little brown bat (*Myotis lucifugus*) at 2 °C is 140 times slower than that of a fully homoeothermic individual (Thomas *et al.*, 1990). This uses just 4 mg of fat per day, from the 2.5 g available to a well-fed bat. In theory, this would keep it going for almost two years! However, a small rise in temperature, or a brief arousal, increases this rate enormously, and 165 days has been estimated to be the maximum, uninterrupted hibernation period possible for this bat. How long can a bat remain in hibernation? Little brown bats have remained torpid for up to 140 days under laboratory conditions (Menaker, 1964). In the wild, hibernation is usually interrupted by frequent arousal.

Fig. 4.6. The location of brown adipose tissue in a microbat.

How do bats arouse themselves? It starts with an increase in heart rate and breathing rate. The increased blood flow is sent in part to the brown adipose tissue (Fig. 4.6, abbreviated to BAT!)—a deposit of fat on the back, which has cells specialised for heat production. The fat cells in the BAT of the bat have an unusually large number of mitochondria, the organelles responsible for turning fat into ATP, the high-energy molecule which powers most cellular processes. In this case, the energy is released directly as heat. BAT is found in many small mammals, and in the young of larger mammals, including humans.

The blood is warmed as it passes through the BAT, and warms the rest of the body. The bat may begin to shiver, once the muscles are warm enough to do so, and the heat generated by this muscular activity speeds up the warming up process. Muscle is only 20–40% efficient at producing mechanical power—the rest of the energy is lost as heat. In 10–30 minutes the bat can be fully active (Fig. 4.7).

Small mammals have high mass-specific rates of heat loss, and during arousal, we would expect them to lose heat more rapidly to the environment than larger heterotherms, and therefore warm more slowly. However, Stone and Purvis (1992) found that mean warm-up rate increased with decreasing body size in heterothermic mammals, a result which runs counter to predictions based on scaling effects. It seems that small mammals have evolved mechanisms to speed up arousal; possibility by having more brown adipose tissue. Furthermore warm-up rate increased as the temperature range over which the animal arouses increased, and surprisingly, warm-up rate was inversely related to resting metabolic rate (although positively related to peak metabolic rate). The mechanisms underlying these interesting relationships are not yet understood, but they all make sound functional sense. Arousal is an expensive process, and mechanisms which minimise the time of arousal reduce the energy wasted. The low RMR reduces the cost of maintaining a high body temperature, and we might expect this trait to be selected for during the

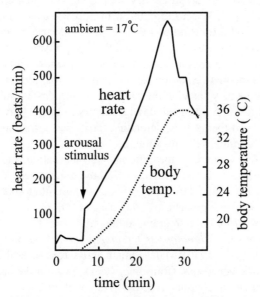

Fig. 4.7. Heart rate and body temperature changes during arousal from torpor in the mouse-eared bat, *Myotis myotis* (from Kulzer, 1967, Fig. 13).

evolution of small heterotherms. The data are too few to interpret them with confidence in terms of natural torpor patterns, but they are certainly thought-provoking.

THE ECOLOGY OF TORPOR AND HIBERNATION

Torpor, used on a daily basis for energy budgeting, or for long periods of hibernation, is an important and integral component of the life history strategy of bats in both temperate and tropical regions. To give a general picture of how torpor can be used, let's briefly look at a year in the life of a temperate microbat, before broadening the discussion to cover all bats. We'll start in spring, with a well fed pipistrelle.

Its fuel tanks, in the form of fat deposits, are full after foraging on several warm, insect-rich evenings. The capricious temperate spring brings in cold, wet weather, and the bat can't forage, so it stays in the roost. It's a pregnant female, with a developing foetus, so it maintains a high body temperature throughout most of the day and night to speed the growth of its baby, using up its stored energy. The bad weather doesn't last, so it is soon out foraging again. A couple of weeks later, there is a longer cold snap. The bat's reserves of fat are reduced to a critical level, and it is forced to become heterothermic to save energy. This slows foetal development, but there is no choice. In a bad year, this may lead to abortion. However, this year the bat is soon feeding again, and spends much of its time in a homeothermic state through gestation, lactation, and into weaning. During this time a nearby male has a different strategy. He hasn't got the worry of a developing foetus, he is probably not defending a territory or attracting mates at that time of year, so he doesn't need to maintain a high body temperature. He can afford to forage only on those nights best suited for foraging, and spends a lot of time in torpor to save energy. An opposing view recently put forward is that he does need energy to produce sperm, and he may not have it quite so easy as previously supposed. This problem was addressed by Hamilton and Barclay (1994) who monitored big brown bats, *Eptesicus fuscus*, with temperature-sensitive radio transmitters. Both sexes made use of torpor throughout the summer, but males used it more frequently, and their torpor was deeper.

Let's jump now to late summer and autumn. Food is plentiful, and the bats are making the most of it. This is the mating season for bats, so they will remain homoeothermic for at least some of the time they spend in the roost. However, despite substantial reserves of fat, the females will spend a lot of the daylight hours in torpor, saving energy. It is the turn of the males to exert themselves, defending territories, attracting mates and mating. This behaviour will continue well into autumn.

It is difficult to define when daily torpor turns into hibernation, and it is probably uninformative and misleading to try. It all depends on the temperature, the food supply, and other demands on the bat's time. However, the bats will go into torpor more often, and for longer periods as the winter approaches. Young bats are still growing, and may not be able to afford the luxury of torpor quite so often, so they may enter hibernation later than adults and at a lower weight (e.g. *Rhinolophus ferrumequinum*, Ransome, 1968, 1990; three *Myotis* species, Ewing *et al.*, 1970). Males remain active for longer than females, and also enter hibernation at a lower weight (Ransome, 1971). Even in the depths of the harshest winter, bats do not remain in continuous torpor. They will arouse at intervals of from days to weeks to drink, move to another hibernation site, or even mate (Ransome, 1971). Males are certainly more active than females in some species (e.g. Avery, 1985), possibly due to the need to compensate for a lower body weight at the onset of hibernation (Ransome, 1990), and to mating activity. In periods of warm weather, common in temperate winters, many bats will come out and feed. In mild winters bats forage right through the winter (Ransome, 1971; Avery, 1985; Brigham, 1987). In horseshoe bats, *Rhinolophus ferrume-quinum*, there is no correlation between mass on entering torpor in winter, and that at the end of hibernation, and they can increase fat reserves substantially during the winter months (Ransome, 1990). These bats can clearly top up their food stores by winter foraging. In captive pipistrelles, *Pipistrellus pipistrellus*, mass loss during torpor is independent of original mass (Speakman and Racey, 1989), and although winter feeding occurs, they do not appear to regulate their body mass in the same way as horseshoe bats—a light bat in a group is always a light bat (Avery, 1985). Speakman and Racey (1989) suggest that they may not need to regulate mass: by regulating fat reserves over the winter they ensure that even late in hibernation they are well above levels which could lead to mortality.

Comparative aspects

Daily torpor is used by many species in the large, temperate branches of the Rhinolophidae and Vespertilionidae. Many temperate, and a few subtropical, species from these two families are known hibernators. It has been suggested that some members of the Molossidae, Hipposideridae, Rhinopomatidae, and Mystacinidae use torpor, but the question is far from resolved. Torpor is characteristic of insectivorous bats, and this is related not only to their small size, but to the ephemeral nature of their food supply. In species which bridge the temperate–subtropical divide, the situation may be more complex than in those confined to temperate regions. The Mexican free-tailed bat, *Tadarida brasiliensis*, ranges from northern California south to Mexico. Populations in northern California do not migrate, are perhaps capable of using torpor, and have been found 'hibernating' in cold sites typical of those used by temperate bats (Pagels, 1975). They do not, however, allow their temperature to drop close to ambient, but maintain a differential of 24–31 °C (Pagels, 1975). *T. brasiliensis* in Arizona also do not migrate, but they are incapable of torpor, and spend the winter roosting in warm chimneys, caves and tunnels. *T. brasiliensis* from other south western states migrates into Mexico.

Some species on the temperate–sub-tropical divide use daily torpor only in the winter months, and seem unable to utilise it at other times, e.g. the western mastiff bat, *Eumops perotis*, in the United States and the greater mouse-tailed bat, *Rhinopoma microphyllum*, in India. Daily torpor is used to a limited extent by many tropical, insectivorous bats whose food supply is unreliable and often low in energy (McNab, 1969; Studier and Wilson, 1970; McNab, 1982).

The fruit-eating megabats are almost exclusively homoeothermic, due in part to their large size, but also to the relative abundance and reliability of their food supply—they can afford the expense of continuous homoeothermy. Large *Pteropus* and *Rousettus* species wrap their wings around their body and tuck in their heads, when temperature is very low, creating large, still air spaces to reduce heat-loss. Conversely, wing flapping, panting, and other behavioural methods are used to keep cool when temperatures are high. One or two small megabats have been shown to make use of daily torpor when ambient temperature is very low. The tube-nosed bats *Nyctimene albiventer* (30 g) and *Paranyctimene raptor* (20 g) from New Guinea can slip into torpor and reduce oxygen consumption four fold at 25 °C (Bartholomew *et al.*, 1970). The African long-tongued fruit bat, *Megaloglossus woermanni*, also enters daily torpor, reducing body temperature to as little as 26 °C at an ambient temperature of 23 °C (Kulzer and Storf, 1980).

The diverse Phyllostomidae of south and central America includes both frugivores and insectivores. However, the over-riding factor determining the thermoregulatory strategy is size. The insectivores are all heterothermic to some degree, as expected, and the fruit-eaters, small in comparison to the average megabat, are also generally heterothermic in the wild. However, when this family was first studied some conflicting results were obtained, one investigation suggesting homoeothermy in the fruit-eaters (McNab, 1969), the other heterothermy (Studier and Wilson, 1970). The problem was resolved when it was realised just how important the nutritional state of the bats was in determining their response to low ambient temperatures. A well-fed bat can afford the luxury of homoeothermy, a hungry bat may not (Studier and Wilson, 1979).

The relatively large size and high energy diet of carnivorous bats should incline them towards homoeothermy. The 150 g Australian ghost bat, *Macroderma gigas*, is homoeothermic over a wide temperature range, and so too is the phyllostomid *Chrotopterus auritus* (100 g) (McManus, 1976). The larger fisherman bat, *Noctilio leporinus* (60 g) does appear to have the capacity for heterothermy, due to its size, and perhaps its mixed diet—it may rely on insects to a large extent in some circumstances (McManus, 1976). In contrast, *Nycteris grandis* (30 g) takes large numbers of vertebrates, but is homoeothermic. The common vampire, *Desmodus rotundus*, (35 g) also appears to be homoeothermic down to very low temperatures in the wild, although capable of heterothermy. The two other vampire species, *Diphylla ecaudata* and *Diaemus youngi* may resort to heterothermy more often. Perhaps the avian blood they feed on is harder to obtain than the blood of the largely domestic prey of *Desmodus*.

Hibernacula

Different species have different microclimatic requirements for successful hibernation, and the success or failure of a bat to survive the winter is dependent to a large extent on it

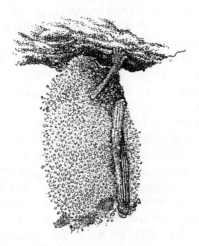

Fig. 4.8.   A hibernating whiskered bat, *Myotis mystacinus*, covered in condensed water droplets.

finding the right conditions—some species have different requirements at different times. Figure 4.8 shows the common perception of a hibernating bat—a whiskered bat (*Myotis mystacinus*), a small vespertilionid, in deep torpor in a cave. Caves selected by bats have several features which apparently make them ideal sites. They are cool in winter, but not too cold: away from the entrance of a cave with limited airflow temperatures are typically 2–10 °C throughout even the harshest temperate winter. The temperature may be very stable in any given location in the cave, although different locations may be quite different in temperature. For example it is cold on the floor, but depressions in the ceiling retain rising warm air and can be considerably warmer than other parts of the cave. Bats roosting in such a depression can raise the temperature further. Different species can therefore select the location which suits them best. Caves can also be damp. Most species benefit from high humidity, since it reduces the amount of water they lose to the air, and they do not need to drink so often. The whiskered bat's glistening coat is due to a covering of condensed water droplets.

Many species habitually select open sites, and often hang free of the rock e.g. horseshoe bats, which characteristically wrap their wings around their body (Fig. 4.9), and

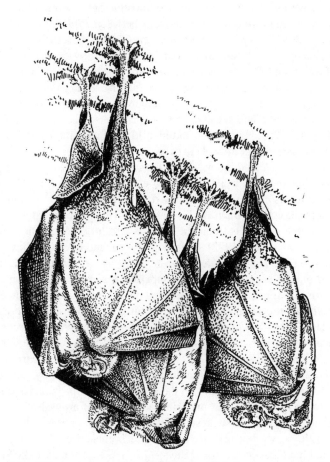

Fig. 4.9.   Hibernating greater horseshoe bats, *Rhinolophus ferrumequinum*.

many *Myotis* species, e.g. mouse-eared and Daubenton's bats, *Myotis myotis* and *M. daubentonii,* in Europe, and the little brown and grey bats, *M. lucifugus* and *M. grisescens*, in North America. Others, e.g. *Myotis nattereri* commonly crawl into cracks to hibernate. The rubble on cave floors is also used by some species. Several species of bat are often found roosting in the same cave, and it is not uncommon to find clusters containing two or more species. Many species have adapted to man-made hibernacula such as mines and tunnels which offer similar microclimates.

The literature on cave-hibernating bats is quite extensive, and a number of general statements can be made about their behaviour. Bats very rarely spend the entire winter in torpor: arousal occurs at intervals dependent upon ambient temperature, the size of the bat, and its roosting habits (Daan, 1973; McNab, 1974b; Ransome, 1990). A number of studies have shown that within a species, the interval between arousals decreases with increasing temperature (e.g. Ransome, 1971; Twente *et al.*, 1985). Small bats also tend to arouse less frequently. At 10 °C, half of the 6 g *Pipistrellus subflavus* in a cave aroused and moved position in 44 days, but at 20 °C half moved in just 1 day (McNab, 1974b). In contrast, half of the 25 g greater horseshoe bats, *Rhinolophus ferrumequinum*, moved in 1 day at 10 °C. To compensate for this effect, larger species will often select cooler locations in caves. As well as the difference in size, roosting habit is important, and probably accounts for some of the difference in behaviour between *Pipistrellus subflavus,* a solitary hibernator and *Rhinolophus ferrumequinum*, which hibernates in clusters. The importance of clustering, independent of size, can be seen by comparing *Myotis lucifugus*, a cluster former, and *Myotis emarginatus*, a solitary hibernator. Both weigh about 9 g, but *M. lucifugus* arouses far more frequently than *M. emarginatus* (McNab, 1974a). Clustering bats tend to maintain higher body temperatures, relative to ambient temperature, than solitary bats, and will select cooler sites in caves (Beer and Richards, 1956). In warm caves (Twente, 1955; Hall, 1962) and in mild weather (Hooper and Hooper, 1956), bats form smaller clusters than in cool caves and cold weather.

Assuming bats have selected the most appropriate natural hibernation sites, how often do they arouse? The short answer is that once every 20 days is a rough mean, but the period between arousals can vary from a few days to many weeks. A number of studies of vesper and horseshoe bats (Daan, 1973; Ransome, 1971; Brack and Twente, 1985) all agree on the point that arousal is frequent. There is also little doubt that some of the bats leave the hibernaculum (Daan, 1973), to drink and feed, and to change hibernation site.

Work by Ransome (1971) on greater horseshoe bats shows that they select sites within a hibernaculum on the basis of ambient temperature and season. Warmer sites were chosen after warm days, presumably to trigger arousal so that the bats could feed during these warm spells. At the same ambient temperature, they choose cooler sites in spring, than in winter (Fig. 4.10)—to compensate for an observed increase in arousal frequency at a given temperature, from winter to spring. Avery (1985) showed that winter flights of the pipistrelle, *Pipistrellus pipistrellus*, occurred more often on warm nights, when insects were more abundant. Their behaviour could be explained by a model based on emergence for food. Laboratory studies on the same species (Speakman and Racey, 1989) give an alternative explanation: that the primary function of arousal in this species is to drink. More recently it has been suggested that the need for water may be responsible for arousal in the little brown bat (*Myotis lucifugus*, Thomas and Cloutier, 1992) and the brown long-eared bat (*Plecotus auritus*, Hays *et al.*, 1992). Thomas and Cloutier showed that more than 99% of water loss was by evaporation across the skin, and suggested that clustering may be an adaptation to reduce water loss.

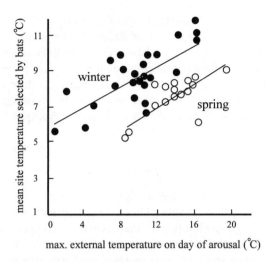

Fig. 4.10. Hibernation temperature selection in greater horseshoe bats, *Rhinolophus ferrume-quinum*, in relation to external temperature and season (from Ransome, 1990).

Some bats, such as the long-eared bat (*Plecotus auritus*) in Europe, are rarely found deep in caves, but may spend part of the winter near the entrance. For much of the winter, long-eared bats hibernate in more exposed sites, often in buildings, or in trees. Few studies have been carried out on tree hibernators. The red bat, *Lasiurus borealis*, has been found in deep hibernation torpor hanging from tree branches, but this and most other tree species hibernate in tree holes. The most extensive study was carried out on the noctule, *Nyctalus noctula*, a 25 g bat found throughout Europe (Sluiter *et al.*, 1973). Bats were kept singly or in clusters of 50 in sections of tree trunk, either in the open or in temperature-controlled rooms. Single or clustered bats survived without food for the duration of the experiment—almost 4 months, and clusters of bats could tolerate ambient temperatures of –16 °C, by maintaining surface body temperature at –9 °C. Between –9 °C and 10 °C, bats aroused every 4–8 days. Temperatures above and below this range often led to daily arousal. Noctules are migratory in parts of continental Europe (Strelkov, 1969): even holes in the thickest tree trunks may not provide sufficient insulation against the extreme temperatures of a continental climate.

Some bats use the most unusual and often puzzling sites for hibernation. Barbastelle bats, *Barbastella barbastellus*, have occasionally been found in the leaf litter among the roots of large trees. Others species have been found in small cavities in the soil, often gaining entry through a bank side. Some species, such as the pipistrelle, *Pipistrellus pipistrellus*, appear to tolerate daily temperature fluctuations of over 20 °C in some of their hibernation sites and just how they deal with this in energetic terms remains a mystery.

BIOLOGICAL CLOCKS

The movement of the Earth brings about environmental changes which influence the behaviour of virtually all organisms. At the most fundamental level, light intensity, temperature, and humidity change on a daily (circadian) and an annual (circannual) cycle. These changes cause complex, but to some degree, predictable changes in the biotic and abiotic environment. Animals have adapted to these cycles by evolving their own internal clocks, which allow them to synchronise their activity patterns with the environmental cycles, and even prepare for changes in advance. There are three main types of internal clock: circadian, circannual, and tidal. I do not think the latter is of any major importance to bats, although vampires will delay evening emergence to avoid moonlight, and the activity of some insectivorous species is also influenced by moonlight (Bay, 1978)—presumably to avoid predators. The circadian and circannual clocks of bats play a crucial role in torpor and hibernation.

Circadian clocks

In the absence of external cues, few biological clocks are accurate—e.g. circadian rhythms are not set to exactly 24 h, but can be several hours longer or, more frequently, shorter. In normal life, they are kept in synchrony with the environmental cycles by external cues, which reset the biological clock each day, entraining it. The most common circadian cue is photoperiod—the most invariant of the environmental cues. The importance of a good circadian clock to a bat is obvious. With the major (night-time) insect abundance peaks occurring at dusk and dawn it's no good if the bat sleeps in and misses them. On the other hand it does not want to arouse too early and waste energy. Some of the best evidence for circadian clocks in bats comes from studies of hibernating microbats.

Figure 4.11 shows the frequency of flights within a cave over a 48 h period, from October to April, of 3 *Myotis* species (Daan, 1973). The frequency of flights is a good indicator of arousal from torpor. In October, the bats arouse in large numbers, with peaks in the late evening. The bats are still feeding outside, and the biological clock is therefore entrained with the environment. As the winter progresses, there is much less activity, the bats remain torpid for up to 20 days at a time, and the peaks are much less evident, since the clocks of most bats are free-running, and no longer entrained. In spring, as the bats come out of hibernation and feed, the clocks are again entrained.

Figure 4.11 does not show that in individual bats the circadian clock can be very stable, even in bats in deep torpor, although clock period can vary considerably. For example, in captive big brown bats, *Eptesicus fuscus*, held in the dark at 2 °C, clock period varied from 13–21 h (Twente and Twente, 1987), but most bats kept good time, and aroused within 2 or 3 hours of dusk. Thomas (1993, 1995) used automatically logged echolocation calls and temperature-sensitive radio tags to study hibernating little brown bats in the wild. In contrast to the laboratory studies, he found no evidence for an endogenous circadian rhythm tightly regulating the timing of arousal. Differences in arousal patterns between laboratory and field studies are common, and are reviewed by Thomas (1995). In many hibernacula temperature may provide no clue to the weather outside, so an ability to maintain a reasonably accurate circadian rhythm through torpor is important if bats are to take advantage of warm nights when feeding might be possible. Failure to arouse means a missed opportunity, and arousal during the day is wasteful of energy. Bats with an intrinsically more stable and reliable circadian clock should have a selective advantage over others. However, as shown in Fig. 4.11, in the absence of external cues the clock free runs, and synchrony between the bat and its environment is lost. Thomas suggests that synchrony of arousal in the laboratory is an artefact, and that wild populations quickly desynchronise.

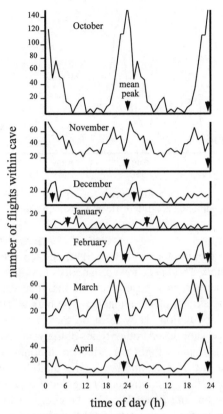

Fig. 4.11.   The frequency of flights of *Myotis* bats within a hibernation cave (from Daan, 1973).

Circannual clocks

Another way of keeping ahead in the survival game is to be prepared for the future. In bats, this could mean preparation for the onset of winter. A circannual clock, free, at least to some degree, of the vagaries of the temperate climate, could be useful to a temperate bat in triggering preparation for hibernation. Do circannual clocks exist in bats?

Figure 4.12 shows the body weight changes in a male pallid bat, *Antrozous pallidus*, over 3 years. The bat was kept under constant conditions of photoperiod (14 h light), temperature (23 °C), and food supply (Beasley, Pelz, and Zucker, 1984). Despite the lack of external cues, it still put on weight from September to December in preparation for a winter which did not come. A similar pattern was seen in many other bats in the study. The clock period varied from bat to bat, and small differences were noted between the sexes, but the mean for all bats was 300 days, significantly less than one year. Food intake and reproductive cycles also showed similar behaviour. The changes in reproductive state and body weight normally seen in male bats in autumn could be induced by the appropriate change in photoperiod, or by subcutaneous implants of the hormone melatonin, which is normally secreted by the pineal gland in response to photoperiod changes (Beasley, Smale, and Smith, 1984). In another experiment (Beasley, 1986), pallid bats

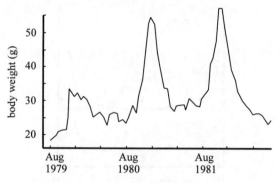

Fig. 4.12. Changes in body mass, over three years, of a pallid bat (*Antrozous pallidus*), kept under constant environmental conditions (from Beasley, Pelz and Zucker, 1984).

were again kept under constant photoperiod (14 h light) and temperature (23 °C), but the food supply was unrestricted. The bats showed patterns of weight change, food intake, and reproductive state comparable to those of a wild bat. The value of this circannual clock should be as obvious as that of the circadian. The bats will need to put down fat reserves in readiness for hibernation. They must do this in the autumn in the face of fluctuating weather and food supplies. At other times of the year, excess weight increases the cost of locomotion and impairs flight performance: the amount of stored fat must reflect the needs of the bat at that time, and not food availability, which may be unpredictable. The bats in essence have a continuously regulated food reserve. The 'correct' amount varies with the season, and is regulated by the circannual clock. This clock can free run, but is normally entrained by environmental factors, principally photoperiod, the most predictable indicator of the season. On top of this the bat has a fine control, determined by a more variable set of physiological and ecological factors, linked to the life history cycle.

EVOLUTION OF TORPOR AND HIBERNATION

It is now generally accepted that torpor evolved in the tropics, probably in small insectivorous bats. We have seen in this chapter how tropical insectivores have lower RMRs than frugivores or omnivores of a similar size, and how they are more likely to resort to facultative torpor due to fluctuations in their food supply and their small size. From their origins in the tropics, bats invaded the sub-tropical and then the temperate zones, and many were pre-adapted to some extent to a heterothermic existence. As they colonised higher latitudes, facultative torpor evolved further, enabling bats to exploit some of the most extreme temperate climates, by hibernating for extended periods. Hibernation occurs in members of at least two microbat families, and possibly evolved independently on several occasions. Interestingly, some temperate bats may have invaded the tropics, and this may explain why tropical horseshoe and vesper bats do not maintain high body temperatures like other tropical insectivorous bats: they may not have there long enough to evolve a 'tropical' thermoregulatory strategy. For a more detailed discussion, see McNab (1969).

5 Reproduction and development

Reproductive cycles, timing the onset of gestation—different strategies. Monoestrous and polyoestrous cycles and the environment. Gestation. Birth, development, and survival. Life expectancy. Infant–mother communication and maternal care. Roost selection and maternal feeding patterns. Mating patterns, sexual dimorphism.

I'll look at reproduction predominantly from an ecological and behavioural perspective, concentrating on how different strategies have evolved to meet different ecological and environmental demands. The detailed physiology of reproduction in bats is very varied, but follows the essential mammalian plan in outline, and I will not cover it in any detail. Hill and Smith (1984) give a good account of the basics. Excellent reviews on all aspects of bat reproduction have been written by Racey (1982), Tuttle and Stevenson (1982), Kunz (1987), Kurta and Kunz (1987), and Ransome (1990).

REPRODUCTIVE CYCLES

Bats are placental mammals. After mating and fertilisation, the egg is implanted in the wall of the uterus and the foetus completes its development over a gestation period characteristic of the species. All nourishment comes from the placenta, which also meets the embryo's other physiological requirements—delivery of oxygen, removal of waste products, and immunological defence. After birth the young are protected and given shelter, fed on the mother's milk, and possibly instructed for a period, before weaning and eventual independence. Within that framework, bats show considerable variation, and this can generally be linked to climate and feeding habits. Before looking at variations in the reproductive cycle, I need to say something about the physiological mechanisms which have evolved to enable bats to adjust the timing of the key stage in reproduction.

Starting gestation at the right time

Bats have evolved a number of mechanisms to ensure that birth is timed to give the greatest chance of survival to both the female and its young. This may mean that timing has to be very precise. For example, in the case of bats at the highest latitudes the summer is short, and the young must be born as early in the year as is feasible to maximise the time for full development before the onset of winter. The females need a good food supply through gestation and lactation, the young must be rapidly weaned, and there must still be time for both mothers and young to fatten themselves up for hibernation. Just how do they achieve this? The temperate summer is not long enough for mating, gestation, lactation, weaning, and prehibernation feeding. The last four factors must follow each other in fairly rapid succession. Once the foetus has begun to develop, most bats have little scope for putting the process on hold, or speeding it up. However, bats have evolved ways of isolating the first step, mating, from the last four steps of the reproductive cycle.

One mechanism was thought to be unique to bats, but it has now been observed in a small number of rodents and lagomorphs, and is probably more widespread still. This is delayed ovulation and fertilisation. It is the most common method used by temperate species, primarily vesper and horseshoe bats. Sperm production reaches a peak in late summer/early autumn, when the females are in oestrus. The bats will mate any time during this period, and mating can continue right through the winter in many species, during periods of arousal from hibernation. However, fertilisation does not occur, because the egg has yet to be released into the oviduct. The sperm are stored and possibly nourished in the oviduct or the uterus right through the winter, and ovulation and fertilisation occur in late winter/early spring, often when the female is arousing from hibernation. This ensures that as soon as the climate is suitable, the bat can leave hibernation, and the foetus can begin to develop. This is a remarkable process, since it means that foreign cells, which would normally be attacked and destroyed by the female immune system, are not only tolerated, but perhaps even nourished, for several months. In those species which can mate throughout the winter, sperm production normally ceases in September–November (in the northern hemisphere) and the males can store viable sperm through the winter.

Another strategy is delayed implantation, a method common to many mammals. In this case, ovulation occurs about the time of mating, and fertilisation occurs in the oviduct. (Ovulation is spontaneous in most bats, but in some it is triggered by copulation.) The fertilised egg then undergoes its first few cell divisions. What happens next depends upon geographical location and climate. In Schreiber's bent-winged bat, *Miniopterus schreibersii*, in the tropics foetal development continues uninterrupted, but in north and south temperate regions it is arrested in its early stages, and the embryo is not implanted in the uterus. After a delay of up to 5 months, implantation occurs at the beginning of the summer and gestation continues.

These strategies are not unique to temperate bats: many phyllostomids use them to synchronise birth with the rainy seasons, as we will see below.

The last strategy, embryonic diapause, appears to be unique to a few species of phyllostomid bats of Central and South America, such as the Jamaican fruit bat, *Artibeus jamaicensis*. In this case the embryo implants in the uterus, but becomes dormant for up to 10 weeks.

Monoestry

In the simplest reproductive patterns, there is a single cycle of oestrus, pregnancy, and lactation each year (Fig. 5.1). This pattern is common in tropical bats, and is found in most pteropodids (e.g. *Pteropus poliocephalus*, Nelson, 1965), and the majority of microbats, e.g. the megadermatids (*Megaderma lyra*, Brosset, 1962b), emballonurids (*Saccopteryx bilineata*, Bradbury and Vehrencamp, 1977b), phyllostomids (*Phyllostomus hastatus*, McCracken and Bradbury, 1977; *Brachyphylla cavernarum*, Nellis and Ehle, 1977) and vespertilionids (*Tylonycteris pachypus* and *T. robustula*, Medway, 1972). The

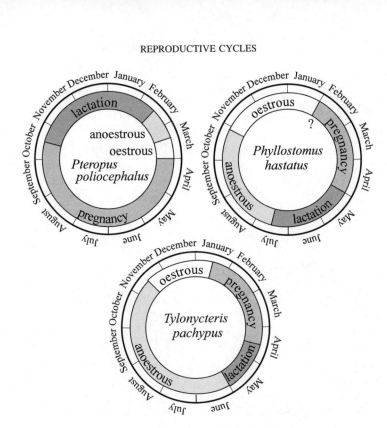

Fig. 5.1. Monoestrous reproductive patterns.

timing of the cycle is presumably governed by a circannual clock and entrained by photoperiod, although firm evidence for this is lacking, but other environmental factors modulate this control. The reproductive cycle is precisely timed, and pregnancy can be delayed after copulation in many species, to synchronise birth with the abundant food available during the rainy seasons (e.g. *Artibeus jamaicensis*). The gestation period is very variable and sometimes surprisingly long: 12–13 weeks in the very small *Tylonycteris pachypus* (4 g) and *T. robustula* (6 g) (Medway, 1972), and this may be an adaptation to the fluctuating insect supply.

Monoestry is the rule in temperate bats, but mating usually occurs in the autumn, and oestrus is 'extended' over the winter by one of the strategies described in the previous section, so that pregnancy begins in the spring. Because of the short summer, the breeding cycle is typically highly synchronous, and births occur over a period of as little as two weeks in a given species at a particular location (Racey, 1982). The females of most temperate species form maternity colonies, and the clusters share the costs of thermoregulation during pregnancy and lactation (Dwyer, 1971). The energy savings are very considerable and foetal and infant growth are accelerated (Herreid, 1963; 1967; Tuttle, 1975). Synchrony is best seen in small species which use cool roost sites, since they make the biggest gains from clustering (Dwyer, 1971). For example, the 7–9 g grey bat, *Myotis grisescens*, occupies the coldest reported summer roosts in North America (down to 13 °C), and birth is highly synchronous (Tuttle, 1975). The little brown bat, *Myotis lucifugus*, is the same size, but roosts at much higher temperatures in the same areas, and shows a lower degree of synchrony than any bat of similar size and distribution

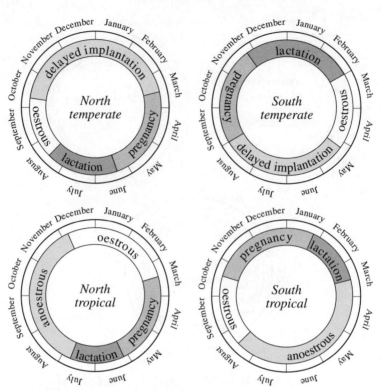

Fig. 5.2.   Reproductive patterns in Schreiber's bent-winged bat, *Miniopterus schreibersii*.

(O'Farrell and Studier, 1973). The largest North American species, the western mastiff bat, *Eumops perotis*, selects warm roosts, and has the least synchronous birth pattern (Barbour and Davis, 1969). O'Farrell and Studier (1973) studied two related species in the same building. In *Myotis thysanodes,* a bat which often uses cooler roosts, births were highly synchronous, but they were asynchronous in *M. lucifugus.*

Bats with a wide geographical distribution show the most varied patterns. In the tropics, foetal development in the bent-winged bat, *Miniopterus schreibersii*, begins immediately after mating: in March in the north and in October in the south. In north and south temperate regions, embryonic development is arrested in its early stages, and the embryo is not implanted in the uterus. After a delay of up to 5 months, implantation occurs at the beginning of the summer and gestation continues (Fig. 5.2) (Richardson, 1977). A similar pattern is seen in the moustached bat, *Pteronotus parnellii*, in the New World.

Polyoestry

In the generally more equable but more variable climates of the tropics, bats exhibit a very wide range of reproductive patterns (see Wilson, 1979; Racey, 1982; Tuttle and Stevenson, 1982, and Hill and Smith, 1984 for reviews from different perspectives). Most tropical species have two or even three annual oestrus cycles, which may be continuous (e.g. *Rousettus aegyptiacus* (Fig. 5.3) and *Eonycteris spaelaea*), interrupted by anoestrous

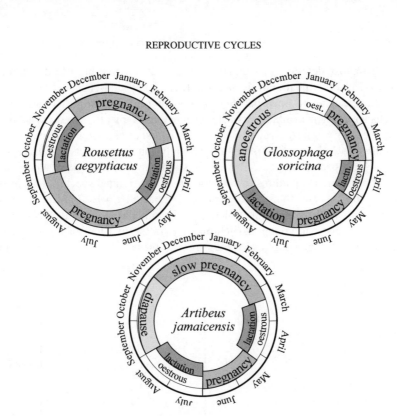

Fig. 5.3. Polyoestrous reproductive patterns.

(*Glossophaga soricina,* Fig. 5.3), delayed implantation (*Miniopterus schreibersii,* Fig. 5.2), or embryonic diapause (*Artibeus jamaicensis,* Fig. 5.3). Individual bats may produce young two or even three times a year.

In the cases investigated, multiple cycles are generally linked to seasonal trends in food supply, which in turn are determined by environmental factors such as rainfall and temperature. Underlying all this is the photoperiod-driven circannual clock. The importance of the clock itself is uncertain and probably varies, being more important at higher latitudes where changes in photoperiod are significant.

Species whose food is not subject to seasonal fluctuations tend to show aseasonal, asynchronous polyoestry. The common vampire, *Desmodus rotundus,* breeds continuously and asynchronously, but each bat has just two litters of single young each year (Fleming *et al.,* 1972). The fruit eating *Artibeus literatus* (Phyllostomidae), and the insectivorous *Taphozous longimanus* (Emballonuridae) and *Myotis mystacinus* (Vespertilionidae) appear to breed aseasonally and asynchronously over much of their range. *Pipistrellus dormeri* fits the same pattern, but from November to February the majority of births are twins, with single young predominant for the rest of the year (Madhaven, 1978). Patterns are discernible in species which at first appear to be asynchronous. The mastiff bat, *Molossus sinaloae,* although asynchronous, has a tendency to show birth peaks twice a year (LaVal and Fitch, 1977). *Myotis albescens* in Paraguay (Myers, 1977) and *M. adversus* in southern Queensland, Australia (Dwyer, 1970a) breed asynchronously for only half of the year, producing two and occasionally three young in separate litters (see also Thomas and Marshall, 1984).

One of the most detailed investigations was that by Bradbury and Vehrencamp (1976a;b; 1977a;b) of emballonurids in Costa Rica. The proboscis bat, *Rhynchonycteris naso*, and the lesser white-lined bat, *Saccopteryx leptura*, forage in habitats with little seasonal change in their availability of insect prey, and typically breed asynchronously more than once per year. The white-lined bat, *Saccopteryx bilineata*, and the sac-winged bats, *Balantiopteryx plicata*, feed more on seasonally abundant insects, and have a single, synchronous birth peak each year. This stresses the importance of food supply, and the flexibility of reproductive patterns, even between closely related species. This flexibility can be seen within species too: the 'big fruit-eating bat', *Artibeus lituratus*, is aseasonal and asynchronous near the equator, synchronously bimodal in Central America, and in Mexico produces just one young, asynchronously, in the first half of the year (Wilson, 1979). This, and other geographical trends are also presumably due to changes in food

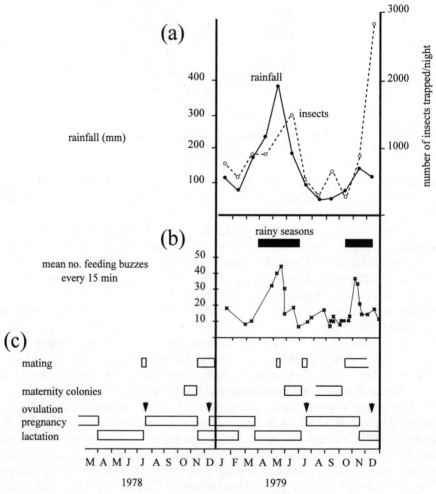

Fig. 5.4.   The reproductive cycle of the African sheath-tailed bat, *Coleura afra,* in Kenya (adapted from McWilliam, 1987).

supply, but most lack detailed investigation. Many bats have birth peaks which coincide with the known or predicted peaks in food abundance, which makes good sense, since the most energetically demanding period for the females is lactation (see Racey, 1982).

Figure 5.4 summarises studies by McWilliam (1987) on *Coleura afra* roosting in coral caves near Mombassa in Kenya, where there is a long rainy season (April–June inclusive) and a short rainy season (November and December) each year. The insect groups most commonly taken by *Coleura* all showed peaks roughly coincident with the rainy seasons, as did 'feeding success', as measured by terminal feeding buzzes on an ultrasound detector. The first pregnancy was coincident with the short dry season (January and February), and nearly all females in the colony gave birth at the onset of the long rainy season. However, the second pregnancy over-ran the long dry season (July–September inclusive) with birth occurring in the middle of the short rainy season, when many females failed to give birth. Their lower body mass early in pregnancy, and at ovulation, relative to that after the long rainy season, suggests this may be due to poor condition. Reproduction in some of the bats is suppressed early in the long dry season, presumably to save energy in those individuals not physiologically fit for the second pregnancy. Also coincident with the rainy seasons were maximum male body mass and testicular activity. Ovulation and mating occurred at the end of each rainy season. Foetal growth occurred at similar rates in the two cycles, but the poorer condition of the females led to an early delay in the short rains pregnancy and a longer gestation period. Early growth rates of the young bats were significantly slower after the short rains pregnancy.

Given the apparent difficulties of the second pregnancy, why do the bats persist with it? The answer lies in survival. The smaller number of young females from the short rains pregnancy survived the short dry season better than the long rains young survived the long dry season. Females become mature in their first year and can breed in the season in which they were born. All long rains females bred in their first season, but the majority of short rains females, like older females, did not breed over the first long dry season, a tactic which may increase their overall reproductive success.

The themes and variations within tropical bats are endless, and many are still poorly understood. For a further glimpse at this complexity, read Bonaccorso's (1979) description of Panamanian bats, Fleming *et al.* (1972) on some Central American communities, Wilson (1979) on the Phyllostomidae, and Thomas and Marshall (1984) on three west African fruit bats.

GESTATION

Determining when gestation actually begins can be a difficult task and so therefore is determining the length of gestation—the period from implantation to birth. As we have seen, bats can make use of sperm storage, delayed implantation, and embryonic diapause. The California leaf-nosed bat, *Macrotus californicus*, can slow foetal development right down, to achieve the same ends. The gestation period is thus very variable in bats, within and between species. As a general rule the larger the bat the longer the gestation period, from about 40 days to 5–6 months. In vampires, it is as long as eight months. The 40–50 days typical of a 5–8 g bat is relatively long: in a similar sized rodent or shrew, gestation is 20–30 days. Foetal growth rates in bats are among the slowest in mammals and are comparable with primates (Racey, 1973). We saw in the last chapter that heterothermic bats have generally low metabolic rates and this may in part explain the low rate of growth.

Variation within species is largely due to environmental factors affecting food supply. European pipistrelles, *Pipistrellus pipistrellus,* kept at 11–14 °C with no food entered torpor, and gestation period increased by 14 days in these bats relative to fed individuals within their natural temperature range (18–26 °C). However, given sufficient food bats remained homoeothermic and gestation period was independent of temperature between 10–25 °C (Racey, 1969; 1973). At 5 °C gestation period increased by 5 days, and at 30–35 °C it was reduced by 2–3 days. In the wild, in two successive years, pipistrelle gestation period (from the end of hibernation to birth) was 41 and 51 days, the variation being due to poor weather and fewer flying insects in the second year (Racey and Swift, 1981). Gestation period in greater horseshoe bats, *Rhinolophus ferrumequinum,* in the wild can be lengthened when bad weather prevents them feeding and forces them into torpor (Ransome, 1973). Low temperature acts in two ways: by reducing insect availability and by increasing the cost of homoeothermy. During periods of poor weather and thus insect availability, delayed birth may be a chosen option, not simply obligatory. Bent-winged bats, *Miniopterus schreibersii,* which typically form large colonies, have been seen to disperse into smaller, cooler roosts late in pregnancy, possibly to delay birth (Dwyer and Harris, 1972). Similar behaviour has been observed in the grey bat, *Myotis grisescens,* by Tuttle (in Tuttle and Stevenson, 1982).

High temperature may also influence gestation. Aestivation has been put forward as a possible cause of delayed birth in the tomb bat, *Taphozous longimanus* (Krishna, 1978). Gestation in this 5 g bat may last for up to four months.

BIRTH, DEVELOPMENT, AND SURVIVAL

Early development

Bats will give birth in the head-down roosting position, but the majority of those studied use a head-up or cradle (horizontal) position. The wings and tail membrane may be used to cradle the baby during birth. At birth, bats are typically around 20–30% of the mother's weight, but in rare examples can be up to 40% (for comparison, those of most other mammals, including humans, are 5–10% adult weight). In a survey of the literature by Kurta and Kunz (1987) the average was 22% adult weight, compared with the average of 8% for other mammals of a similar size range. However, total litter weights were 26 and 25% respectively: bats have bigger babies because they have less of them. Small bats with low wing loadings tend to have relatively bigger babies/larger litters, but there is considerable variation among the smaller species: similar to the situation in non-flying mammals. Size and degree of development at birth are quite variable even within a species, and depend upon maternal size, nutritional and hormonal state, and the size of the litter: the combined weight of twins is generally significantly larger than that of a single baby from the same or a related species (Kurta and Kunz, 1987), but the degree of development may be similar (Ransome, 1973). At birth, megabats have a good covering of fur, their eyes are open, and they are alert. Most microbats are proportionally larger, but are naked with closed eyes (Orr, 1970). However, their skin rapidly pigments and grows fur, and the eyes open within a few days. The phyllostomids are unusual among

Fig. 5.5. Mother and young of the mouse-tailed bat, *Rhinopoma hardwickei*

microbats in giving birth to advanced young. All bats are born with milk teeth, and quickly find the nipple and take a firm grasp. They have the ability to climb and cling to their mother, but are otherwise relatively helpless. Why do bats have such large young? Kurta and Kunz (1987) put forward several ideas: a longer period of protection in the uterus, better thermoregulation, reduced mortality, a more advanced developmental state, and the simple fact that female bats have unfused pelvic girdles, and are therefore able to give birth to bigger young. The relative importance of these factors will be very variable, and is still largely unknown.

Most bats produce just one young per litter, and only in the Vespertilionidae are multiple births at all common. Most vesper bats produce a single young, a significant minority can produce twins, a few up to three young, and four species of *Lasiurus* give birth to three, four, and sometimes five, although only the red bat, *L. borealis*, produces more than two with any frequency (see Tuttle and Stevenson, 1982, for references). Older more experienced females tend to have the larger litters. Some species which produce only one young in part of their range may typically produce twins elsewhere. For example the European pipistrelle, *Pipistrellus pipistrellus*, and noctule, *Nyctalus noctula*, usually have a single baby in Britain and twins in parts of Europe: *Eptesicus fuscus* has one baby in western North America, and twins in the east. Season and variation in climate from year to year also play a role. Myers (1977) found that *Eptesicus furinalis* generally has twins in its first annual cycle in Paraguay, but the second litter of the year, when food supplies are diminishing, invariably contains just one young (see also Madhaven, 1978, p. 137 above).

Growth rates are lower in megabats than in microbats, but relative to other mammals they are all fast, and bats achieve independence rapidly, aided also by their high birth weight. They generally need to reach 90–95% of adult skeletal size (70% mass), and their wings must achieve close to adult dimensions, before they fly, but this can take as little as 2–3 weeks (Kunz, 1987). The greater horseshoe bat, *Rhinolophus ferrumequinum* (25–30 g) is typical of microbats, and several colonies have been intensively studied by Ransome for over the last 30 years (Ransome, 1973; 1990; Hughes *et al.*, 1989). In this species, young are capable of flight in as little as 15 days, and are competent flyers at 24 days. Over this brief period, rapid growth of the wing reduces wing loading by 30%, and it continues to decrease to day 40, by which time the young are becoming independent. They are generally weaned some time between days 45 and 62. Echolocation calls increase in frequency and length to reach adult values around day 30. This rapid development is essential if the bats are to meet the aerodynamic constraints of flight at an early stage and give themselves time to become fully independent, and their mothers time to recover and mate, in preparation for hibernation. In the greater horseshoe bat, large females tend to give birth to larger young. Young which are born large and which grow quickly into large bats tend to have the greatest chance of survival. Interestingly, reproductive success increases in females up to the age of eight, and can continue to be high even at 20 years (Ransome, 1990). The cause of this success in older bats is not yet known, but large babies which develop quickly are produced by well nourished mothers.

Development after birth depends primarily on two external factors: the microclimate of the roost, and food availability and the environmental factors which influence it. The most important aspect of microclimate for most species, particularly those from higher latitudes, is temperature. At low temperatures, the metabolic cost of thermoregulation is high, and less energy can be put into growth. Many species choose warm roosts and/or form large colonies which reduce the cost of thermoregulation by clustering (Dwyer, 1963; Kunz, 1973). Tuttle (1975) has shown that the early growth rate of the grey bat, *Myotis grisescens*, increases with increasing temperature, and at a constant roost temperature it increases as colony size increases. Very young bats do not thermoregulate, hence the importance of roost temperature, and all of the energy goes into growth in the first few days (Kunz, 1987). By choosing roosts which receive radiant heat from the sun, or which are warmed by the bats themselves, high temperatures can be maintained (Kunz, 1982; 1987, see below). Rapid growth requires regular feeding for the mother for milk production. Strong winds, heavy rain, fog, drought, and low temperature all reduce insect availability or foraging success (Tuttle and Stevenson, 1982; Kunz, 1987).

Balancing the energy budget during reproduction

Bats go into torpor when adverse conditions prevent feeding, and this option is open to bats during pregnancy and lactation too: do they take it? The energy demands of reproduction are high, and a pregnant bat could respond by providing this energy by eating more or by utilising stored fat. Alternatively, it could reduce its overall energy requirements by becoming heterothermic. However, heterothermy may have the disadvantage of slowing down some stages of reproduction. Several studies suggest that in the wild females do make use of torpor during reproduction, but to a lesser extent than males (Hamilton and Barclay, 1994), and considerable interspecific variation is seen in its use.

In the greater horseshoe bat, *Rhinolophus ferrumequinum*, (Ransome, 1973) and the little brown bat, *Myotis lucifugus* (Studier and O'Farrell, 1976), females are heterothermic during early pregnancy, but homeothermic in mid-late pregnancy, before reverting to heterothermy just prior to birth and during lactation. A similar pattern was observed in free-living brown long-eared bats *Plecotus auritus* (Speakman and Racey, 1987), although they remained homeothermic right up to birth. Audet and Fenton (1988), using temperature-sensitive radio transmitters attached to big brown bats, *Eptesicus fuscus*, found that females were more likely to be heterothermic during pregnancy than during lactation. Speakman and Racey also measured energy expenditure, and compared it with that predicted on the basis of continuous homeothermy. Energy costs were significantly lower than predicted overall, and from a low level during early pregnancy they rose rapidly to exceed the predicted level at the time of birth, before falling to lower than predicted levels during lactation. Why don't the bats remain heterothermic and save energy throughout the cycle? Presumably, the foetus cannot develop sufficiently rapidly under these circumstances. Lactation however does not seem to be compromised by heterothermy. Perhaps the female remains homeothermic long enough to produce milk and feed its offspring, before entering torpor until its next foraging trip.

Is energy intake by the female the factor which limits litter size and development?

Barclay (1995) has recently made the interesting suggestion that calcium requirements, rather than energy intake, limit litter size and growth. Since the overall litter weight is the same for bats and other mammals of a similar size (Kurta and Kunz, 1987), prenatal constraints do not appear to be the crucial factor—bats put their effort into a single young, rather than several small ones. Young bats and birds are both large when they achieve independence, and this appears to be a constraint imposed by flight. Swartz *et al.* (1992) have shown that the forces acting on the wing bones of bats in flight are very high, and fully calcified bones may be required before young bats can fly: hence the production of a single baby, which must grow to adult size before independence. Until the youngster is flying, the female must supply all of its nutritional needs, and the diets typical of almost all bats (insects, fruit, pollen, and nectar) are low in calcium. (Birds and terrestrial mammals get calcium from various organic and inorganic sources.) Bats can usually meet their energy demands during lactation, but not their calcium requirements, so the female must put calcium into the milk from her own reserves. A number of testable predictions arise from this hypothesis, and it will be interesting to see how the story develops. If flight does demand large fledgling size, then this has important consequences to the life-history strategy of bats: the short life, large litter pattern seen in other small mammals is not an option for them.

Barclay (1995) raises another interesting point. There is a big debate as to how much size alone plays in determining variation in mammalian life-history patterns (see e.g. Promislow and Harvey, 1990). Big mammals tend to live for a long time, and produce few, slow growing, slow developing young. In contrast, small mammals live life at a fast pace, producing lots of rapidly developing youngsters, before dying young. How much of this variation is due to size alone, rather than to phylogenetic, ecological, or other factors? Some biologists argue size is everything (or almost everything), but most studies under-represent or even neglect altogether the bats, the second largest group of mammals. Bats are an effective argument against the over-riding importance of size.

Size does have a profound effect on growth rate. In a recent review of the available data, Kunz and Stern (1995) found a strong negative relationship: big bats grow slowly. After removing the effects of size no apparent effects on growth could be attributed to diet, phylogeny (megabat vs microbat) or resting metabolic rate. Temperate insectivorous bats did, however, grow faster than their tropical counterparts. Intraspecific differences in growth rate could be attributed to gender, litter and colony size, climate, latitude, and food abundance in certain instances.

Later development and survival

Survival rates vary with the stage in development. During preflight development survival rates are very high: Tuttle and Stevenson's (1982) review of the literature yielded a figure of 0–12% mortality, with a mean of about 3%, and Ransome (1990) arrives at a similarly low figure. However, in exceptionally poor conditions, e.g. prolonged bad weather during early pregnancy, the females may abandon the roost to ensure their own survival (to breed the following year), and mortality may be 100% (e.g. Nellis and Ehle, 1977; Stebbings, 1988). Typical causes of mortality include maternal stress, predation, and falls from the roost (although females will often retrieve young).

The time to first flight shows enormous variation within and between species, and is dependent on a wide range of external factors, reviewed by Tuttle and Stevenson (1982). For example, first flight times of *Myotis lucifugus* in different studies ranged from 14–15 days to 21–30 days. Differences in colony size and temperature led to first flight times of 24 and 33 days in *Myotis grisescens*.

Large megabats fly at 9–12 weeks of age, with weaning at 15–20 weeks. In microbats the figures are 2–6 and 5–10 weeks, respectively. Early flight and weaning are associated with weight loss in the young (Tuttle and Stevenson, 1982; Kunz, 1987). Stored fat is mobilised to carry the bat over this difficult period, and in bats with a short weaning period (e.g. in *Myotis* species) fat deposits are greater than in those with long weaning periods (e.g. *Eptesicus* and *Antrozous*) (Kunz, 1987). During this time the young must perfect their flight and (in the case of microbats) echolocation skills, learn to catch prey, and familiarise themselves with foraging sites. Mortality over this period is hard to assess, and there are few published values. It appears to be comparable to preflight mortality in some cases, but is more variable and can be high (10 to >50%) (Tuttle and Stevenson, 1982; Ransome, 1990). Young, unskilled flyers are particularly susceptible to predation and accidents. Other factors influencing mortality include weather, proximity of foraging sites to the roost, the level of maternal care, and pesticide poisoning.

In both microbats and megabats, sexual maturity is normally reached in 1–2 years. In some microbats, females may be mature in only 3 months. In half of the species studied females mature before males, but males are only rarely ahead of females. Early maturity is most common in polyoestrous species.

Life expectancy

How long do bats live? This question has been addressed in detail by Tuttle and Stevenson (1982), so I will be very brief. Data on mortality rates after birth are variable, and in many cases unreliable, but the general trend is always the same; mortality is high in the first year and decreases rapidly over the next few years. A good start in life is important. An early birth, a roost with the right microclimate, and good foraging close to the roost have been shown to be critical factors (Tuttle, 1976a; Ransome, 1990). I have already mentioned that young bats enter hibernation late, since they are still feeding and growing as winter approaches. Bats tend to be rather long-lived for their size. If it gets through its first year, a typical microbat has a 40–80% chance of surviving to 7 or 8 years, and there are many instances, from a wide range of microbats and megabats, of wild individuals living for 10–30+ years.

INFANT–MOTHER COMMUNICATION AND MATERNAL CARE

The rearing of young is carried out exclusively by the females. The bond between young and females is established at birth, and vocalisation plays a major role in this bonding. Communication between mother and offspring has been studied in greatest detail in the microbats. Fenton (1985) has reviewed this, and other aspects of bat communication. On returning to the roost after foraging, the females of many species emit special search calls, to which the young have specific replies. In microbats, these calls are often ultrasonic, and resemble segments of the foraging calls: they become increasingly complex as the young develop (Jones et al., 1991). There is now considerable evidence that calls emitted by an individual bat are sufficiently reproducible, and calls between bats sufficiently varied, to enable mother and youngster to identify each other (e.g. Balcombe and McCracken, 1992; Scherrer and Wilkinson, 1993), and behavioural studies confirm that the mothers respond to the calls of their own young (Balcombe, 1990). Scherrer and Wilkinson's (1993) study of evening bats, Nycticeius humeralis, has shown that the calls are heritable, and carry information about family identity. The young do not learn the calls from their mothers (although this has been suggested for other species), but use them within minutes of birth. This is important if proper mother–offspring bonding is to occur, since the mothers may leave the roost to forage within hours of giving birth, and will need to find their own youngsters on their return. Isolation calls are not the only means of identification. Visual and olfactory cues are also important (Fenton, 1985; Gustin and McCracken, 1987).

In most microbats, the young are left in the roost when the females leave to forage. Foraging, insectivorous microbats would pay too high a penalty in terms of loss of flight performance and cost of transport (Hughes and Rayner, 1993). The young of many species, e.g. Tadarida brasiliensis, Macrotus californicus, and Miniopterus schreibersii will cluster when left in the roost, reducing the costs of homeothermy. Very young bats are poor regulators, and may not be able to maintain high body temperatures without clustering. The females of these species roost separately, unless they are suckling young. Female fringed myotis (Myotis thysanodes) and little brown bats (M. lucifugus) are said to baby-sit young while the rest of the colony is foraging.

Communal behaviour does not appear to extend to suckling young as frequently as was once thought. For example, it was widely accepted to be the case in the Mexican free-tailed bat, Tadarida brasiliensis, but in a study by McCracken (1984) 83% of sampled females were feeding their own young. Kin selection or reciprocal altruism are unlikely to be operating in the 17% of cases where bats are feeding young other than their own, since the youngsters move appreciable distances between feeding bouts, and individuals within a given area are unlikely to constitute a kin or reciprocation group. The still significant degree of indiscriminate suckling observed may simply be due to the enormous size of maternity roosts, and the difficulties mothers have in finding their own offspring. In this species, maternity roosts frequently contain millions of bats: the largest known roost has around 20 million individuals. Wilkinson (1992) studied the evening bat, *Nycticeius humeralis,* which forms colonies of only 15–300 females. Evening bats are weaned around 40 days after birth. Communal nursing was never seen before day eight, but increased slowly to a peak over the last two weeks, when the youngsters were beginning to forage for themselves. During this period females suckled young other than their own 18% of the time. As in the case of the Mexican free-tailed bat, kin selection and reciprocal altruism are not operating. Interestingly, the females tended to accept non-descendent female young, but rejected males. Wilkinson makes the intriguing suggestion that the females may feed non-descendent youngsters to dump excess milk and reduce wing loading prior to foraging. Why should they restrict feeding to female youngsters? Since females generally return year after year to the roost in which they were born, this strategy may help to maintain colony size, and hence information transfer between females about foraging and roosting sites. In a review of the literature Fenton (1985) found that the vast majority of species studied appeared to nurse only their own young most of the time.

In the later stages of lactation some species which feed on vertebrates take prey back to the roost, like raptors, to feed their young, for example *Megaderma spasma* and the Australian ghost bat *Macroderma gigas*. In the wild, the pallid bat, *Antrozous pallidus*, is known to feed its young on arthropods, and African sheath-tailed bats, *Coleura afra*, return to the roost with cheek pouches full of insects. Captive *Molossus ater* feed their young on insects, as do *Noctilio albiventris*. In captivity the common vampire will regurgitate blood for offspring (see Racey, 1982 and Fenton, 1985 for references). This practice may be more widespread than is generally thought, although it has not been observed in many extensively studied species. Once they are flying, youngsters may accompany mothers on foraging flights (*Myotis adversus*, Dwyer, 1970b; *Cardioderma cor*, Vaughan, 1976). Young vampires will feed with adults, and the young of some insectivorous microbats (e.g. lesser white-lined bats, *Saccopteryx leptura*) will shadow their parents, mimicking every twist and turn, even copying echolocation calls to the terminal feeding buzz (Bradbury and Emmons, 1974). Observations of the pallid bat, *Antrozous pallidus*, suggest that young may learn to forage from their mothers (O'Shea and Vaughan, 1977). This is not the case however in the little brown bat (Buchler, 1980). Radiotracking of greater horseshoe bats, *Rhinolophus ferrumequinum*, has shown that after weaning mother and offspring leave the roost separately, and forage apart (Jones *et al.*, 1995). However, survival of the mother is a major determinant of juvenile survival over the following year (R.D. Ransome, pers. comm.).

Many maternity colonies include males as well as females, but the males do not appear to play any part in rearing the young. Male *Phyllostomus discolour* are often found with youngsters sleeping on their backs (Bradbury, 1977b), but to what extent there is bonding is unknown.

ROOST SELECTION AND MATERNAL FORAGING PATTERNS

This topic is really part of the next chapter, but one or two points are perhaps most relevant here. First of all, roost selection is critical to reproductive success. As we have

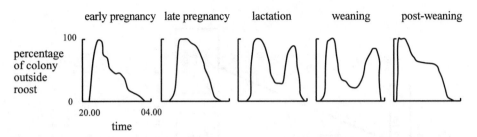

Fig. 5.6. Activity patterns of the pipistrelle, *P. pipistrellus* during pregnancy and lactation (adapted from Swift, 1980).

seen above, roost microclimate is one of the most important factors influencing growth and development. Suitable roosts may not be available close to the best foraging sites, and commuting distance may influence the foraging success of the adults. Tuttle (1976a) showed that as commuting distance increased, the mortality of young grey bats, *Myotis grisescens*, making their first flights also increased.

Weather permitting, the females will forage every night during pregnancy and lactation, to feed the growing young. Few data are available from individual bats, but studies of whole colonies can, if interpreted with caution, give some insights into behaviour.

Figure 5.6 shows the percentage of female pipistrelles out of the roost at different times during the night, over a Scottish summer (Swift, 1980). Early in pregnancy, the females do not need to forage for long. They all leave at sunset, but soon start to come back, and few bats are out in the early morning. As pregnancy progresses more bats stay out late. During lactation and weaning, when the demands on the females by their growing young are greatest, they go out to feed twice, at dawn and dusk. Once the youngsters start to fend for themselves, the females need to feed less, and the activity curve reverts to its unimodal form. This pattern has been observed in a number of species, and illustrates how reproduction can influence foraging activity, but there is considerable variation. Once the youngsters are weaned, the colony can begin to break up at any time. From now until hibernation, the adult bats are preoccupied initially with mating, and later with preparation for hibernation. The young must become competent foragers, familiarise themselves with roosting sites, complete their growth, and prepare for hibernation.

MATING BEHAVIOUR

Bats probably show more forms of mating behaviour than any other mammalian order. The bewildering range of patterns seen must have its origin in natural selection. If we can understand how the different mating strategies work, why a particular species has evolved to use a particular strategy, and the selective pressures operating on each system, then some form of order should come out of the confusion. Bradbury (1977a) has described mating systems in some detail, and Bradbury and Vehrencamp (1977a) developed a general model of mammalian mating systems based on their studies of emballonurid bats. These are still the most thorough reviews on bats. In a more recent general review of mammals Clutton-Brock (1989) identified the most important factors influencing mating strategy, and related them to the patterns observed in nature. Figure 5.7 summarises mating systems and the ecological/behavioural characteristics of females

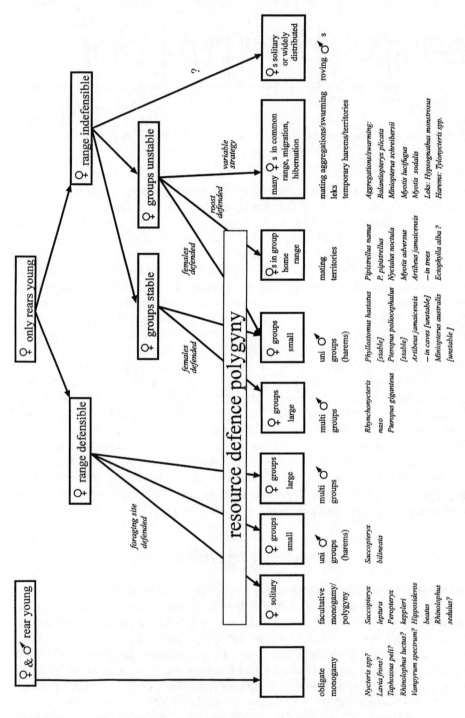

Fig. 5.7. Mating patterns in bats (adapted from Fig. 1, Clutton-Brock, 1989).

normally associated with each system. It is based on the scheme set out by Clutton-Brock, with some modification to fit the observed patterns in bats. It is widely recognised that it is the social and ecological characteristics of the females which are largely responsible for the mating strategy which has evolved in the males. A common strategy in bats is that known as resource defence polygyny, in which males defend a resource against other males, which enables them to copulate with a large number of females. This resource may be a foraging area, a roost site, or the females themselves. Although a widely recognised strategy, few studies actually identify the resource being defended. In Fig. 5.7 the different resource defence strategies are listed separately. I will briefly describe the patterns first, and then look at examples.

Mating patterns

Obligate monogamy (males mating with a single female in a given season) commonly arises when the young can only be successfully reared with the help of the male, or when male help significantly increases breeding success. This situation is not yet known in bats. Males do not appear even to participate in rearing—they are certainly not essential in any species of bat studied. Monogamy may occur in *Hipposideros beatus* and *Rhinolophus sedulus* (see Heller *et al.*, 1993), but requires confirmation and further study.

All other patterns arise when the male is dispensable as far as rearing is concerned. He is thus more of a free agent, and able to pursue other females. The main factors become the range and social behaviour of the females. If the home range of the females can be defended by a male, then three main systems may arise, depending upon the size of the female groups: *facultative monogamy* (or *polygyny*), *unimale (harem) groups,* or *multi-male groups*. All involve males holding a territory and defending the female(s) within it. If the female group is large enough, then more than one male may be involved. All three systems are seen in bats, particularly in the tropics.

If the females' range is too large or too mobile to be defended, then female group stability is the next determinant. With stable groups, *harem* and *multimale groups* form, based on defence of the group, rather the territory. If the female groups are unstable, males typically defend small *mating territories* at sites frequented by females. As female density increases, male territories become less dispersed, ending in *leks* at the highest densities of females: small, adjacent male territories from which males display to compete for passing females. Some mammals mate on migration or at the onset of hibernation, and behaviour is flexible: defence of individuals, (transient) harems, mating territories, and swarming are all common. Again, all are seen in bats. Finally, if females are thinly or unpredictably distributed males rove in search of individual females. I have not seen this documented for bats, but I suspect is does occur.

Some examples

Too few species of bats have been studied in sufficient detail to give many examples of each pattern, and to place them in a category with any certainty. In fact the various categories are not mutually exclusive, and many bats show elements of several strategies. I have categorised them, sometimes tentatively, on the basis of the most prevalent strategy.

Obligate monogamy has yet to be verified in any bat, but a number of species are routinely found in pairs or family groups, and possible candidates include the African slit-faced bats (*Nycteris* spp.), the African yellow-winged bat (*Lavia frons*), the neotropical phyllostomid *Vampyrum spectrum,* and the Old World bats *Taphozous peli* and *Rhinolophus luctus* (see Bradbury, 1977a for references), but all could be facultative. Why should it occur in these species, assuming that the male does not have to participate in rearing? Foraging area defence by single females and large home ranges used by females could both lead to the evolution of monogamy, since it would be energetically costly for males to chase several females. Both could be factors for carnivorous bats such as *Vampyrum spectrum.*

The neotropical emballonurids *Saccopteryx leptura* and *Peropteryx kappleri,* two of five species studied by Bradbury and Vehrencamp (1977a), defend feeding territories used by females and typically form monogamous pairs. Foraging areas are small, females roost singly or in small, stable groups and they are thinly scattered through their wet forest habitat. It is therefore feasible for males to defend feeding territories, but in so doing they will defend only one or perhaps a few females. The main resource appears to be the foraging area, which is defended by males and females, but the females themselves may also be defended against other males. When groups (colonies) are large (7–9 bats in this species) the group territory is not subdivided by the pairs.

In contrast, *Saccopteryx bilineata* roosts in large but unstable groups (up to 40 bats) and forms harems of one male and up to 8 females within the group (Bradbury and Vehrencamp, 1977a). Although the individual bats present in a group turnover quite frequently, the roost site is used for long periods. Each male defends part of the colony's feeding territory and the tree buttress roost site against other males in the colony, and competition for females is intense. However, males do not attempt to retain females which leave their territory. Mating occurs at the day roost, so males can only benefit if the females which roost with it are the only bats allowed into its its feeding territory. The males can presumably recognise individual females.

A fourth emballonurid, *Rhynchonycteris naso* feeds along rivers in the same part of the world. Group size is similar to that of *S. bilineata*, but stable. However, bats frequently change roost. Female rather than resource defence would therefore be the predicted strategy, and that is what is seen (Bradbury and Vehrencamp, 1977a). Multi-male groups form, and males only defend territory against males from other colonies. Within the colony, individual males will follow foraging females if they move feeding site.

The fifth species, *Balantiopteryx plicata*, forms very large colonies: up to 10 000 bats. Group stability is low, and roosting and foraging sites change frequently. Defence of foraging site, roosting site, or females by the males would be impractical and costly. Although it was difficult to study this species in detail, the evidence suggests male mating aggregations or swarming during the short copulation season is the mating strategy. This pattern is common in temperate bats which mate prior to hibernation, frequently in large colonies, e.g. *Miniopterus schreibersii* (Dwyer, 1966, in Australia) and *Myotis lucifugus* (Thomas *et al.*, 1979, in Canada). The social bat *Myotis sodalis* mates largely over a 1–2 week period (Barbour and Davis, 1969, in the United States). The sexes are segregated in the cave during the day and the females invade male occupied areas at night.

Another strategy which has evolved in the face of large numbers of mobile females within a common home range is lek formation. This could be thought of as an extension of the mating territory strategy to high densities, so I will deal with the two together. If

Fig. 5.8.   Male pipistrelle, *P. pipistrellus*, in songflight.

female groups are moderately large and unstable, but females forage within a well-defined home range, males may set up mating roosts within foraging areas or on commuting routes, and attract passing females, defending the roost and a small airspace around it. This is common among European temperate bats: males occupy tree roosts and call from their roost (*Nyctalus noctula*, Sluiter and van Heerdt, 1966), or use a songflight (*Pipistrellus pipistrellus*, Gerell and Lundberg, 1985) to advertise their presence (Fig. 5.8).

Tropical species also make use of mating territories, e.g. *Pipistrellus nanus* in Africa (O'Shea, 1980), *Myotis adversus* in Australia (Dwyer, 1970b), and *Artibeus jamaicensis* in the neotropics (Morrison, 1979). When *A. jamaicensis* roosts in trees, single males defend holes in the trunk or branches against other males (Morrison, 1979). Groups of females (4–11) roost in these holes, but group composition is very variable. Their food source (*Ficus* species) is dispersed but abundant, trees fruiting asynchronously for 1–2 weeks each year. Females disperse to feed, preventing their defence by the male. Instead he spends 90% of the night flying within 50–100 m of the roost, chasing males and escorting returning females back to the hole. This flight is fuelled by occasional foraging trips for fruit, which is carried as much as 1.5 km back to the roost for consumption (Morrison and Hagen-Morrison, 1981). Females feed close to the fig tree providing the fruit. The male may expend 30% of his daily energy budget on roost defence.

As the density of females increases, male territories may become smaller and more closely packed. Ultimately this grades into a lek: females visit groups of males occupying small adjacent territories, and the male display to the females, who choose a mate for copulation. No resource is defended, but some males are more successful than others at attracting females, due to some quality of their display. The African epomophorine megabat, *Hypsignathus monstrosus* (hammer-headed bat) is undoubtedly the best example (Bradbury, 1977b). The males have an enormous larynx (20% of body cavity) which enables them to emit loud, low frequency honks. As many as 90 males line up along river banks, one every 50 m, and honk continuously to passing females. The bats honk at a rate of 50–120 honks per min, and beat their wings. When females approach, honk rate and wing flapping increase. The specific cues which win female attention are not known, but the call must have an important role.

The behaviour of *Artibeus jamaicensis* in tree roosts was described above. This species is interesting in that it frequently roosts in caves, when its behaviour is different. Kunz *et al.* (1983) found that the favoured sites were solution cavities in the cave roof. Unlike the tree holes used by the bats in the Morrisons' studies, these cavities were not in limited supply: only 13% were used at any one time, and the females frequently changed roosts. The cavities are clearly not a defensible resource: are the males defending the females instead? If so, they should move from cavity to cavity with the females, but fidelity of males to particular female groups has yet to be demonstrated, and there is switching of females between groups. Whatever the strategy, it is not that used by the tree roosting members of the species studied. A similar system seems to be operating in *Miniopterus australis* in Borneo (Medway, 1971). Males are found with harems of up to 6 females,

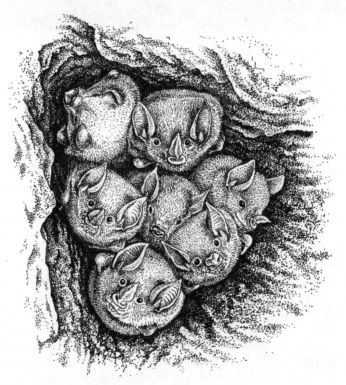

Fig. 5.9.   Harem of greater spear-nosed bats, *Phyllostomus hastatus*.

but roost fidelity and group stability are both low. Roost defence is unlikely, but female defence would involve frequent changes of the females defended.

In the neotropical *Phyllostomus hastatus*, the case for female defence is clear (Fig. 5.9). Single males defend harems of 7–25 females (18 on average) in their cave roosts, in some cases for several years (McCracken and Bradbury, 1977, 1981). Female groups are very stable: turnover is low and comparable to the annual mortality rate. This stability is maintained even through changes of harem male.

Defence of one or more females is also typical of many megabats. In *Pteropus polio-cephalus* in Australia, single males select one or more females, and the group as a whole defends its small territory on the camp tree (Nelson, 1965). Elements of both roost and female defence are therefore present, although the latter is perhaps the most important. Male *Pteropus giganteus* in India are very possessive of females in the vicinity of their defended tree roost, but bonding does not occur, and females move around the camp tree to some extent.

Sexual dimorphism and sexual signals

I have mentioned songflights in microbats and lekking behaviour in megabats already. The hammer-headed bat, *Hypsignathus monstrosus,* shows an extreme form of sexual dimorphism: the enlargement of the larynx and other structures for honking gives the males a grotesque and distinctive head (Fig. 5.10).

Males of many epomophorine species are larger than females, and have display markings, typically on the head and shoulders. They often go in for wing shaking to attract the females, and mutual grooming. The shoulders of these and other bats have glandular sacs which put out an odour to attract females. Quite a few bats have courtship songs, or rather courtship screams, grunts, and bellows. Sexual dimorphism is seen in microbats too: females are commonly larger than males. A very striking example is the large crest of the male African crested free-tailed bat, *Chaerephon* (*Tadarida*) *chapini* (Fig. 5.11). A more detailed look at this subject, and other areas of communication can be found in Fenton (1985).

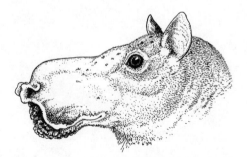

Fig. 5.10.   Male hammer-headed bat, *Hypsignathus monstrosus*.

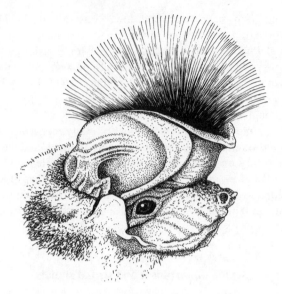

Fig. 5.11.   Male crested mastiff (free-tailed) bat *Chaerephon* (*Tadarida*) *chapini*.

6 Behavioural ecology

Roosting ecology—the importance of finding the right roost. Advantages and disadvantages of communal roosting. Where do bats roost; caves and crevices, trees, foliage, tent making bats, man-made roosts. Feeding ecology: the diversity of feeding habits and adaptations, with diversions into reciprocal altruism, optimal foraging, and convergent evolution. Information transfer. Interactions between habitat, food, foraging, and social structure and behaviour. Migration and navigation.

ROOSTING ECOLOGY

The importance of finding the right roost

Bats spend most of their lives in their roosts. Roosting habits influence local and global distribution, densities, foraging and mating strategy, social structure and seasonal movements, and even the morphology and physiology of bats. An understanding of their roosting ecology is therefore fundamental to an understanding of bats. The most wide ranging and thorough review is that by Kunz (1982). I have already talked a little about roosting ecology when we covered hibernation and reproduction. In this chapter I will take a broader view, and look at the great diversity of roosting adaptations and show how they relate to other aspects of bat biology. By choosing a suitable roost, bats can gain many advantages. Here are the most important potential benefits:

- protection from the weather
- protection from predators—the selfish herd (Hamilton, 1971)
- cheaper thermoregulation—energetic savings during roosting
- reduced commuting costs to foraging sites
- improved mating opportunities
- improved maternal care
- information transfer—knowledge of foraging and roosting sites
- competition avoidance—few other vertebrates can make use of most bat roosts

The processes involved in roost selection are complex, with many mutually dependent interactions. The availability of suitable roosts, for example, will influence foraging behaviour, but roosting behaviour itself may be influenced by the abundance and dispersal of food, and both have an important role in determining the social structure of intra- and interspecific bat communities.

Before looking at some of these interactions I want to review the enormous diversity of roosting behaviour. There are some general trends, and there are many exceptions to all of them, but here are the broadest. Bats in the tropics are known to use exposed roosts: in the harsher temperate climate exposed roosts are rare. Bats which roost in the open tend

Brown long-eared bats, *Plecotus auritus*, roosting in the roof of a building

also to be large. Bats in high latitudes tend to roost in larger groups. Opportunistic (adaptable, generalist) roosters tend to be more widespread than specialists. Bats utilising stable roosts such as caves are frequently very faithful to these sites, over many years and many generations. Ephemeral roosts such as those in foliage may increase local movements, but bats may still be faithful to particular locations. Within this broad framework is a wealth of fascinating detail.

Where do bats roost?

Caves and crevices

Caves

Let's start with caves, the most stable and persistent roosts. Bats are the only vertebrates to really make use of caves for permanent shelter, although there are a few notable exceptions among fish and amphibians. We have already looked at the advantages offered by caves to hibernating bats, and it may have been an extension of their use of warmer caves

Fig. 6.1. Cave bats. Summer roost of Schreiber's bent-winged bat, *Miniopterus schreibersii*.

in the tropics which led bats to use caves as hibernacula, as they spread to higher latitudes. Caves are a scarce commodity in most landscapes: when present, few may be suitable for bats, and of those that are, only part of each cave may offer the appropriate microclimate. It may be these factors, together with the obvious thermoregulatory advantages of communal living, which have led to the formation of vast colonies by some species. As an order, bats are undoubtedly the most gregarious and social of mammals. A single colony of the Mexican free-tailed bat, *Tadarida brasiliensis*, (in Bracken Cave in the south eastern United States) has contained 20 million bats (Davis *et al.*, 1962). Several species across the world assemble in roosts of 100 000 to over 500 000 (e.g. *Hipposideros caffer* in Africa, Brosset, 1966; the bent-winged bat *Miniopterus schreibersii* in Australia, Dwyer and Hamilton-Smith, 1965; the grey bat, *Myotis grisescens* in the United States, Tuttle, 1976a), and populations in some remote caves have yet to be estimated. Many caves harbour a number of different species: Bateman and Vaughan (1974) estimated that four species of mormoopid in a Mexican cave totalled 800 000 bats. At the other extreme, caves are home to many species which roost in small groups and even individually.

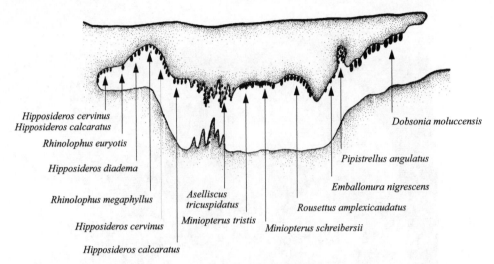

Fig. 6.2.   Distribution of bats in a cave in Papua New Guinea (from Hill and Smith, 1984).

The varied formations and microclimates found within a single cave can encourage colonisation by several species, each with their own particular requirements. Temperature, humidity, and cavity size are the most important factors, but precise requirements have been worked out for few species. A large and varied cave in the tropics will frequently be home to more than ten species. Figure 6.2 shows the distribution of bats in a cave in Papua New Guinea, from Hill and Smith (1984).

The cave dwelling megabat, *Dobsonia moluccensis*, roosts in the large and well-lit entrance. Few megabats venture far into caves, but echolocating members of the megabat genus *Rousettus* will penetrate the darker regions and roost in the roof void. Emballonurids are also found in relatively well-lit areas, and vesper bats will use crevices close to the entrance. Vesper bats roost in the dark regions of the cave, and hipposiderids and rhinolophids are typical of the deepest regions. Tropical caves show only minor variations in microclimate, and few caves are uninhabited by bats. In temperate regions microclimate is strongly influenced by cave structure. Cold air falls into descending caves, and these are rarely used by bats at any time of year. Caves with little or no air flow are also frequently too cold for summer use. The most commonly used caves have several entrances, significant movement of air, and a variety of different temperature regimes. In sub-tropical and warm-temperate zones caves can make suitable maternity, mating, and hibernation roosts. At higher latitudes caves are rarely used by maternity colonies, although small numbers of bats may be present all year round.

Bats can alter roost microclimate

Bats which form large maternity colonies can have a significant impact on cave microclimate, raising the temperature in roof cavities by as much as 10 °C. Some species, such as the grey bat, *Myotis grisescens*, in the United States (Tuttle, 1976a) successfully rear young in cool caves. This said, only 2.4% of the 1635 known caves in the cave-rich state of Alabama were used by the grey bat in summer (Tuttle, 1979). The increased temperatures generated by one species can benefit another. *Miniopterus australis* is always found in association with larger colonies of its more populous relative, *Miniopterus schreibersii*, in the southern limit of its distribution in New South Wales, Australia (Dwyer, 1968). In the warmer north, they are not usually found together. A similar advantage may be gained by the grey bat in the United Sates, where it associates with *Myotis austroriparius*. Postnatal growth rates, and postflight survival are very low if the grey bat colony is too small (Tuttle, 1976a), so reproductive success may be greater in mixed roosts.

In large numbers, bats alter their cave habitat in other ways. A large colony produces a lot of urine and guano, leading to massive accumulations of nitrogenous waste on the cave floor, and high ammonia concentration in the air. Species diversity in a cave may be reduced by the presence of large numbers of some species: few bats can tolerate the high ammonia levels generated by a large colony of the Mexican free-tailed bat, *Tadarida brasiliensis*. The bats, and their piles of guano, have evolved their own unique ecosystems, including the parasites and diseases of the bats themselves. The increased incidence of pests and disease is one of the two major disadvantages of community life: the other is the possible increased competition for food in the vicinity of the roost. A large colony of Mexican free-tailed bats must forage over a very wide area.

Cave dwelling bats are frequently very faithful to their roost sites, occupying one cave for life. Alternatively a small number of sites may be used by a colony, and one or more sites will be in use at any one time, depending on cave microclimate, food availability, and physiological requirements.

Rock crevices

From crevices in caves, it is a short flight to crevices in rock outside the cave. Rock crevices rarely offer the same thermal stability as caves, or the same degree of protection, but they are more common. Availability facilitates, and unstable microclimate often necessitates, mobility in crevice dwelling bats. Although many are faithful to particular roosts, many are not. Because of this, and the fact that they roost in small groups, they are difficult to find, and their roosting ecology is not well understood. All manner of crevices are used, and the general trend is for the bats to move around, within, and among cracks choosing temperatures appropriate to their immediate needs. Vaughan and O'Shea (1976) studied the roosting ecology of pallid bats (*Antrozous pallidus*) in the semi-arid desert of Arizona, a habitat typical of many crevice roosting bats. In the spring and autumn groups of up to about 20 bats occupied vertical crevices which showed large diurnal variations in temperature (Fig. 6.3).

For most of the day temperature was below 20 °C, and the torpid bats conserved energy. The afternoon sun raised the temperature in these crevices to 32 °C, more than 10 °C above outside, ambient temperature, warming the bats prior to their evening emergence. Deep, horizontal crevices at 14–18 °C were not used by the bats at this time of year. However, groups of up to 176 bats did occupy these crevices in the hot summers, when crevice temperatures were a stable 28–33 °C: the thermal neutral zone of the bats. Outside the roost the diurnal, summer temperature varied between 18 °C at night, and 38 °C in the daytime shade (50 °C on rock faces). In addition to moving around within the system of crevices, bats would cluster when necessary to reduce heat loss and conserve metabolic energy. Mexican free-tailed bats, *Tadarida brasiliensis*, and Yuma myotis, *Myotis yumanensis*, occasionally shared these roosts. Bats did not use the sites in winter, when the mean daily ambient temperature was as low as 6 °C. Many bats make use of

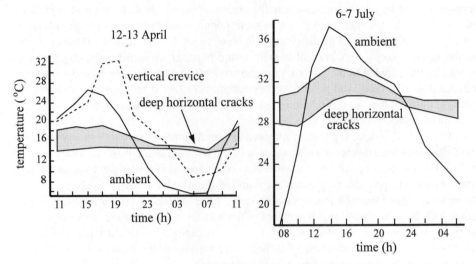

Fig. 6.3.   Temperature variation in rock crevices used by the pallid bat, *Antrozous pallidus* (from Vaughan and Thomas, 1976).

rock crevice roosts in the more arid regions of the United States, from the 70+ g western mastiff bat, *Eumops perotis* (Vaughan, 1959), to the 6 g western pipistrelle, *Pipistrellus hesperus* (Hayward and Cross, 1979).

In their study of pallid bats, Vaughan and O'Shea (1976) described a pattern of behaviour which is typical of many species. More time was spent in the day roost than in foraging and night roost occupation combined—about 13–16 hours in each 24 hour period. The bats emerged earlier, and returned later, on summer nights. On their return large groups of bats circled the roost entrance for up to 45 min before entering. During this time they would make frequent brief landings close to the entrance crack, and emit regular 'directive' calls which attracted other bats. This rallying behaviour has been widely reported, although often without the directive calls, but its function remains uncertain. Vaughan and O'Shea suggest that the scent cues on landings allow the bat to confirm that it is at the right entrance. The rallying itself may enable the bats to refresh their knowledge of the detailed topography of the roost. Rallying has also been described for the common European pipistrelle, *Pipistrellus pipistrellus* (Swift, 1980), the southeast Asian bamboo bats *Tylonycteris pachypus* and *T. robustula*, (Medway and Marshall, 1972), the New World *Tadarida macrotis* (Vaughan, 1959), and many other species.

Crevice dwelling bats often show anatomical adaptations to this way of life. Bats tend to be dorsoventrally flattened for aerodynamic reasons, but some crevice dwellers show a more extreme flattening, notably of the skull in certain molossids of the genera *Platymops* and *Neoplatymops* (Peterson, 1965). *Platymops setiger* is probably the most extreme example of this trend in bats.

Tree roosting bats

Tree-bark cracks are used by many species in all parts of the world, but there are few detailed accounts. I have found solitary males of the European pipistrelle under the bark

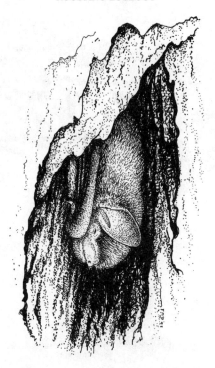

Daubenton's bat, *Myotis daubentonii*

of trees in Britain, and at one location several were found (singly) under the thick bark of imported North American giant sequoias, in the grounds of a large house which held a large maternity colony. Cervený and Bürger (1989) found small numbers of male Daubenton's bat, *Myotis daubentonii*, and Bechstein's bat, *M. bechsteinii*, under the bark of alder trees in spring. Small maternity colonies of the Indiana myotis, *Myotis sodalis*, roost under the bark of the bitternut hickory, and in the winter, the thicker bark of the shagbark hickory is preferred (Humphrey *et al.,* 1977). The tiny African vespertilionid, *Mimetillus moloneyi*, and the larger *Laephotis wintoni*, also roost behind tree bark (Kingdon, 1974). The common name of the former, Moloney's flat-headed bat, points to its adaptation to this way of life.

Cavities in the trunk and branches of trees offer roosts which are both more durable and thermally more stable than bark crevices, and they are widely used in both temperate and tropical regions (see Bradbury, 1977a, and Kunz, 1982, p. 7, for references). Cavities vary enormously in size and position, and in the size and location of the entrance holes. A roost site very common in the tropics is the large cavity which forms inside the bole of many trees, as the inside rots out. The temperature and humidity inside these cavities can be remarkably stable. Smaller cavities form where branches have fallen.

The baobab tree in Africa is a first class bat roost (Fig. 6.4), and home to some of the big carnivorous megadermatids such as *Cardioderma cor*, which forms groups of up to 80 individuals (Vaughan, 1976). The large New World carnivore *Vampyrum spectrum* also roosts in tree cavities (Vehrencamp *et al.,* 1977). Many other phyllostomids use tree cavities (Tuttle (1976c) noted 28 species), as do molossids, vesper bats, and noctilionids.

Fig. 6.4. Bat roost in a baobab tree, *Adansonia digitata*.

It is also common to find more than one species in a tree roost: *Saccopteryx bilineata* with *Vampyrum spectrum* (Vehrencamp *et al.,* 1977), and the common vampire, *Desmodus rotundus* with phyllostomids such as the fringe-lipped bat, *Trachops cirrhosus* and *Carollia perspicillata* (Tuttle, 1976c). These cavities are used as maternity roosts, mating roosts, and night feeding roosts.

Trees with hollow trunks are very prevalent in nutrient poor soils in the tropics, and Janzen (1976) has suggested that this may be an adaptation to encourage bats and other animals, providing the trees with valuable nitrogen and minerals from the faeces. If Janzen is correct then bats may have an important role in tropical forest nutrient cycles.

In temperate regions, tree cavities are widely used by vesper bats. Cervený and Bürger (1989) found 5 species using tree holes in a small study site in Czechoslovakia: *Myotis nattereri, M. bechsteinii, M. daubentonii, Nyctalus noctula,* and *N. leisleri.* The two *Nyctalus* species were found roosting together, and both were also found with *M. daubentonii.* Colonies of the last species numbered over 85 individuals, and Gaisler *et al.* (1979) found colonies of up to 70 *N. noctula.* Bats are found in trees at all times of year, using cavities as maternity, mating, and night feeding roosts, and as hibernacula.

The most unusual tree hole bat is the endemic short-tailed bat of New Zealand, *Mysticina tuberculata.* In addition to using natural holes, it burrows into dead and rotting kauri trees, *Agthis australis,* (Daniel, 1990). Groups of up to 200 bats line up like peas in pods in these burrows, where they can raise the temperature to 39 °C, and the humidity to 100%.

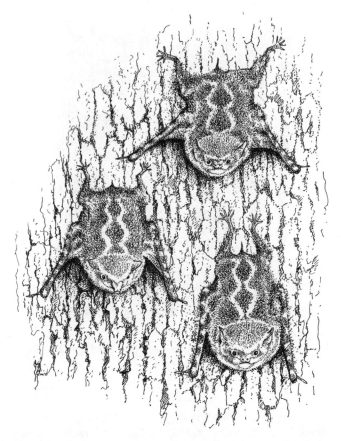

Fig. 6.5. *Rhynchonycteris naso*, the proboscis bat, on a tree bole.

Some species roost in the open against the trunk or branches of trees. The proboscis bat (*Rhynchonycteris naso*), a small (4–5 g) neotropical emballonurid, is typical. It is frequently found on branches which overhang water, and has a speckled yellow-grey colouration which resembles lichen, making it difficult to see (Bradbury and Vehrencamp, 1976a; Bradbury, 1977a). Small colonies of 5–11 bats are typical, and they often space themselves in a vertical line, 2–4 cm apart (Fig. 6.5).

Despite the open nature of the roost, colony size can be as great as 45, and in addition to their cryptic colouration, the bats remain quiet and still to avoid detection. Other microbats known to roost on exposed trees trunks or branches include the related *Saccopteryx leptura* (Bradbury and Vehrencamp, 1976a) and the African Butterfly bats of the genus *Glauconycteris* (Kingdon, 1974). *Glauconycteris variegata* has a beautiful reticulated pattern on its wings which strongly resemble leaves. Some of the smaller megabats also roost on tree trunks, and have cryptic colouration, e.g. *Nyctimene major* in south-east Asia (Walker, 1975).

Although bamboos are not trees, they can be large and relatively long-lasting, so they are best dealt with in this section. Two species of bat are known to use bamboo stems:

Fig. 6.6.   *Tylonycteris pachypus*, the bamboo bat, roosting in a bamboo culm.

Tylonycteris pachypus and *T. robustula*, the small bamboo bats of India and south-east Asia (Fig. 6.6).

They roost inside the stem (culm) of the large bamboo, *Gigantochloa scortechinii* (Medway and Marshall, 1970; 1972), entering through the internodal emergence holes of a chrysomelid beetle, which has pupated in the culm. Both species have fleshy pads on their wrists and ankles which help the claws to grip the inside of the culm (Fig. 6.5), in which they roost in the typical upside down posture at the top of the internodal cavity. Both also have flattened skulls, which allow them to enter the narrow hole left by the beetle.

Foliage and other temporary roosts

Foliage roosts are often very freely available, but they are also very short-lived. Many bats use foliage roosts: most are solitary or roost in relatively small groups, and most are tropical. The exceptions to the first rule are the larger megabats. They have few natural predators and will roost in large camps, frequently of several thousand individuals, in the canopies of large trees (e.g. Nelson, 1965; Kingdon, 1974). The camps are frequently noisy, smelly, and very conspicuous, and can be made more conspicuous by the defoliation often caused by these large colonies. Many megabats, and most foliage roosting microbats, are less conspicuous, particularly smaller species or those roosting in smaller groups. Many have cryptic colouration (Fig. 6.7) and adopt distinct postures to avoid detection.

Camouflage is achieved by several means. Multi-coloured fur, e.g. in the vespertilionid genus *Kerivoula* (Walker, 1975), can resemble moss, lichen, dead foliage, and other

Fig. 6.7. The hoary bat, *Lasiurus cinereus*, has fur of several colours, and a grizzled (frosted) appearance, which may help to camouflage it when roosting.

backgrounds, although it is not known where these bats roost. Specific patterns may match specific substrates or mimic leaves or fruit. It has been suggested that light coloured heads and shoulders in pteropodids act as countershading. The white lines common on the body and head of many foliage roosting phyllostomids may disrupt the outline of the bats against a background of leaf veins and shafts of light penetrating the foliage (Fig. 6.8). The white coat of the white bat, *Ectophylla alba*, takes on a green hue when lit through foliage.

Exceptions to the tropical rule for foliage roosting bats are members of the genus *Lasiurus*. In North America, the hoary bat, *Lasiurus cinereus*, roosts in trees and has a long, thick coat of grizzly fur (i.e. frosted, like the grizzly bear), which is clearly cryptic against many backgrounds (Fig. 6.9). Some tropical foliage roosters also have long, thick fur, presumably for insulation, e.g. *Lavia frons*, the yellow-winged bat of Africa. Externally roosting bats also tend to have good vision, to keep an eye open for predators, although in some cases it is also for visual hunting. This is seen particularly well in the phyllostomids. Some phyllostomids have transparent windows in the dactylopatagium (handwing), so that they can see what is going on even when the wings are wrapped around the head and body (Vaughan, 1970). One species, the wrinkle-faced bat, *Centurio senax*, also has a translucent chinfold, which can be lowered over its face (Goodwin and Greenhall, 1961).

The Thyropteridae, two species of neotropical disk-winged bats, roost inside furled leaves of *Heliconia* and similar plants in Central America (Findley and Wilson, 1974). The single species of sucker-footed bat (family: Myzopodidae) of Madagascar has been found in rolled leaves of the palm *Ravenala*. All three species have very well developed adhesive disks on their wrists and feet, which stick on the smooth inside surface of the leaves (Fig. 6.10). This adaptation may be so specialised that it restricts the bats to this sort of roost, and Findley and Wilson suggest that competition for unfurled leaves may limit the distribution and numbers of *Thyroptera tricolor*. These roosts are abandoned as the leaves begin to unfurl, so bats move frequently. Similar, but usually less well developed

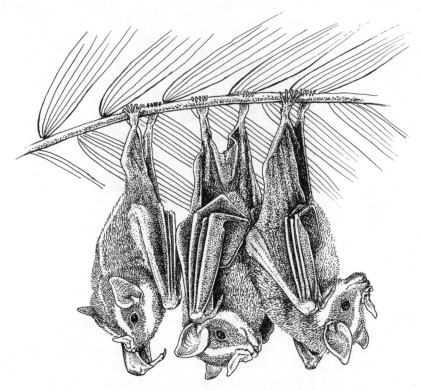

Fig. 6.8. The phyllostomid, *Vampyrodes caraccioli*. The white lines may serve to break up the bats' outline and help to camouflage them.

Fig. 6.9. The hoary bat, *Lasiurus cinereus*, frequently roosts in the open and has thick, insulating fur which covers the tail membrane and part of the wings.

(a)

(b)

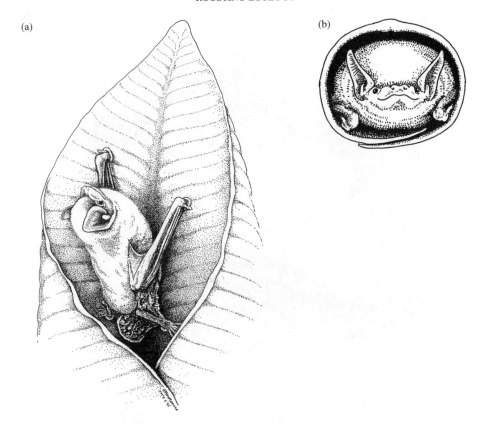

Fig. 6.10. (a) The New World disk-winged bat, *Thyroptera tricolor,* roosting in a rolled leaf, and (b) the African banana bat, *Pipistrellus nanus*, which lacks disks, in a tightly rolled leaf.

pads are found on at least 11 species of vespertilionid bat (see Kunz, 1982 for references). One species in Gabon, *Myotis bocagei*, has been found roosting inside the flowers of the water arum, but it is more commonly found in banana leaves (Brosset, 1976).

Tent-making bats

The final word in roosting behaviour is found in those species which make their own roosts. Tent-making, or at least tent-use, has evolved independently in 3 families of bats: in the neotropics, India/Indonesia, and the Philippines. As many as 14 phyllostomids, 2 pteropodids, and one vespertilionid, are believed to modify the leaves under which they roost to make tents (e.g. Kunz, 1982; Rickart *et al.*, 1989; Brooke, 1990; Foster, 1992; Charles-Dominique, 1993; Balasingh *et al.*, 1993), although the evidence is often circumstantial. All use the same basic technique: the veins or midrib of large, broadleaved, and often pinnate leaves are partially chewed through, causing the leaf to collapse. The partially enclosed tent thus formed gives protection from the weather and predators. Figure 6.11 shows the phyllostomid *Ectophylla alba* in a tent.

Palm, and *Heliconia* are the most commonly used plants, but there are some unusual variations: e.g. in India the pteropodid *Cynopterus sphinx*, in addition to making more

Fig. 6.11. The white bat, *Ectophylla alba*, and a *Heliconia* tent.

typical tents, makes a structure resembling an upside down bird's nest from the stems of the creeper *Vernonia scandens* (Balasingh *et al.*, 1993). The extent to which tent making is innate or learned is unknown, and probably varies from species to species. In a study of the white bat, *Ectophylla alba*, in Costa Rica (Brooke, 1990) 57% of all tents were found to be made from two species of *Heliconia*, but at least 26 other plants species were used for the 361 tents located. Despite this diversity, all showed the same pattern of perforations, suggesting that the construction technique is largely innate. Tent-making in *Uroderma bilobatum* is more flexible, it uses several plants of several leaf forms. Until recently tents from this and other species, were made from single leaves. Recently Choe (1994) has found *U. bilobatum* making tents from up to 14 leaves of young, unbranched *Coccoloba manzanillensis*. Bats start by collapsing the bottom leaf and work up the plant over several days.

Tent construction has to be time consuming and energetically expensive, so the cost must be offset by some clear adaptive advantage. Can a single bat make a tent in one night, or is construction a group venture? Only *Cynopterus sphinx* has been observed making a tent, and in this case the harem male did the work. A tent may be used for as little as 1–2 consecutive nights, but most tent bats make several tents, and will utilise many of them for several weeks or months. They are used as day roosts by maternity groups, harems, and solitary bats, and at night to consume fruit in safety (Brooke, 1990; Charles-Dominique, 1993). Roosting groups range from 1–80 depending upon species, and there is evidence for considerable year to year fidelity to specific locations, despite the short life of the tents themselves. Tent bats are often highly localised, being dependent upon the number and distribution of suitable plants. The dependence of foraging behaviour, social patterns, and mating systems of tent bats on the distribution of tent plants and food plants is an interesting topic barely exploited to date.

Man-made roosts

By now it will be clear that many bats are very adaptable and opportunistic roosters. This adaptability has enabled bats to exploit a wide range of man-made structures throughout the world. Many are obvious analogues of natural sites: mines, tunnels, tombs, and similar structures are used by cave bats: roof cavities in wooden buildings substitute for tree cavities, as do the numerous smaller cavities found in buildings. Crevice dwellers occupy cracks in the stonework of buildings and bridges, or the expansion joints of more modern structures. Some species have become so well-adapted to man-made sites that they are now rarely found in natural roosts: the serotine and pipistrelle, *Eptesicus serotinus* and *Pipistrellus pipistrellus*, in Britain, the big and little brown bats, *Eptesicus fuscus* and *Myotis lucifugus*, in North America (Barbour and Davis, 1969), *Mollosus molossus* and *Myotis nigricans* in the neotropics (Greenhall and Stell, 1960; Wilson, 1971), and *Taphozous melanopogan* and *Megaderma lyra* in India (Brosset, 1962a, c).

FEEDING ECOLOGY

The feeding habits of bats are almost as varied as those of the mammals as a whole, and this dietary diversity is responsible for much of the morphological, physiological, and ecological diversity seen in bats. Bats feed on insects and other arthropods, including freshwater and marine species, mammals, birds, reptiles, amphibians, fish, blood, carrion, fruit, flowers, nectar, pollen, and foliage.

A comprehensive review of the feeding ecology of bats would need a large book in itself. I am going to go through the list, briefly cover the basics, and highlight some features I find particularly interesting or informative.

Natterer's bat, *Myotis nattereri*.

Insectivory

Although insects are the dominant component of most bat's diet, spiders, scorpions, crustacea, and other arthropods are eaten. For simplicity I use the term insectivorous to describe all of those species which feed on insects and other arthropods. Around 70% of all bats are insectivorous: all but a few microbats. Arthropods are an abundant and widespread food, and it is likely that their diversification was a primary driving force for the evolution and diversification of bats. The vast majority of insectivorous microbats are small, and catch their food on the wing. Their small size gives them the manoeuvrability and agility necessary to catch flying insects detected by their short-range echolocation system (Barclay and Brigham, 1991). Size is important in other ways: it is a generally accepted ecological rule that the size of the predator is related to the size of its prey. Optimal foraging theory predicts that predators, and in particular carnivores (including insectivores), should, under certain conditions select prey which are most profitable in terms of energy intake per unit handling time. An insect which is too big may take a disproportionately long time to catch, subdue and eat, and this may incur a considerable energy cost in itself. If the insects are too small, it may not be possible to catch and eat sufficient to meet daily energy requirements. The number and size of teeth, the size of the jaw, the size of the cranial crest where the chewing muscles are attached, and other morphological features, can all be related to diet (e.g. Freeman, 1981; Findley and Black, 1983). Bats which eat hard-cased insects like beetles have strong jawbones, large jaw muscles, and few, large teeth.

Several species eat scorpions: members of the Nycteridae, the slit-faced bats, in the Old World tropics, and the pallid bat, *Antrozous pallidus*, in North and Central America. The fish-eating bats, *Noctilio leporinus* and *Myotis vivesi* take crustacea: *N. leporinus* in Puerto Rica are known to eat lots of fiddler crabs (Brooke, 1994), and in this population insects were more important in the wet season, and fish and crustacea in the dry season.

Optimal foraging

In Chapter 3 I discussed the subject of prey selection in relation to the perceptual abilities of echolocation. I want to raise it again, in the context of optimal foraging. There is considerable debate among bat biologists as to whether bats do indeed select their prey: studies can be cited in support of both selective and opportunistic foraging. Fenton (1990) and Jones (1990) provide interesting insights into the debate. The problem, like many in ecology, is a very complex one, with many factors likely to influence the foraging strategy adopted by a bat. Let's review some of the more important, and then see if the observed behaviour of bats can be explained with reference to them. Unfortunately, few studies really address the question of optimal foraging in bats, and far more questions are asked than answered. However, in the next few years we will probably see major advances in this field.

Optimal foraging can involve both selective and opportunistic foraging, a point sometimes missed in the literature on bats—selective feeding is confusingly associated with optimal foraging. A selective bat (a specialist) will take only the most profitable prey, but it may spend a lot of time and energy looking for them. An opportunist (generalist) will spend little time and energy looking for particular prey, and many will give it little energy in return, but its rate of food intake may still be high. An optimal forager will adjust the time it spends using each strategy to maximise its net energy intake (MacArthur and Pianka, 1966). Let's assume the bat is feeding, and taking profitable prey, when it encounters a slightly less profitable insect. Should it expand its diet and eat it? The answer is yes, if it increases its overall net energy intake rate—more specifically, if the profitability of that item, (the ith) is greater than the expected rate of energy intake if it ignores this item and continues to search for its more profitable prey. The profitability of its new item is:

$$\frac{E_i}{h_i}$$

where E_i is its energy content, and h_i its handling time. The rate of energy intake on the present diet is:

$$\frac{\bar{E}}{(\bar{s} + \bar{h})}$$

where $\bar{E}$ is the average energy content of the present diet, $\bar{h}$ the average handling time, and $\bar{s}$ the average search time. The bat should therefore take this ith item when:

$$\frac{E_i}{h_i} \geqslant \frac{\bar{E}}{(\bar{s} + \bar{h})}$$

Searching and handling—generalist or specialist?

There are two major components to any foraging strategy: searching and handling. If search time is long in relation to handling ($s>h$), then the bat should be a generalist or opportunist, because E_i/h_i will be large for a wide range of insects, and $\bar{E}/(\bar{s} + \bar{h})$ small. Once it has found a prey item, it might as well eat it. All bats which feed on the wing are relatively small, and encounter prey quite frequently (1–20 each minute, with a capture success rate of about 40%, reviewed by Fenton, 1990). Prey are predominantly small, and handling times will be short, so theory predicts that these bats will be generalists. Published evidence is contradictory (see Jones, 1990; Fenton, 1990), with studies suggesting both generalist and specialist strategies, even for the same species (e.g. *Myotis lucifugus*, Anthony and Kunz, 1977; Belwood and Fenton, 1976). However, the generalist strategy does appear to be that most commonly adopted.

If handling time is long in relation to search time, then it may be energetically more advantageous to reject some prey items and search again. This is because when $\bar{s}$ is small, the bat must effectively maximise $\bar{E}/\bar{h}$: i.e. keep eating only the most profitable prey. It has been suggested that this specialist strategy is used by the larger aerial insectivores. For example, the hoary bat (*Lasiurus cinereus*) takes only large prey, when small insects are known to be available (Barclay, 1985). This has been noted for a number of species (see Barclay and Brigham, 1991), although again, exceptions have been noted (Rydell, 1986). It may be true that this is selection for profitable prey, but Barclay and Brigham (1991) present an alternative and persuasive hypothesis. They note that insectivorous bats are small, even by comparison with insectivorous birds, suggesting that aerodynamic constraints alone (small size confers increased manoeuvrability and agility) do not explain their small size. They argue that because bats use echolocation, a short-range orientation system, prey are detected only when the bats are very close, giving them little time to change flight path. This makes adaptations for manoeuvrability and agility even more important: hence the strong selective pressure for small size. Bigger bats are less manoeuvrable and agile, since they have higher wing-loadings, and hence faster flight speeds. They compensate for this by having lower frequency echolocation pulses, which are attenuated less in air, and can thus detect prey at greater distances. However, the penalty for this is a decrease in resolution; they cannot detect small insects, and this may be the reason why many large bats (but by no means all) only take large prey—selection may not enter into the equation.

The relative lengths of searching and handling times will depend upon the habitat, the behaviour of the prey, and the nature of the prey itself. Compare for example a slow flying, small, soft moth in an uncluttered airspace with a large, hard, fast moving, stinging scorpion that must be gleaned from a cluttered ground habitat.

Foraging style

Several styles have been identified in bats, but for the purpose of this discussion, I'll consider two extreme categories: aerial hawking and flycatching (perch-hunting). In the former bats detect, pursue, and eat their prey on the wing; in the latter prey may be detected from a perch, pursued, and caught, and then eaten back at the perch. Jones and Rayner (1989) compared the feeding behaviour of the closely related and morphologically similar 7 g lesser horseshoe bat (*Rhinolophus hipposideros*) with that of the 25 g greater horseshoe bat (*R. ferrumequinum*). Although both had very flexible foraging styles, the lesser horseshoe bat was predominantly an aerial hawker, and was never observed flycatching. Greater horseshoe bats often spent much of their time flycatching. This is a common trend among bats—large nycterids (slit-faced bats), and megadermatids are typically flycatchers. As I said above, large animals take large prey, and it may be the difficulty of handling large prey in flight that makes these bats return to a perch. Why should they hunt from a perch in the first place? The cost of flight is around 20 times resting metabolic rate for an insectivorous bat, that of flycatching may be only 3 times. Large prey items generally occur at lower densities, so search times and flight costs will be high. Flycatching—sitting and waiting for large prey, is likely to be a cost-effective strategy. Foraging in clutter, as many of these bats do, demands low aspect ratio wings and low wing loading for slow manoeuvrable flight—characteristics which make flight even more expensive. This large difference in energy cost between the two strategies must be a major factor in determining which style is adopted, as the density and type of prey being sought changes through the night and with the seasons. There are a number of descriptive accounts of bats changing foraging style during the night.

Prey density

Search time, $\bar{s}$, will increase as prey density decreases, and this should lead to the adoption of a generalist strategy. Some of the apparent contradictions seen in the literature may be resolved if future studies take this into account.

Perception and pursuit of prey

As we saw in Chapter 2 bats differ in their flight performance, and in Chapter 3 we saw that they differed in their perceptual abilities in terms of the size of prey they can detect, their ability to function in cluttered environments, and the detailed information that echolocation gives them about their prey. All of these factors must be taken into account when trying to explain foraging strategy.

The predator as prey

Even if all of the above could be quantified, a bat may not conform to the rules of optimal foraging—its behaviour may be influenced by other factors, such as avoiding being eaten itself.

Carnivory

A carnivorous bat is generally thought of as one which takes small vertebrates (excluding fish) as a significant component of its diet. Only 10 species are confirmed carnivores (Norberg and Fenton, 1988): four species of false vampire (Megadermatidae)—

Megaderma lyra and *M. spasma* (India & South East Asia), *Cardioderma cor* (East Africa), and *Macroderma gigas* (Australia); four phyllostomids—*Trachops cirrhosis, Vampyrum spectrum, Phyllostomus hastatus,* and *Chrotopterus auritus* (Central and South America); one nycterid—*Nycteris grandis* (Africa) and one vespertilionid—*Antrozous pallidus* (southern United States and Central America). None are small bats (all weigh more than 20 g) and all but one have low aspect ratio wings and low wing loadings—all useful attributes for catching and carrying large ground dwelling prey. The exception is *Phyllostomus hastatus*: although it does take vertebrates, its higher aspect ratio and wing loading have led Norberg and Fenton (1988) to predict that they do not make up a significant part of this species' diet. *Vampyrum spectrum* and *Macroderma gigas* are the biggest microbats, with a wingspan of almost 1 m, and a mass of 130–180 g (Fig. 6.12). Another feature common to all is the use of low intensity, broadband echolocation calls, and/or prey-generated sound cues when hunting. None appear to be exclusive carnivores, and a very broad diet characterises most.

Megadermatids will eat arthropods, other bats, small rodents, birds, lizards, and frogs. *Vampyrum spectrum, Trachops cirrhosus,* and *Chrotopterus auritus* have similar diets. The foraging behaviour of *Vampyrum spectrum,* studied by Vehrencamp *et al.* (1977) in Costa Rica is probably typical. They roosted in small groups in tree holes, and left and returned singly during the night. They probably therefore foraged alone. Foraging time was very variable, and on some nights they did not forage at all. This is consistent with the high energy content of the predominantly avian prey of this bat—one 75 g bird every second or third night may meet its energy requirements. Food was sometimes taken back to the roost, possibly for consumption, for a mate guarding its pup, or even for feeding the pup. The only clue is the observation that a captive male provided food for a female. The bats specialised in birds which roosted communally and/or had strong body odours. Vehrencamp *et al.* (1977) make the interesting comment that these two characteristics have been put forward as anti-predation mechanisms. They clearly do not work against the bats, but may be more effective against other predators. Other studies suggest a more varied diet, and a very broad diet has been reported for *Nycteris grandis* (see Norberg and Fenton, 1988 for references) and *Megaderma lyra* (Audet *et al.*, 1991).

Fig. 6.12. Linnaeus' false vampire, *Vampyrum spectrum.*

Carnivory almost certainly evolved from insectivory and most carnivorous bats still take large numbers of arthropods: little modification of the teeth was necessary to deal with the new prey. Relatively large size may be a prerequisite of carnivory, and also a consequence permitted by the rich diet.

Piscivory

Piscivory is really a specialised form of carnivory, and probably evolved in trawling insectivorous bats. Like carnivores, fish-eating species do still take insects. Two species are confirmed fish-eaters—*Noctilio leporinus* (60 g, Noctilionidae) and *Myotis vivesi* (25 g, Vespertilionidae), from the tropics and sub-tropics of the Americas. This is another good example of convergent evolution. Both species have long legs and huge feet for effective fishing and long, sharp claws for gaffing fish. They have high aspect ratio wings for efficient flight over water: flight is free from clutter, making long wings practical, and lift is gained by flying close to the surface. Finally, both have a low wing loading, an adaptation for slow flight, and for carrying large prey (Fig. 6.13). The smaller noctilionid, *N. albiventris* (30 g), although predominantly insectivorous, also takes fish. Other insectivorous trawlers are known to take fish to varying extents, as do *Megaderma lyra* and *Nycteris grandis*.

   N. leporinus has a strong, long calcar which can be folded forward to lift the tail membrane clear of the water as the bat swoops to lift fish. They search for fish breaking the water surface using characteristic echolocation calls in high (20–50 cm above water) or low (4–10 cm) search flights, dipping the feet in only in an attempt to catch located fish. Alternatively they can trawl randomly in areas of high fish activity, dragging their feet through the water in up to 10 m straight lines without targeting a specific fish (Schnitzler *et al.*, 1994).

Fig. 6.13. *Noctilio leporinus*, the fisherman bat.

Sanguivory

This is the habit which has given bats their undeserved bad image. Ironically, only three species feed on blood. They all belong to the Desmodontinae a sub-family of the large and diverse Phyllostomidae. By far the most abundant is the common vampire, *Desmodus rotundus*.

It is widespread in the tropical and sub-tropical areas of the New World, and just extends into the southern United States. The other two, the white winged vampire (*Diaemus youngi*) and the hairy-legged vampire (*Diphylla ecaudata*) (Fig. 6.14), are much less common, and much less widespread. *Diphylla ecaudata* apparently has a strong preference for bird blood. *Desmodus* on the other hand has a preference for large mammals, and the introduction of domestic horses, cattle, and pigs, has probably led to a dramatic increase in its numbers over the last 300 years. The booming human population also provides an occasional food source in some areas.

Vampires roost in colonies of up to 100 or so individuals in caves or hollow trees. They locate their prey by a combination of smell, sound, echolocation, and possibly heat. They are remarkably agile on the ground, and will often land near their prey, run up to it, and jump onto the foot or leg. They have heat-sensitive cells in the nose to help them locate capillary rich areas of skin, which they nick with their razor sharp, blade-like, upper incisors. The wound is kept open by an anticoagulant in the saliva, and the bats lap up the blood as it flows—they do not suck. It takes them 20–30 min to take in around

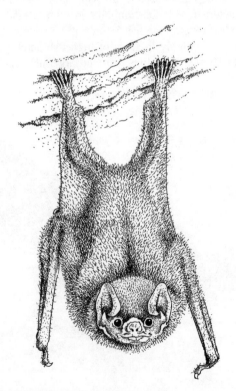

Fig. 6.14. *Diphylla ecaudata*, the hairy-legged vampire.

25 ml of blood—a large quantity for a bat which weighs only 30–35 g. They can be so heavy that they are unable to take off: their specific name, *rotundus*, is therefore appropriate to their after-dinner appearance! Fortunately for the bat, since this situation leaves them open to predation, they have very efficient kidneys: if the meal is a long one, they begin to urinate excess plasma from the ingested blood before they finish feeding. In the subsequent digestion of this protein-rich diet, they have to cope with very high concentrations of nitrogenous waste, and the kidney switches from a water expelling to a water conserving mode.

Reciprocal altruism

Perhaps the most interesting thing about vampires is their social behaviour, studied to great effect by Wilkinson (1984, 1990). Examples of reciprocal altruism, in which animals return favours to their mutual benefit, have been put forward for many years. Most however turn out to be either false, or examples of kin-selection, where the individuals are really protecting their own genetic interests. In vampires we find one of the few cases of reciprocal altruism which stands up to scrutiny. Within a colony of females (males roost separately, defending territories), there are groupings of 8–12 individuals, which roost close together on a regular basis over several years. If bats do not get their 25 ml of blood on a regular basis they rapidly deteriorate: 2–3 nights without a meal leaves a bat close to starvation. However, within these social groups, bats which did get a meal on a particular night will regurgitate blood back at the roost for those which did not, and this behaviour is reciprocated on later nights. Genetic analysis of blood samples from bats within a group showed that although there are sibling and parent/offspring groupings, many of the bats within groups are not related. Study of the blood sharing behaviour showed that bats regurgitated blood for related and unrelated bats in the group, and that sharing occurred between unrelated bats only if they roosted together regularly—in other words with those bats likely to do the same for them on a later occasion. Vampires therefore provide us with an example of both kin-selection and reciprocal altruism. When the field studies were followed up by laboratory experiments, it was shown that the bats in fact tended to set up buddy systems, with pairs of bats forming the tightest blood-sharing associations.

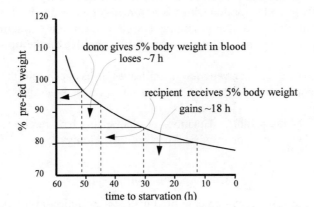

Fig. 6.15. Weight loss curve after feeding in *Desmodus*, the common vampire. A cost–benefit analysis of blood-sharing (adapted from Wilkinson, 1984).

Figure 6.15 shows the weight loss curve of a vampire after returning to the roost with a good meal inside it. Weight loss is initially rapid, and slows to a starvation point after 60 hours. If a donor gives just 5% of its body weight in blood to a buddy, then it loses the equivalent of 7 h of its time to the starvation point. However the recipient, if it is relatively close to starvation, gains 18 h. Computer simulations showed that the buddy system will work well only if donors give to their buddies when the recipients have 24 h or less to live, and this is just what happened in the laboratory experiments.

Wilkinson (1987) has studied other phyllostomids, concluding that both kin-selection and reciprocal altruism are plausible mechanisms governing aspects of the social behaviour in those bats with stable group composition and/or a high degree of relatedness among individuals in the group. Future research on the behaviour of other species with varied social systems are likely to be very informative in this context—no other group of mammals can boast of such a diverse social organisation.

Bats that eat plant products

The Old World megabats feed almost exclusively on fruits, flowers, pollen, and nectar, and appear to have done so from their beginnings. In the New World, in the absence of competition from megabats, plant-eaters evolved from insectivorous microbat ancestors, and the evidence suggests they evolved independently several times. All microbat plant-eaters are from the family Phyllostomidae. It is assumed that in taking insects from fruit and flowers, they developed a taste for the vegetation underneath. Many of the phyllostomid species are probably less than committed vegetarians, taking insects to varying extents. *Phyllostomus hastatus,* although it eats predominantly fruit, takes the occasional vertebrate in addition to insects: perhaps protein-limited lactating females do this. Conversely, several species thought of as insectivores eat nectar and pollen on a seasonal basis.

Pollen and nectar provide a rich diet. In addition to carbohydrate, bat nectar is often rich in lipids, and pollen has a high protein content. 70–75% of the diet of *Leptonycteris curasoae* (*sanborni*) is nectar, and a much smaller amount of pollen provides all the necessary protein. The hair on the head and shoulders of some bats is rough and scaly to collect pollen which is groomed off and eaten back at the roost. The long tongue is useful for pollen grooming as well as for nectar extraction. The latter is made more efficient by the evolution of brush-like papillae on the tip of the tongue in some species.

Some megabats have been reported to eat leaves. It has been said that they are probably an unimportant part of the diet, but this has recently been questioned (Kunz and Ingalls, 1994).

More details of the feeding adaptations of plant-eating bats can be found in Hill and Smith (1984): I want to go on to other aspects of their biology.

Convergent evolution again?

We might expect to see a classic case of convergent evolution in the megabats and the phyllostomids, and at first glance we do. For example, species which feed almost exclusively on nectar and pollen are found in both families, and they exhibit many similarities.

The Macroglossinae (megabats), like their counterparts in the phyllostomids (e.g. Glossophaginae) are small, and some hover like hummingbirds in front of flowers. Members of both groups have long muzzles for probing flowers, and long tongues to extract nectar. Since they have little use for teeth, they are often reduced, although a sharp pair of incisors may be retained to puncture nectaries. However, the Old and New World environments differ in many respects, and the plant-eaters in the two worlds evolved in different ways to meet the challenges posed by their habitats. Fleming (1986; 1993; and Fleming *et al.*, 1987), argues that the key lies in the diversity and ecology of the food plants, which have led to two fundamentally different strategies. Both families are large and evolutionarily successful (Pteropodidae = 42 genera, 175 species; Phyllostomidae = 51 genera, 147 species), and Fleming was able to study their adaptive radiation by examining a number of morphological traits at the generic level of each family, in relation to those of the most primitive genus in each (*Rousettus* and *Macrotus*). The results are summarised in Fig. 6.16.

Average size has not changed over the course of the evolution of both families, but megabats are bigger. Since the mass-specific cost of flight decreases with increasing body size, megabats fly more efficiently. As they evolved, the wings of megabats increased in aspect ratio—long narrow wings are aerodynamically more efficient, and with a high wing loading, lead to fast, efficient flight. Phyllostomids, in contrast, are relatively small bats, with low aspect ratios and wing loadings, for slow, manoeuvrable flight. The New World tropics have a greater diversity of food plants, and show less

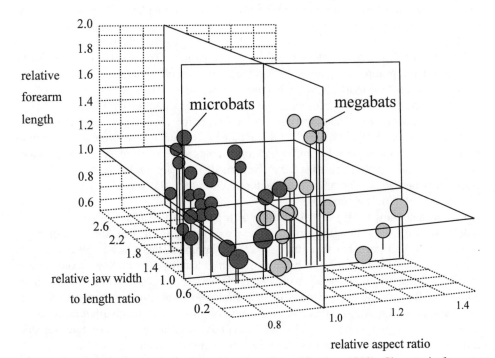

Fig. 6.16. Adaptive radiation in plant-eating bats (from Fleming, 1993). Changes in forearm length, wing aspect ratio and jaw shape relative to bats of the most primitive megabat (*Rousettus*) and phyllostomid (*Macrotus*) genera.

spatial and temporal patchiness, than those of the Old World. In the Old World, a smaller number of food plant species are generally more scattered, and a greater proportion go in for 'big bang' flowering or fruiting, i.e. they flower or fruit explosively over just a few days. Megabats may commute 50 km or more in their search for fruiting trees, hence their adaptations for rapid, efficient flight. Phyllostomids, with a richer and more predictable source of food, rarely range more than 10 km from the roost, and frequently much less. The jaw structure of megabats appears to have diverged little from that of their ancestors, since they must remain generalist feeders in order to exploit any flowering or fruiting tree they encounter in their long foraging trips. The richer habitat of the phyllostomids has enabled them to specialise, and many are specialist frugivores or nectarivores, with jaw structure to match. The divergence resulting from these two different strategies, the large, wide ranging generalist versus the small, home range specialist, can be seen in Fig. 6.16.

Optimal foraging again

Studies of *Leptoncteris curasoae (sanborni)* by Howell (1979) and Howell and Hartl (1980) revealed one of the most fascinating illustrations of optimal foraging seen in the mammals. This bat spends much of its time feeding on nectar from the large flower panicles of the agave, *Agave palmeri,* a desert succulent of Mexico and the south-western United States. It is a medium-sized (17 g) bat which roosts in groups of 20–100 individuals, and after dusk they forage as a group. When one bat finds a panicle which has flowers full of nectar, all of the other bats join it and circle round the plant. They then leave the circle at random and take turns to dip into the flowers for nectar. At some point, one of the bats leaves this panicle, and flies in search of another. All of the remaining bats will follow and make no further attempt to feed on that panicle. The first bat to leave can be any one of the group, and there is no evidence of a social hierarchy within the flock. Why do the bats feed in flocks, and what makes them suddenly leave?

Having observed the bats closely in the field, and measured the distribution of nectar volumes in flowers before and after bat visits, an experiment was set up in a large outdoor enclosure. Artificial glass flowers in a mock panicle contained an appropriate amount of nectar. A group of temporarily captive and trained bats were released and allowed to feed at this artificial agave. Each time they abandoned it the amount of nectar left in each flower was measured. The amount of nectar taken at each dip was also determined and this turned out to be very constant.

Howell and Hartl (1980) argued that the distribution of nectar levels after a visit is a reflection of the bats' foraging strategy, and this strategy must obey some set of rules. How do you find out what that strategy is? The approach taken was to devise sets of rules which might govern the bats behaviour, such as leaving after finding a fixed number of empty flowers in total, or so many empty flowers in a row, or simply after a fixed number of flowers had been visited: 42 such strategies were tested. A computer simulation, based on each of these rules was then run 100 times, and the distribution of nectar levels was compared with that left by real bats. Only two rules gave statistically satisfactory fits, and one in particular best described the pattern produced by the bats: leave the panicle when a total of 8 flowers have been found empty (Rule 13). This may not be what the bats are actually doing, but it is the statistical equivalent, and it fits very well. The investigators had a strategy, but was it an optimal foraging strategy? In other words, if all

Fig. 6.17. *Leptonycteris curasoae* (*sanborni*) at an agave panicle.

of the bats adopt this strategy, and then feed randomly in flocks, do they maximise the return (nectar eaten) on their investment (foraging cost)? To answer this, we need to know the cost C of actually working the flower panicle, in terms of the number of flower visits. This can be found again from the computer simulations and videotapes of actual bats. To produce the nectar distribution left by real bats at the end of their visit, each computer bat in the group made an average of 23 visits. Computer bats never fail to sample the flower, but real bats do. Since real bats make an average of 35 visits, the number of misses is 35–23 = 12. Add 1 or 2 for the initial flight to the panicle, and 1–6 for occasions when 2 bats approach the flower and one gives up, then the cost C = 14–20 visits. The return R, in terms of mouthfuls of nectar is given by:

$$E \, \frac{Y}{C + V}$$

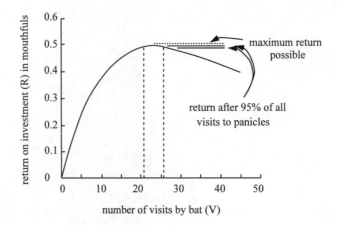

Fig. 6.18. Optimal foraging in nectar feeders. The calculated return in mouthfuls of nectar in relation to the number of visits to an agave panicle, by a simulated flock of six *Leptonycteris sanborni* (from Howell and Hartl, 1980).

where E is the expectation, Y is the total yield in mouthfuls, V is the number of flower visits to obtain yield Y, and C is the cost of working the panicle in numbers of visits. All 42 strategies were compared, and the strategy giving the best return R for a cost C of 14–20 visits was Rule 13—it does appear to be an optimal foraging strategy. How good a strategy is it ?

Figure 6.18 shows the calculated return R for a 6 bat flock, for a value of C of 17. The curve has a maximum at 23.2 visits per bat, when R = half a mouthful per visit on average, the maximum theoretically possible. With rule 13, the bat would abandon the panicle after 21–26 visits 95% of the time. Over this range, R is very close to its maximum value: the strategy is a very good one. What does half a mouthful of nectar do for the bat? For a cost of 0.003 kJ in circling the panicle (6.1 m), it gets 0.84 kJ of energy—sufficient to power a flight of 0.25–0.5 km—not a bad return.

There are other important points to note—by foraging in flocks the bats enhance their chance of finding the next panicle unexploited, and hence with full flowers—essential for the successful operation of their foraging strategy. The bats can thus switch with minimal risk of making a bad decision. Note that in this example, the bat is optimising energy input in a 24 hour period: this may not always be the most important consideration (see Heithaus, 1982, p. 355).

INFORMATION TRANSFER

Given the gregarious nature of bats, we might expect them to have well developed communication skills, and to intentionally and unintentionally share information about roost sites, foraging areas, etc. Although communication in bats has received considerable attention (see Fenton, 1985), information transfer in particular has been neglected in the past. A recent review by Wilkinson (1995) provides a timely summary of the current state of the field, and points the way to future research. Wilkinson describes four basic mechanisms of information transfer: local enhancement, social facilitation, imitative learning, and intentional signalling.

Local enhancement

Local enhancement involves unintentionally directing another organism to a particular part of the habitat. Insectivorous bats quickly gather round patches of prey, presumably as the echolocation calls of feeding bats attract other bats in the vicinity. Barclay (1982) showed that little brown bats (*Myotis lucifugus*) flew to loudspeakers broadcasting calls of both little (*Myotis lucifugus*) and big (*Eptesicus fuscus*) brown bats: good evidence for eavesdropping behaviour. Bats may also find good foraging sites by following other bats. Wilkinson (1992) has shown that the foraging success of evening bats, *Nycticeius humeralis*, is increased by following behaviour. These bats exploit insect patches which persist for several days. It appears that bats which have failed to find these patches will follow at random another member of the colony on its next flight from the roost, and in doing so reduce their chance of returning without a meal. This system will be most beneficial to those bats making frequent foraging trips from the roost in a given night—notably females during lactation.

Social facilitation

Social facilitation is an increase in individual foraging success brought about by group foraging behaviour. Some degree of co-ordinated behaviour has been reported for a number of group-foraging bats, e.g. proboscis bats, *Rhynchonycteris naso*, follow each other when feeding on insects (Bradbury and Vehrencamp, 1976a), and *Phyllostomus discolor* visit flowers in turn (Heithaus *et al.*, 1974), but whether this improves foraging success, and by what mechanisms, is largely unknown. Wilkinson (1995) suggests that the decrease in frequency of echolocation pulses in the feeding buzz observed in some species may serve to advertise prey and increase group size.

Imitative learning

Whilst a number of studies have looked for evidence that bats can learn foraging techniques from other bats (notably their mothers) most are far from conclusive. The most persuasive case can be made for the common vampire, *Desmodus rotundus*, in which feeding ranges of mother and yearling-daughter overlap significantly more than expected (Wilkinson, 1985). The long period of association between mother and young perhaps facilitates this. There is considerable evidence to show that the social and echolocation calls of young bats can closely resemble those of their mothers (e.g. Mexican free-tailed bats, *Tadarida brasiliensis*, Balcombe and McCracken, 1992; greater horseshoe bats, *Rhinolophus ferrumequinum*, Jones and Ransome, 1993). Although it has been shown that isolation calls are heritable and very specific even in bats just 2–5 days old (evening bats, *Nycticeius humeralis*, Scherrer and Wilkinson, 1993), Jones and Ransome (1993) provide some evidence to suggest that echolocation call structure in greater horseshoe bats does have a learnt component.

Intentional signalling

Intentional signalling can take many forms: mating calls, territorial calls, alarm calls, and food calls have all been reported in bats. The most spectacular mating calls are those of the epomophorine megabats (Bradbury, 1977a,b). Since call rate increases when females approach the calling males, the intentional nature of this signal is clear. Mating calls are also made by microbats, e.g. the European pipistrelle, *Pipistrellus pipistrellus* (Lundberg and Gerell, 1986) and the white-lined bat, *Saccopteryx bilineata* (Bradbury and Emmons, 1974). We do not know how (or if) females make their choice of mate on the basis of these calls. Territorial calls are widely described for temperate and tropical insectivores, e.g. the European pipistrelle (Racey and Swift, 1985) and the white-lined bat (Bradbury and Vehrencamp, 1976a). The Australian ghost bat, *Macroderma gigas*, (Tidemann *et al.*, 1985) and the spear-nosed bat, *Phyllostomus hastatus* (Wilkinson, 1995) both call at feeding sites in the absence of territorial behaviour, suggesting advertisement of food. *Phyllostomus hastatus* appears to use such calls to attract bats into foraging groups as they leave their cave roosts.

INTERACTIONS BETWEEN HABITAT, FOOD, FORAGING, SOCIAL STRUCTURE, AND BEHAVIOUR

Over the last two chapters we have looked at mating systems, roosting ecology, feeding ecology, and information transfer. Can we pull all these aspects together, and say something about the way they interact to give a bat a particular life history? This is an essential task if we are to really understand the biology of bats, but it is a difficult task which few researchers have tackled.

Several questions are of fundamental importance. What roosting sites are available? What is the life span of these roosts? How abundant is the food supply? Is it evenly or patchily distributed? How does food supply vary in time? Where are the roosts in relation to foraging sites? What are the risks of predation? When we have answers to these questions we can begin to piece together the story.

The importance of food distribution can be best illustrated with some extreme examples. If the food supply of a bat is widely and densely distributed, and does not vary with the seasons, the bat need only travel a short distance from its roost to find food, and it can return again and again to those sites it knows well. Such sites may offer other benefits in addition to low transport costs and commuting time, e.g. a reduced risk of predation. Such a bat may forage most effectively if it forages alone. An abundant food supply need not be defended: it may even be energetically unfavourable to expend time and energy on defence rather than on feeding. An abundant and invariant food supply may also enable the bat to specialise on a small number of food types.

At the opposite extreme, we have a species which relies on a patchy source of food, which undergoes large seasonal or even unpredictable changes in abundance. This bat may need to travel considerable distances in search of food, and it will have to change its foraging sites to locate new sources. Foraging in this species may be more effective in groups, since a group can search a wider area, and when one individual finds food, others may be attracted to it, intentionally or unintentionally. Whether or not a patch of food is defended by the group, or small patches by individuals, will depend upon how rich the food supply is, and how defensible the patch. For example, a very rich but difficult to defend patch is not worth defending—best to just tuck in and eat. A patchy and ephemeral food supply may encourage a generalist feeding strategy, with bats taking a wide range of transiently available food.

This is just the simple tip of a complex iceberg: there's much more under the surface. If the patchy food of our group forager undergoes rapid changes in abundance and distribution, then any group of bats is likely to be as successful as another. If patches persist for days or weeks, then stable groups, within which information about patch locality and abundance can be shared, may be more successful foragers. Should a bat or group of bats combine foraging and commuting, or separate these tasks? It would make sense to combine them if food was abundant and uniformly distributed. Conversely, in getting to a known, rich patch of food in an unpredictable environment, commuting by the shortest route without foraging is likely to be the optimal strategy. Predation risk may also play an important role, but it is difficult to generalise, since the risk will be determined not only by the foraging style of the bat, but also by the strategy of the predator. As an example, long flights combining commuting and foraging will make bats particularly vulnerable to aerial predators: other bats and owls? The proximity and availability of roosts will also influence strategy: cave roosts are relatively scarce, and may necessitate long commuting flights irrespective of the spatial and temporal distribution of food. Tree and foliage roosts are generally more abundant, and will enable bats to roost close to their food source. The use of special night roosts, or the ability to return to the day roost between foraging excursions will influence foraging style, and the level of information transfer between group members. Night roosts used for resting or food consumption may also reduce the risk of predation. The size of the bat species may be important, since small bats have high energy requirements, which may necessitate a high energy content diet, and a specific foraging strategy. It is clear that all of these factors, and many others, determine the foraging strategy of an individual bat: whether or not the bat will forage as part of a group, the degree of compositional stability of that group, home range or territory size, and fidelity to particular roost sites. As we have seen in the last chapter, it is these factors which in turn determine mating strategy. In a species which forms stable female groups, which show a high fidelity to a particular roost site, then a male will find it easy to defend a harem against other males. If the females forage as a group, the male or males may forage with them, and the group may even defend a territory. When female group composition varies, and roost sites change frequently, other strategies must be adopted, such as mating roost defence or lekking. Finally, the social status of the bat is important. A dominant male will spend time in defence of a roost or harem or in advertisement, and this may necessitate changes in foraging strategy. I could go on, but the point has been made, and I think it is time to look at some specific examples, and see if there is any evidence to suggest that bats conform to any of these rules.

Insectivores

Bradbury and Vehrencamp (1976a; b; 1977a; b) studied five species of emballonurid in Costa Rica. The food supply of all species was spatially and temporally variable, so we might expect group foraging, and possibly stable social groups. Of course life is rarely that simple, and this study is a good lesson in how the complexity of real situations makes it difficult to uncover the basic rules governing behaviour. Important aspects of the biology of the five species are summarised in Table 6.1.

There was no obvious relationship between social structure (colony size and stability) and group foraging. The three smaller species all frequently foraged in groups, the larger

Table 6.1. Aspects of the biology of five species of emballonurids in Central America (based on Bradbury and Vehrencamp, 1976a, 1976b, 1977a)

Species	weight (g)	colony (group) size mean, range	group compositional stability	mating system	foraging dispersion, territory defence, territory size, mean density of bats	foraging strategy/ habitat habitat	roost site
Rhynchonycteris naso	4.5	7.8, 5–11	high	Multi-male groups, female defence by males	f: group beats, at territory centre m: solitary, at territory periphery colony territory defended, 1.1 ha, 8 bats/ha	specialist, over water, rarely pasture wet forest river	tree boles near water, move around 3–6 sites
Saccopteryx leptura	5.0	3.6, 1–9	high	Monogamous pairs (?), resource /female defence by male	solitary and group beats common colony territory defended, 0.14 ha, 2.5 bats/ha (Costa Rica)	specialist, below mature or riparian forest canopy at dusk, moving above canopy with insects later in the night wet forest	tree boles in forest, move around several sites
Balantiopteryx plicata	6.1	?, 50–2000	low	swarming (?) male strategy unknown	solitary and group beats, defended, unknown but large, unknown	opportunistic: pasture, swamps, woodland in highly seasonal areas dry seasonal savannah	caves and crevices, no movement

Table 6.1. *Continued*

Species	weight (g)	colony (group) size mean, range	group compositional stability	mating system	foraging dispersion, territory defence, territory size, mean density of bats	foraging strategy/ habitat	roost site
Saccopteryx bilineata	7.7	6.8, 2–32	low	temporary harems, resource defence by male	solitary beats, clustered to form colony territory, females of harem forage on adjacent patches, and harem territory defended by male (against males) and females (against females), 7 ha, 0.7 bats/ha	opportunistic: all habitats, as insects peak seasonally wet ↔ dry forests	tree buttress and trunk cavities, no movement
Peropteryx kappleri	9.0	4.3, 1–7	high	Monogamous pairs (?), resource defence by male	solitary beats, unknown, 0.6 bats/ha	sub-canopy of mature forest wet forest	fallen logs, tree buttress cavities, some movement between roosts

two were always solitary feeders. Clearly, we need to look deeper. What about the habitats and the way the bats used them?

There are two dominant habitats, 'wet' and 'dry'. Wet habitats are characterised by high plant species diversity, a heterogeneous mix of plants, and a high plant activity (i.e. high turnover of foliage, flowers, and fruit), with minimal seasonal variation. Since there is little synchrony of activity among plants, mean plant activity within a patch is relatively low. Since insect abundance is related to plant activity and dispersion, these habitats are characterised by small, low density patches of insects around active plants, and these small patches are densely packed: a 'fine-grained' insect dispersion. In contrast, dry habitats have lower plant species diversity, and a tendency towards monospecific stands of low activity. Plants often releaf or flower in synchrony, so within a patch, plant activity levels can be seasonally very high. Dry habitats are therefore characterised by large, well separated patches of insects, which can be of very high density: a coarse-grained dispersion. How does this influence the dispersion of the bats? First of all, Bradbury and Vehrencamp (1976b) persuasively argue that food supply is the major determinant of population density in these insectivorous bats, and that the bats should minimise the size of their foraging territory, such that it contains only one active feeding site. The smaller the territory, the better the bat's knowledge of the site and the food patches within it. On this basis, the wet habitat bats should have high overall density, and a fine-grained dispersion, i.e. many small colonies with small territories, to exploit the many small insect patches in close proximity to each other. In dry habitats, large seasonally rich insect patches will support large colonies, but these will be well separated (coarse-grained), and overall population density will be low.

So much for the theory, what about the practice? The fit is surprisingly good. The wet habitat bats, *Rhynchonycteris naso* and *Saccopteryx leptura*, do indeed live in small colonies, forage in small territories and have high population densities. In contrast, the dry habitat *Balantiopteryx plicata* lives in very large colonies and forages several kilometres from the roost. Unfortunately, population density is unknown. *Saccopteryx bilineata* moves between the wet and dry forests over the seasons, exploiting larger, more dispersed insects when in the wet forest—hence the coarse-grained, low density dispersion. *Peropteryx kappleri* is something of a puzzle—a wet forest bat with a fine-grained dispersion, but low population density.

Are any other features of Table 6.1 worth closer study? We can divide the five species into two groups, *R. naso, S. leptura*, and *P. kappleri*, the wet forest species and *B. plicata*, and *S. bilineata*, the dry habitat species. The wet forest bats are all specialist foragers, adapted to feeding in specific habitats. They utilise several roosts sites within their small territories, group composition is very stable, and there is a tendency towards monogamy. Dry habitat bats are opportunistic foragers, utilising a wide range of habitats in their large territories. They use a single roost site, group composition is very unstable, and mating is by swarming or harem formation. These patterns can't be explained with real confidence, but here is one possible scenario for debate. In the wet forest species, the small territory size gives bats an intimate knowledge of their feeding sites. In combination with the small, low density food patches, it is therefore more profitable to forage singly or in small groups. The stability of the wet forest environment allows bats to specialise at foraging in particular habitats. Since females forage singly or in small groups, males can only defend small groups, hence the tendency towards monogamy and stable group composition. Small colony size enables them to exploit a wide range of roost sites, and they may

occupy the site closest to active food patches. Dry habitat bats must be opportunistic foragers to contend with the marked spatial and temporal variation in food supply. The large
colonies of *B. plicata* limit choice of roost, and bats must disperse over a wide area to
find sufficient food. Female defence is perhaps not possible in the large cave aggregations, hence the swarming mating strategy, and the unstable groups. It is more difficult to
suggest reasons for the use of a single roost site for *S. bilineata*. Although females forage
singly, they do form groups and individual members forage on adjacent beats. Males can
thus defend a number of females, to form harems.

I know of no other comparative studies of this nature, and we must piece together
examples mainly from studies of just one or two species. Barclay (1991) gives a very
interesting example of how food availability and foraging style influence the distribution
of related species. The little brown bat, *Myotis lucifugus*, and the long-eared myotis,
M. evotis, are the two most common species on the eastern slopes of the Rocky
Mountains in Canada. Both are small (5–8 g), hibernate in caves and mines, and form
maternity colonies in trees or buildings to rear their young. However, Barclay noted that
over 90% of *M. lucifugus* caught in harp traps and mist nets in the summer were males,
but the sex ratio in *M. evotis* was 1:1. He argues that differences in foraging style, in a
habitat of cool nights and relatively low insect abundance, are responsible for the very
different sex ratios.

M. lucifugus typically forages opportunistically over water, feeding on the wing on
small prey, notably chironomids (Fig. 6.19a), which are very abundant, but only for the
first couple of hours after sunset (Fig. 6.19b). *M. evotis* forages along paths and within
forests, where insect abundance is lower than over water, but remains relatively constant
throughout the night (Fig. 6.19c,d). *M. evotis* forages by hawking and probably also by
gleaning: it has the low intensity echolocation calls and low wing loading characteristic
of confirmed gleaners, and captive individuals used prey-generated sounds to take stationary moths. In the wild it preys primarily on moths (Fig. 6.19a), despite their low
abundance, but by doing so is exploiting a temporally more reliable food source. Barclay
suggests that with their more flexible foraging style and more reliable food source, female
M. evotis can meet the high energy demands of reproduction, and can therefore breed
successfully in the region. Female *M. lucifugus* must double their nightly foraging time
from 2 to 4 hours to meet the high cost of reproduction, a strategy unlikely to pay in the
cool mountain habitat studied. They must therefore move to habitats with a higher insect
abundance, the warmer prairies to the east, where maternity colonies are found in large
numbers.

Parallels can perhaps be drawn between Barclay's work and our own study of three
vespertilionids in England. Park, Masters and Altringham (1996) noted very different
patterns in the social structure and mating systems of the pipistrelle, *Pipistrellus pipistrellus*, brown long-eared, *Plecotus auritus,* and Natterer's, *Myotis nattereri*, bats which
used artificial roost boxes in the same forest. *P. pipistrellus* is an opportunistic hawker of
a wide range of small insects around forest rides, edges, and clearings. In contrast,
P. auritus and *M. nattereri* are predominantly gleaners within the forest and take disproportionately large numbers of moths.

Roost box use by *P. pipistrellus* is predominantly by solitary males during spring and
summer (sex ratio, m/f = 5.1). In the autumn solitary males defend territories and each
attracts small groups (1–10) females (sex ratio = 0.54). Recapture rates (Fig. 6.20a) indicate that the female population is the more transient: many of the males are resident

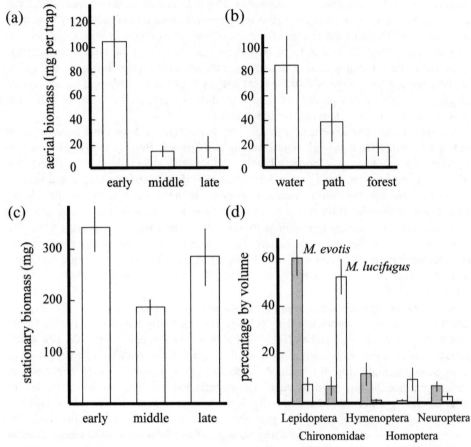

Fig. 6.19. Temporal and spatial patterns in food supply, and the diets of two vespertilionid bats. Biomass and spatial distribution of aerial prey available to *M. lucifugus* and *M. evotis* in eastern Canada (a, b). Biomass of stationary prey on vegetation (c), and the diet (% by volume of prey) of the two species (d) (from Barclay, 1991).

throughout the summer. In contrast, the sex ratios of *P. auritus* and *M. nattereri* are 0.59 and 0.40 respectively and vary little over the seasons. Recapture rates are similar for both sexes and the most common social groups, which are significantly larger than those of *P. pipistrellus*, include several adults of both sexes (Fig. 6.20b).

Both gleaning species form maternity colonies in the roost boxes, but *P. pipistrellus* does not. Is it possible that the two gleaning species are able to forage more effectively in the forest, and thus find it advantageous to breed there, whereas *P. pipistrellus*, which forages only on the periphery, does not? As suggested by Barclay (1991), the gleaners may have a more reliable food supply and a more flexible foraging style, enabling them to exploit the woodland more efficiently. Maternity colonies of *P. pipistrellus*, like those of *M. lucifugus* are usually in buildings.

P. auritus, and *M. nattereri*, with their emphasis on relatively large prey, probably have to deal with a more distributed and patchy food supply than *P. pipistrellus*.

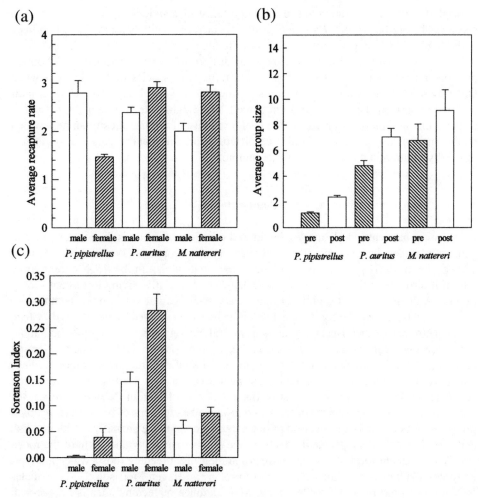

Fig. 6.20. Social structure of three temperate insectivorous bats in an English woodland. (a) Overall recapture rates of males and females from artificial roost boxes. (b) Average group size in pre- and post-parturition periods. (c) Degree of fidelity between individuals (Sorensen Index).

Following the arguments of the previous paragraphs about foraging style and group stability, we might expect the gleaners to have the more stable social groups, since they have more to gain from information exchange and group foraging. There is indeed a low level of group fidelity observed among female *P. pipistrellus* in harems, and a high stability among female groups of *P. auritus* and *M. nattereri* (Fig. 6.20c). We would therefore predict low defensibility of female *P. pipistrellus*, hence the defence of a mating roost by males, rather than defence of the females themselves. Individual males have defended the same boxes for up to five successive years. High group stability in *P. auritus* and *M. nattereri* enables males to defend females, and relatively high fidelity between males and female groups was found. Whether or not the foraging patterns of these three species agree with predictions remains to be determined.

Brigham (1991) drew attention to the importance of geographical variation within a species. The big brown bat, *Eptesicus fuscus*, formed maternity colonies in tree hollows in the semi-arid Okanogan valley of British Columbia, and bats consistently foraged over a short stretch of river up to 4 km from their day roosts, where swarms of Trichoptera provided more than half of their diet. In contrast, the same species studied near Ottawa in Ontario used buildings for maternity roosts. Since these were close to the centre of their foraging ranges bats flew less than 1 km to feed, but foraging sites varied nightly. The use of buildings in Ontario is probably due to the scarcity of natural sites in an area which retains little of its native woodland. The different foraging pattern presumably reflects insect distribution in this more temperate region.

Plant-eaters

Plant-eating bats eat a wide array of wild and commercial fruits including figs, kapok, pepper, mangoes, bananas, peaches, and even young coconuts and cocoa pods. At least 188 species from 64 genera are exploited by megabats alone. In the tropics, trees come into fruit throughout the year, and are well distributed spatially, giving a constant supply of food. Although the food supply is available all year, it can be very patchy, both temporally and spatially, and the foraging habits of the bats are moulded by the plants they feed on. As with many other aspects of bat behavioural ecology, we know only a little about only a few plant-eating bats. Early work has been summarised and interpreted by Fleming (1982), and can be supplemented by several recent studies. The phyllostomid *Artibeus jamaicensis* is a widespread and numerous species with a very flexible frugivorous diet. However, in the moist tropical forest of Barro Colorado Island in Panama, it relies primarily on two abundant species of fig which produce heavy crops of fruit (*Ficus insipida* produces 40 000 fruits over a period of one week, once or twice annually). With this rich and predictable food supply, individuals forage singly, usually within 1 km of the roost, and make frequent forays between fig trees and their night feeding roosts which are typically about 200 m away (Morrison, 1979; Morrison and Hagen-Morrison, 1981). Females only return to the roost to suckle young. Male defence of feeding sites is impractical, given their ephemeral and rich nature, as is the defence of females, since they disperse to forage and roosting groups are unstable. The males in fact defend tree hole roosts, which are in short supply. Males have a very different foraging strategy: they spend 90% of the night in roost defence, feeding only when the females are absent on foraging trips. When they do feed, they bring their food back to the roost to eat it, necessitating long commuting trips. Defence flights and long commuting flights dramatically increase the energy demands of the males, which they cover by eating more fruit (Morrison and Hagen-Morrison, 1981).

Phyllostomus hastatus has a more varied and flexible diet, opportunistically feeding on fruit, pollen and insects (McCracken and Bradbury, 1981; Willig *et al.*, 1993). Some particularly profitable food items may be thinly and unpredictably distributed. McCracken and Bradbury (1981) have shown that this bat forms very stable groups of unrelated females. Males form harems by defending a female group, whose composition may remain unchanged for several years. McCracken and Bradbury considered a wide range of possible benefits which might arise from group formation, ruling out all but co-operation in foraging and foraging site defence. Although bats from a particular group left and returned to the roost alone, each group had its own feeding territory, within which each bat had its own beat. They also noted that all of the bats would occasionally leave their own beats to forage together, and that they were very vocal when foraging. Group foraging was observed around flowering *Hymenaea* trees and fruiting *Lecythis* trees. Bloedel (1955) reported group feeding on termites. Although some crucial evidence was lacking, McCracken and Bradbury concluded that the driving force for the establishment of these stable groups was reciprocated group foraging, with successful bats alerting group members to rich patches of food. Very recently Wilkinson and Boughman (cited in Wilkinson, 1995) have shown that females use low frequency calls to attract group members as they emerge from caves to forage, and when feeding (Fig. 6.21).

Bats screech when leaving the cave, but almost never on returning. Screeching bats are accompanied by other group members more often than expected by chance alone. Again, harem males behaved differently, spending most of their time in or close to the roost, and foraging for as little as one hour each night. Bachelor males also form groups, but they are unstable, foraging sites are scattered, and they forage for significantly longer than either harem males or females, suggesting a rather different foraging strategy.

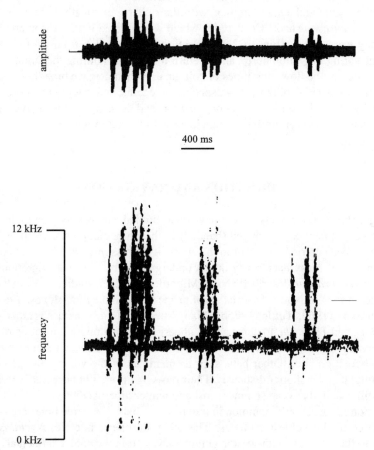

Fig. 6.21. Social screech calls of *Phyllostomus hastatus* used to attract co-members of social groups (from Wilkinson, 1995).

To end this section, we will look at two more phyllostomids and a different aspect of the link between food and behaviour. Most nectarivorous bats live in the tropics and sub-tropics, where food can be found all year round, but a number of phyllostomids are migratory, spending the summer in the deserts of the south western United States, and the winters in Mexico, feeding on route during their unhurried migration. Fleming *et al.*, (1993) used a novel approach to discover which plants the migratory *Leptonycteris cura-soae* fed at over the year, and compared its diet to non-migratory populations in Baja California, and the non-migratory *Glossophaga soricina* in southern Mexico. Plants utilise carbon dioxide in a number of different ways during photosynthesis, leading to characteristic differences in the ratio of the two stable isotopes of carbon, ^{13}C and ^{12}C, in their tissues. By analysing the $^{13}C/^{12}C$ ratio in the tissues of the bats, it was possible to determine which plants they fed at. The rate at which the carbon is taken up is dependent upon the rate of turnover of the tissue in question. By studying 3 mg skin and muscle samples a snapshot of each bat's diet over the previous two months was obtained. *G. soricina* fed mainly on C3 plants throughout the year: members of the Bignoniaceae, Bombacaceae, and Leguminosae in particular (Fig. 6.22a).

Resident *L. curasoae* in Baja California specialised on CAM plants, the desert succu-lents of the cactus and agave families, with their characteristically higher $^{13}C/^{12}C$ ratio. Migratory *L. curasoae* had $^{13}C/^{12}C$ ratios which were related to the season and latitude at which they were caught (Fig. 6.22a), indicating a slow switch from C3 to CAM plants during the spring migration north, and a return to C3 plants during the autumn migration south. A study of the flowering times of columnar cacti and agave broadly fits the pattern of bat migration (Fig. 6.22b). Four species of cactus and one agave flower roughly sequentially along the spring migration corridor, and as many as nine agaves are known to flower later in the year, probably coincident with the autumn migration.

MIGRATION AND NAVIGATION

The long distance movements of bats have been studied extensively, due to the ease with which large numbers can be ringed (banded) in their hibernation sites, and huge ringing studies have been carried out. Prior to this work, it was assumed that bats did not migrate. Although true of many bats, many others undergo lengthy seasonal migrations, such as *Leptonycteris curasoae* described above. Migration has been studied most extensively in temperate species in North America and Europe (e.g. Findley and Jones, 1964; Griffin, 1970; Strelkov, 1969; Tuttle, 1976b). Many species in the genera *Nyctalus, Lasiurus, Pipistrellus,* and *Tadarida*, to name a few, undergo seasonal migrations of up to 1700 km, in a generally north–south direction. Most migrations are between summer roosts and winter hibernation sites. Other bats, such as members of the widespread genus *Myotis*, usually migrate over shorter distances. Their movements are not necessarily north–south, but are still usually between summer roost and winter hibernaculum.

Migration is particularly common in tree roosting bats, since tree holes are poor hiber-nation sites in the coldest climates. The 30 g European noctule, *Nyctalus noctula*, migrates to the south or south-west in autumn, away from the cold, continental interior, to warmer regions under the moderating influence of the Atlantic Ocean (Fig. 6.23). Not all bats in a particular population migrate, and they often disperse to different locations,

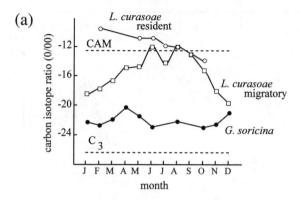

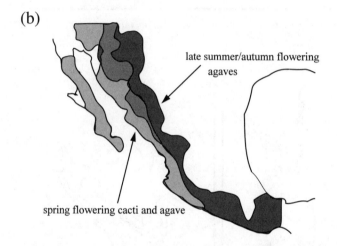

Fig. 6.22. The food plants of migratory and non-migratory nectarivores. (a) The $^{13}C/^{12}C$ ratio of tissue samples from two nectar feeding phyllostomids during the year. High ratios indicate dependence on CAM plants (desert cacti and agaves) low ratios on C3 plants. (b) The flowering patterns of CAM plants on the Pacific coast of Mexico and the south western United States, which provide a food corridor for migrating bats (from Fleming *et al.*, 1993).

from 80–1600 km away. Nathusius' pipistrelle, *P. nathusii*, although much smaller (6 g) undertakes similar migrations over the same geographical area.

A similar picture is seen in North America. Figure 6.24 shows the seasonal distribution of the tree roosting hoary bat, *Lasiurus cinereus* (Findley and Jones, 1964). Like the noctule, it is a large bat for temperate regions, and a strong flier, and has been reported to migrate in substantial waves, sometimes accompanying migrating birds. Populations travelling the shortest distances do so to hibernate, whereas those migrating to the southern end of their range will have a short or non-existent hibernation period. This pattern is common to several other *Lasiurus* species, and bats of other genera. We saw in Chapter 4 how migration/hibernation patterns of the Mexican free-tailed bat, *Tadarida brasiliensis*, are dependent upon the geographical location of a particular population.

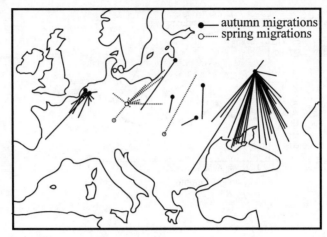

Fig. 6.23. Migration patterns of the noctule, *Nyctalus noctula*, in Europe (adapted from Strelkov, 1969).

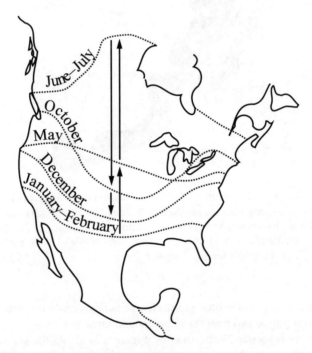

Fig. 6.24. Migration of the hoary bat, *Lasiurus cinereus*, in North America (adapted from Findley and Jones, 1964).

The grey bat, *Myotis grisescens*, has been extensively studied, and it typifies seasonal migrations in many North American and European house and cave bats. About 90% of the grey bats in the south-east hibernate in just three caves (Fig. 6.25): 375 000 in two caves in Tennessee, and 1 500 000 in a single cave in northern Alabama (Tuttle, 1976b).

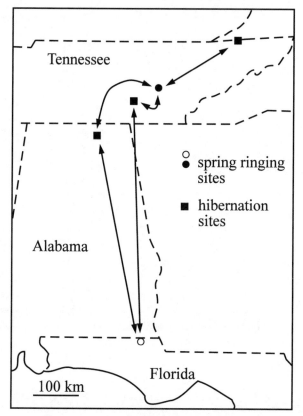

Fig. 6.25. Migration patterns of the grey bat, *Myotis grisescens*, in the southern United States (adapted from Tuttle, 1976b).

The bats show almost perfect fidelity to these caves. Of 3110 bats banded in one cave in winter, none were found in either of the other caves during a 14 year study, despite high recovery rates. Of 6486 bats ringed during hibernation only one was recovered at a different site. In spring they disperse to summer roosts up to 525 km away, perhaps covering the ground in just a few days. Fidelity to their summer roosts is equally impressive.

These long distance flights consume a lot of energy: navigation must be accurate, and flight efficient. We know that bats use both vision and echolocation for orientation and short-range navigation between roosts and foraging sites, but what senses are used for longer migrations. Echolocation provides little information beyond 100 m at best, and bats are known to migrate at much greater altitudes than this. However, they clearly migrate with skill, and homing experiments have shown that bats will return to a roost even if persistently removed, often to locations well outside the home range (e.g. Davis and Cockrum, 1962). Experiments designed to look at the relative importance of vision and echolocation are often equivocal, but many do suggest vision is important. The release of bats inside planetaria with an artificial post-sunset glow shows that this is used by bats to orientate themselves (Buchler and Childs, 1982). Many species can detect light sources equivalent to stars, but we do not yet know if they navigate by the stars. Magnetic orientation has not, as far as I know, even been looked at.

7 Community ecology and the interactions between bats and other organisms

Global distribution, density, and species richness. Communities and guilds. Predators and prey, arms races. Bats and plants, adaptive radiation, pollination and dispersal, coevolution and mutualisms.

GLOBAL DISTRIBUTION, DENSITY, AND SPECIES RICHNESS

Patterns in the global distribution of animals and plants have been recognised for a long time, and research aimed at explaining these patterns has been fascinating and rewarding. Until recently, bats had rarely been studied in this context, but Findley's recent review (1993) may act as a stimulus to research.

Latitude

What patterns do we see in the distribution of bats? The most obvious pattern is the decrease in species richness with increasing latitude, clearly seen in Fig. 7.1a which shows the decrease in the number of species in 500 × 500 km quadrats at each latitude in the New World (Willig and Selcer, 1989). The pattern is also obvious for the whole world in Fig. 7.1b (Findley, 1993) and Fig. 1.11. This increase in species richness with proximity to the equator is common to much of our flora and fauna. The simple explanation rests on the increase in primary biological productivity as light intensity, temperature, and growing season increase. The increased productivity leads to an increased range of resources, and this supports more species. This hypothesis is difficult to test, and is a source of considerable debate among ecologists, but it is supported by a number of studies—none of which include bats. Two other factors which promote equal controversy are seasonal climatic variation and environmental harshness. Although organisms can adapt to predictable seasonal fluctuations in the environment, it is argued that these place constraints on the degree of specialisation possible in a community. Harshness is a difficult concept to define, but the low species diversity of the arid Sahara is clearly seen in Fig. 1.11, and there is no questioning the harshness of polar regions—unless you are a species adapted to such conditions! The last major suggested contributor to the observed latitudinal gradient is the age of tropical habitats—during long periods of stability communities are presumed to increase in richness through colonisation and evolution. This idea was prompted by the belief that the upheavals caused by the temperate glaciations contrasted with the ancient stability of the tropics. However, this is too simplistic: glaciation led to a movement of the temperate zones towards the equator, and a contraction of tropical forests into a number of small refuges. The argument that prolonged stability

(a)

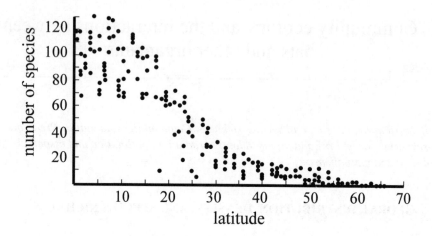

(b)

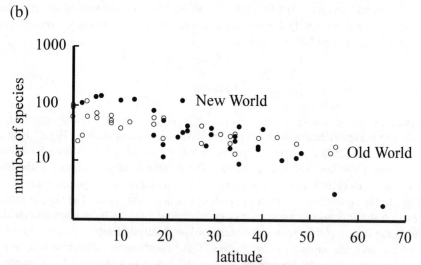

Fig. 7.1. Number of bat species in relation to latitude. (a) In the New World, and (b) in the world. (From Willig and Selcer (1989) and Findley (1993).)

enhances species richness also has its problems: disturbance may promote the evolution of new species to fill vacant niches. A very good general account of the complexity of this and related issues can be found in Begon *et al.* (1990).

Regional variation

Species richness, the measure used above, is just one indicator of bat diversity. Before going further we should decide if it is the most useful tool with which to study patterns in bat distribution. Table 7.1 summarises data from Findley (1993) which looks at diversity

Table 7.1. Summary of bat diversity indices in the Old and New Worlds. See text for full description. Adapted from Findley (1993)

	New World		Old World			
	Neotropics	Nearctic	Ethiopian	Oriental	Australian	Palaearctic
Families						
number	9	3	8	9	6	8
$N2$ (number of very speciose families)	2.7	1.8	4.4	3.5	3.5	1.8
J' (evenness of species distribution)	0.6	0.69	0.8	0.75	0.8	0.47
Genera						
number	67	16	44	57	48	23
$N2$ (number of very speciose genera)	44.4	8	23.6	15.7	19.1	10.6
J' (evenness of species distribution)	0.92	0.74	0.84	0.57	0.65	0.72
Species						
number	221	40	186	268	166	85+
Trophic modes						
number	7	6	6	6	6	5
$N2$ (number of important modes)	3.9	1.7	2.1	2.4	2.8	1.4
J' (evenness of species distribution)	0.8	0.51	0.63	0.69	0.79	0.52

at the family, genus, and species level. Trophic diversity is also measured by dividing bats into 7 broad (and frequently overlapping) categories: gleaners of invertebrates, aerial insectivores, carnivores, fish-eaters, frugivores, nectarivores, and vampires (Wilson, 1973). Hill's number, $N2$ is an indication of the number of families or genera which include numerous species: the higher the number, the more diverse the bats are. Pielou's J' is a measure of the evenness of distribution of species at each level. When this value is high, species are spread more evenly across, for example, the family: a value of 1 indicates an equal number of species in each family. The first thing to note is the striking difference between tropical and temperate regions. Relative to the tropics, the nearctic and palaearctic regions have fewer families, genera, and species. Temperate bat communities are dominated by a few very speciose families.

Within the tropics, three geographically distinct centres of species richness can be seen in Fig. 1.11: the tropical forests of South America and South-East Asia, and the savannahs of East Africa. These regions are compared in Table 7.1. The Old and New World tropics have similar numbers of families, but the palaeotropics have more very speciose families, with a more even spread of species among them. The neotropical bat community is dominated by the diverse Phyllostomidae, which accounts for 51 of the genera and 147 species. In contrast, the neotropics are by far the most diverse at the generic level: most genera are very speciose, and the species are spread very evenly across them. So which is the more ecologically diverse community: that of the Old or the New World? In terms of their feeding mode, the neotropics are perhaps the more diverse, with bats of all 7 modes. Most include many species, and the species are evenly distributed across the modes. Given the foraging flexibility of most bats, and the enormous diversity seen *within* many of the modes, this last conclusion has to be viewed cautiously. Do we have any other indicators of diversity that might be more reliable?

Findley (1993) points to the all-pervading concept of form matching function. We know that there is going to be little or no dietary overlap between some (but by no means all) sympatric aerial insectivores because of differences in their size, wing loading, aspect ratio, and echolocation call structure: they will take variously sized insects, in different parts of their habitat, using various foraging techniques. It is widely accepted that morphological variation is a good predictor of ecological diversity. Findley used multivariate analysis to study morphological variation in relation to the diversity indices described above, and came to the conclusion that morphological diversity reflects trophic diversity, and that the best indicator of trophic/ecological diversity is species richness.

Now that we have some evidence that species richness is our most reliable ecological indicator, let's look at regional patterns in more detail. Although the palaeotropics has more bat species (Table 7.1), the number of bat species per unit area is highest in the neotropics, lower in South-East Asia, and still lower in east Africa (Figs 1.11, 7.1). Why might this be the case? If we assume that differences due to habitat variation between the regions are unimportant (perhaps debatable, since East Africa is dominated by savannah), three major factors are likely to have influenced species richness: the length of time it has existed, its particular history, and the size of the region.

Age

The longer an area has been available for colonisation, then the more species it is likely to support, until some sort of equilibrium is reached, when competition or other factors

prevent an increase in species number, either by immigration of evolution. All three tropical regions in question have probably been present throughout the adaptive radiation of
bats, and there is no fossil or geological evidence to suggest that any one bat community
is older than another, so age is not likely to be a factor.

History

As stated above, tropical forests contracted and fragmented during periods of glaciation,
and coalesced between glaciations. Refuge theory predicts that the generation of these
fragments or refuges promotes speciation, and refuge formation has been claimed to be
partly responsible for tropical forest diversity (Prance, 1982). The evidence suggests that
more refuges were formed in the neotropics than in Africa, although numbers vary
depending upon the animals or plants studied (neotropics, 4–32; Africa, 3–13, see
Findley, 1993, p. 135). South-East Asia presents rather a different case, in that the tropical forest is fragmented on islands now, and there is no evidence to suggest that the
number of refuges was any greater during glacial periods.

Area

We have known for some time that small islands contain fewer species than larger ones,
and that both have fewer species than comparable areas of mainland. It is also apparent
that this principle applies not just to true islands, those surrounded by water, but also to
bodies of water surrounded by land, mountain tops, isolated forests, etc. We can go
further and say that even within the same homogeneous region the number of species
increases with area. In Fig. 7.2, the number of species is plotted against area for temperate and tropical regions, and for tropical forests (Findley, 1993): in all cases there is a
strong positive correlation. Findley (1993, p. 136) suggests that 80% of the variation
between the number of bat species in tropical forests around the world can be accounted
for by differences in area, and the remaining 20% by differences in the estimated number
of refuges, despite the great uncertainty over estimates of the latter. In turn, species richness in a forest region appears to be the main determinant of species richness at a given
locality.

   Several ecological theories have been put forward to explain species–area relations. All
may play a role, but their relative importance will vary. Habitat diversity is thought to be
the most important factor: bigger areas contain more habitats and can support more
species. The number of species will also be determined in part by the balance between the
rates of immigration and extinction. Small islands are small targets for immigrant species,
and small populations on small islands will be more vulnerable to extinction (MacArthur
and Wilson, 1967). Increasing remoteness from the source of new species will also
decrease immigration rate. Finally, speciation rates may vary with island size, but this
factor is only likely to be important for small islands.

   Can the distribution of bats illustrate or test any of these concepts? In formulating a
conservation action plan, Mickleburgh *et al.* (1992) compiled all available information on
the distribution and status of megabats, and I have used their report to address these questions. Some of the islands have yet to be surveyed thoroughly, but I have had to assume
that all of the species present on each island are now known. At least one species which
has recently become extinct is also included.

(a)

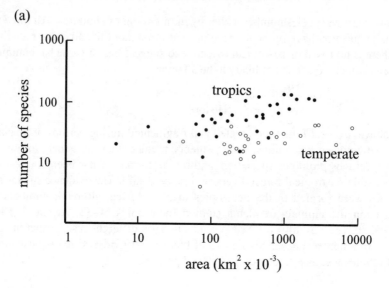

(b)

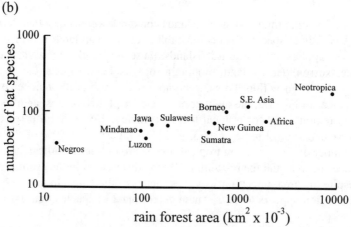

Fig. 7.2. Species–area relationships for bats. (a) In the world, and (b) in tropical forests (from Findley, 1993).

Figure 7.3a includes data from Indonesia, Papua New Guinea, and the Philippines, where there is as random an assembly of islands of different sizes as one could hope for. Some of the scatter is due to large numbers of species on small islands which lie very close to larger, species-rich islands. There is a convincing species–island area relationship for megabats. This can be compared with the species relationship in Fig. 7.3b, for central Africa. I have excluded the Saharan countries and those north of them, together with those which cross the 20°S parallel, to avoid major climatic or habitat effects. Again, there is a significant positive relationship between area and the number of species. If the 'island effect' is important, then the number of species should decrease faster with decreasing area on true islands, and very small islands should have fewer species than

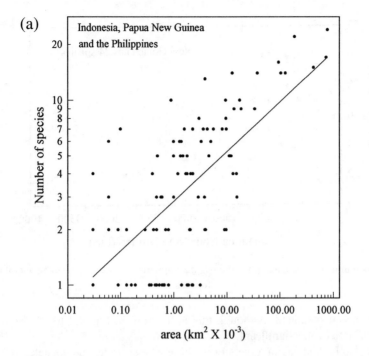

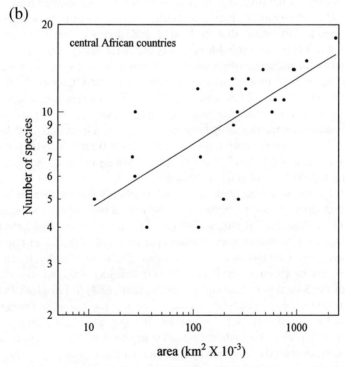

Fig. 7.3. Species–area relations for megabats. (a) On Pacific islands (Indonesia, Papua New Guinea, and the Philippines) and (b) in central African countries.

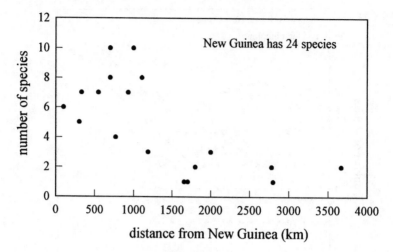

Fig. 7.4.   The number of species on Pacific islands in relation to distance from New Guinea. See text for details.

equivalent areas of mainland. Although this is the case in Fig. 7.3 the differences are small and not statistically significant.

We could also look at habitat diversity on these islands, to test the idea that increasing area simply increases habitat diversity. If there is no correlation between area and diversity, then area alone is important. Previous studies on other organisms suggest that we would find evidence indicating that both area and diversity have a role to play. Unfortunately, I don't know of a suitable diversity index for Pacific islands.

Figure 7.4 shows the influence of remoteness. The numbers of species on islands east of New Guinea have been plotted against distance from New Guinea. I included all islands with areas between 2 000 km² and 10 000 km². The species–area relationship for this region gives an area-induced change in species number of just 1–2 species in this range. Smaller islands almost invariably have just 1–2 species, irrespective of distance. (I did include New Caledonia, the only larger island, at 16 000 km²: despite its size, it has fewer species than predicted.) Clearly migration has a strong influence, with the number of species falling rapidly beyond about 1 200 km.

The arguments so far have been ecological: they implicitly assume that the bats do not evolve. Evolution does of course occur, and the appearance of new subspecies and endemic species is favoured on isolated islands. There are many indications of the importance of evolution in moulding distribution patterns. All of the larger Pacific island archipelagos have large numbers of endemic species. The ratio of endemic:total species does not change very much across the Pacific from Indonesia (24:63) and the Philippines (10:24), through the Solomon Islands (8:20) and Vanuatu (2:4) to Fiji (1:4). In contrast, only one African country has an endemic species: *Pteropus voeltzkowi* in Tanzania, and it is found only on Pemba Island! Pacific island archipelagos also have a large number of subspecies: Fig. 7.5 shows the distribution of subspecies of the endemics *Pteropus rayneri* and *P. anetianus* on the Solomon Islands and Vanuatu.

Figure 7.6 lists the species found on each major island group, with distance from New Guinea increasing from left to right. The first column indicates those species found in

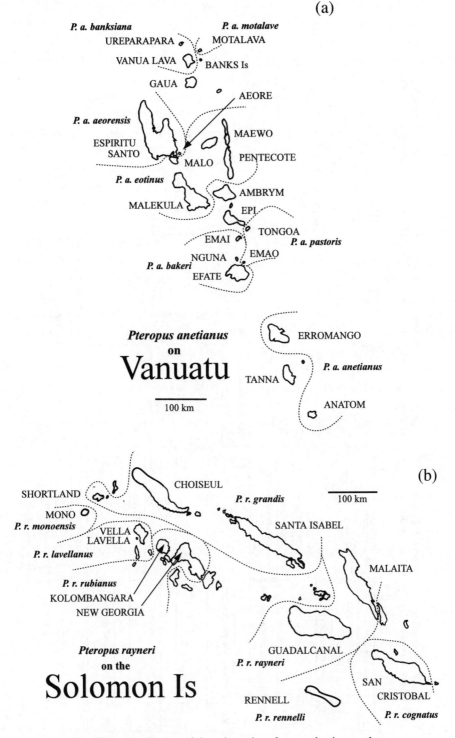

Fig. 7.5.   Distribution of the subspecies of two endemic megabats.

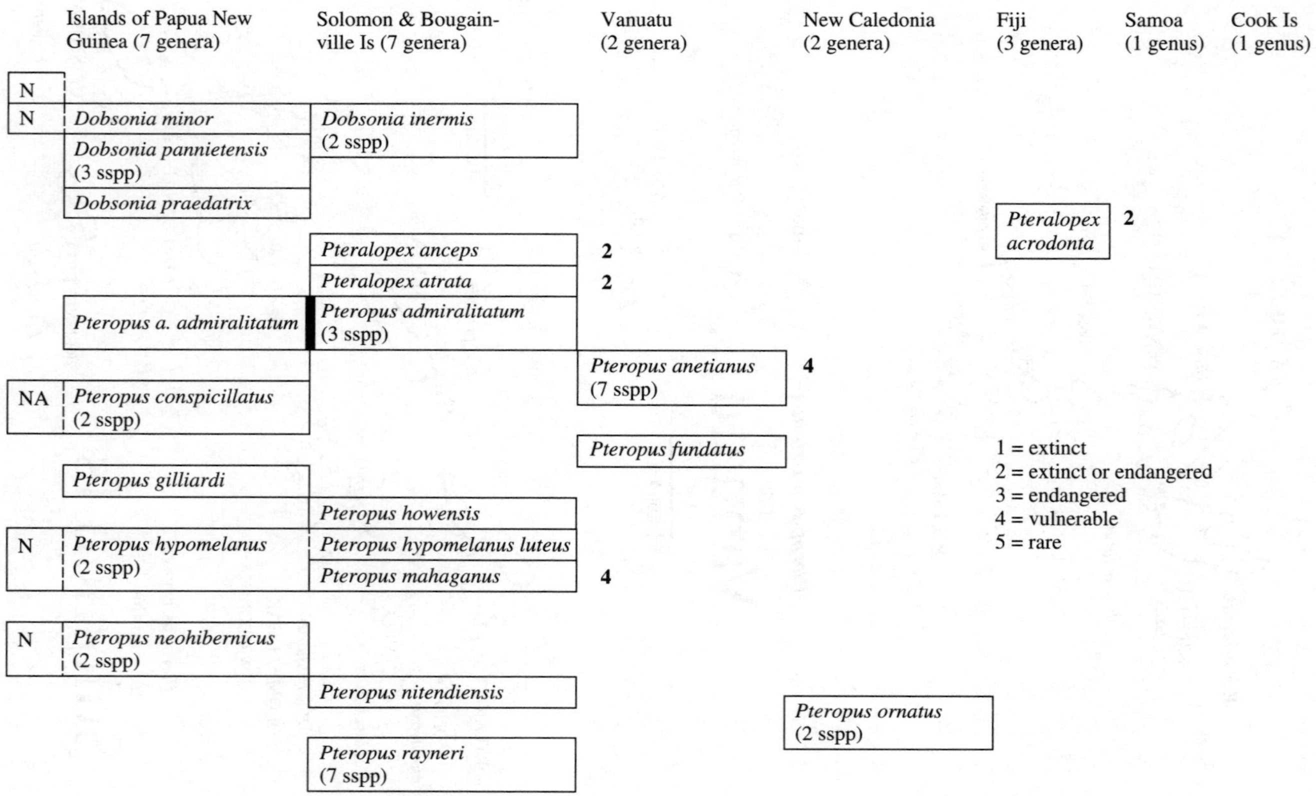

Distribution of Pteropodidae across island groups

Islands of Papua New Guinea (7 genera)	Solomon & Bougain- ville Is (7 genera)	Vanuatu (2 genera)	New Caledonia (2 genera)	Fiji (3 genera)	Samoa (1 genus)	Cook Is (1 genus)
N Dobsonia minor	Dobsonia inermis (2 sspp)					
N Dobsonia panniensis (3 sspp)						
Dobsonia praedatrix						
	Pteralopex anceps **2**					
	Pteralopex atrata **2**			Pteralopex acrodonta **2**		
Pteropus a. admiralitatum	Pteropus admiralitatum (3 sspp)					
NA Pteropus conspicillatus (2 sspp)		Pteropus anetianus (7 sspp) **4**				
		Pteropus fundatus				
Pteropus gilliardi	Pteropus howensis					
N Pteropus hypomelanus (2 sspp)	Pteropus hypomelanus luteus					
	Pteropus mahaganus **4**					
N Pteropus neohibernicus (2 sspp)	Pteropus nitendiensis		Pteropus ornatus (2 sspp)			
	Pteropus rayneri (7 sspp)					

1 = extinct
2 = extinct or endangered
3 = endangered
4 = vulnerable
5 = rare

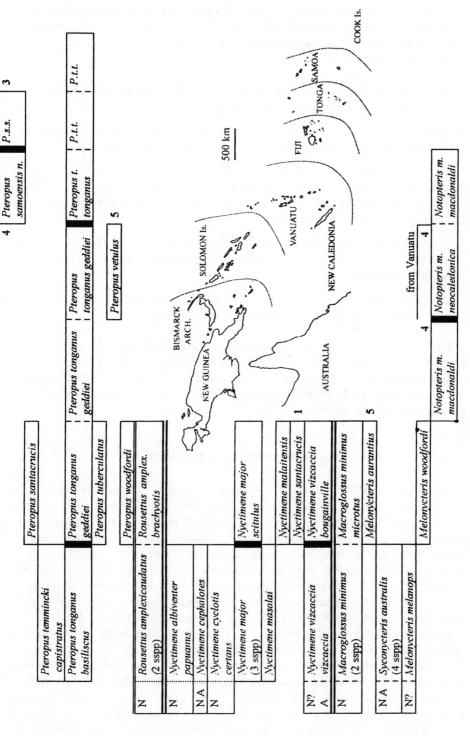

Fig. 7.6. Distribution of megabats on the major island archipelagos of the Pacific Ocean.

New Guinea (N), the original sources of species to the islands by migration and/or Australia (A). Where a species has reached the next island group unchanged (i.e. it is the same subspecies), boxes are bridged by a dotted line. The solid bars indicate migration with presumed, subsequent evolution into a new subspecies.

There are several striking features:

1. Only one species is found on all island groups—*Pteropus tonganus*. It has evolved into three subspecies, and is not found on New Guinea.

2. Most species are found on just one or two island groups (and nowhere else in the world). Their limited distribution means that many are now endangered.

3. Few species appear to have made a step along the chain. Those that have appear generally to have evolved into new subspecies after migration. (Alternatively, a new subspecies could evolve before migration, and then die out on the parent island group, but I think this is far less likely.)

4. Even the short step from New Guinea to nearby islands appears to have been made by few species without subsequent evolution into new species, or (less likely?) extinction on the parent island.

5. There is a sharp decline in the number of genera going east from New Guinea, and only two *Pteropus* species have penetrated beyond Fiji.

Without very detailed knowledge of the inter-relationships between this group of megabats, we cannot read too much into Fig. 7.6, but we can say that the current distribution of megabats in the Pacific is probably as much a result of evolution as of migration. Further insights could perhaps be gained from a more detailed study, and from a look at the more numerous and diverse microbats.

COMMUNITIES AND GUILDS

A community is a group of species co-existing at a given site, a guild a group of species which exploit a similar resource in a similar way. The distinction between the two must therefore be a little blurred in many cases, and I will not discuss the two separately. In earlier chapters we saw how flight morphology, echolocation call structure, and other factors, influenced foraging style and food preference of particular species. Lets look now at how groups of bats live together, and see what we can learn about the rules which govern their co-existence. Important questions include: is there evidence of competition for resources, and if so, is this competition a contributing factor to niche separation? Are the niches occupied by different bats discrete, or is there overlap between niches?

Attempts to study the structure of insectivorous bat communities/guilds have frequently been based around differences in flight morphology and its presumed, or observed, effect on flight characteristics and in turn, the microhabitat used. McKenzie and Rolfe (1986) studied 15 insectivorous species feeding in the mangrove forests of northern Western Australia. Flight morphology was expressed in terms of wing loading (WL = body mass/wing area) and aspect ratio (AR = wingspan^2/wing area). The importance of these variables is discussed in detail in Chapter 2: briefly they determine flight speed, efficiency, and manoeuvrability. In addition, foraging bats were placed in one or more of five microhabitat categories (by direct observation or mist netting), in relation to the mangrove stands.

A plot of WL against AR for all species in the area shows considerable overlap in morphological space (Fig. 7.7a). However, within the guilds observed at each of the six sites studied, little or no overlap was seen (two examples are shown in Fig. 7.7b). A comparison with randomly generated guilds strongly supported the view that the natural guilds had not arisen by chance. Attempts to add other species known to occur in the area to guilds almost invariably led to morphological overlap. WL and AR were good predictors of microhabitat niche (Fig. 7.7b). We can tentatively conclude that we have evidence for a non-random, structured bat community, and in this instance, one with little morphological, and apparently niche, overlap. This clear separation of members of a guild solely on the basis of flight morphology has not been seen in other studies, but it is clearly one of the dominant factors in niche separation, as we shall see.

In several studies, echolocation call structure has been studied alongside flight morphology and foraging behaviour. Aldridge and Rautenbach (1987), in a study of 26 insectivorous species in the Kruger National Park, South Africa, measured three flight morphology indices (WL, AR, and wingtip shape index) and five call parameters (highest and lowest frequencies, frequency of maximum intensity, search phase call shape, and

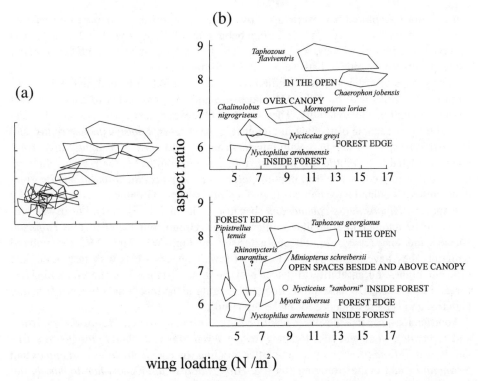

Fig. 7.7. Wing loading plotted against aspect ratio for an insectivorous bat community in an Australian mangrove forest. (a) All species in the region. (b) Examples of two of the six guilds studied, with the microhabitats in which each species foraged (adapted from McKenzie and Rolfe, 1986).

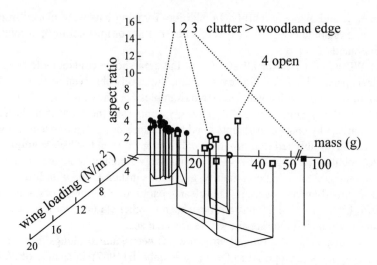

Fig. 7.8. 3-D plot of mass in relation to aspect ratio and wing loading for a South African insectivorous bat community. The different symbols refer to the four classes discussed in the text (adapted from Aldridge and Rautenbach, 1987).

call duration). Captured bats were also flown through an obstacle course to provide an index of manoeuvrability. The foraging behaviour of light tagged individuals was observed in different habitats, which were ranked in order of increasing clutter. Finally, faecal pellets from captured bats were analysed for prey size.

Four groups of species were identified on the basis of WL, AR, and mass (Fig. 7.8). Group one species had low WL, AR, and mass, and were calculated to have low fight speeds and high manoeuvrability. They also had clutter-resistant echolocation calls, and should thus be capable of feeding in clutter (e.g. *Nycticeius, Eptesicus, Pipistrellus,* and *Hipposideros* spp.). Group two, with intermediate WL and mass, and slightly higher AR were calculated to be a little less manoeuvrable, and in conjunction with their echolocation calls, were predicted to feed in both clutter (*Rhinolophus hildebrandti*) and intermediate clutter/woodland edge habitats (e.g. *Scotophilus* spp.). Group three comprised only one species, *Hipposideros commersoni,* because of its high body mass, but it was predicted to be another intermediate clutter species. Group four included five *Tadarida* species and one *Taphozous,* all characterised by high WL, high AR, and pointed wingtips: they have narrowband FM calls of low frequency—bats with fast, agile, and efficient flight, and an ability to detect prey at some distance, and therefore likely to forage in the open. Do these predictions of foraging niche match the observed foraging patterns, and is there evidence for niche separation?

Four habitat-use strategies were identified: open foraging (by e.g. *Tadarida condylura* and *T. pumila*), woodland-edge foraging (by e.g. *Nycticeius schlieffini, Eptesicus capensis,* and *Pipistrellus nanus*), intermediate-clutter foraging (by e.g. *Scotophilus borbonicus* and *S. dingani*), and clutter foraging (by e.g. *Hipposideros caffer* and *Rhinolophus hildebrandti*). Habitat use therefore correlated well with manoeuvrability index and with flight morphology. Although each species appeared to have flight and echolocation characteristics well suited to its foraging style, most were flexible, using several of the seven habitat categories defined. Each niche was also occupied by several species. Furthermore,

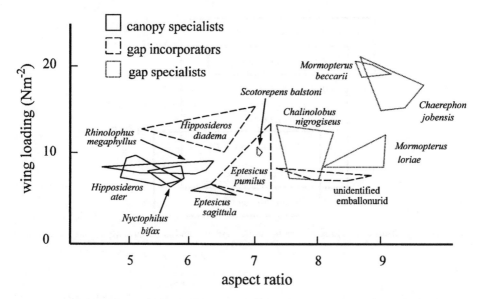

Fig. 7.9. Wing loading in relation to aspect ratio for another Australian insectivorous bat community. See text for details (adapted from Crome and Richards, 1988).

although larger bats tended to eat larger insects, larger species also took a larger size-range of prey, and there was little evidence for partitioning on the basis of prey. In contrast to the mangrove community studied by McKenzie and Rolfe (1986), we have here a community with considerable overlap of prey and microhabitat between species. McKenzie and Rolfe (1986) argue that the clear-cut patterns they observe may be due to the particular stability of the mangrove habitat: the influx/efflux of species due to seasonal and long term habitat changes are likely to blur boundaries in community and guild structure.

Crome and Richards (1988) looked at partitioning between rain forest canopy and artificial gaps (0.03–0.07 ha) created by logging in Queensland, Australia. Four species were confined to the closed canopy, five more to the gaps, and the remaining three foraged in both (Fig. 7.9). Again, flight morphology and echolocation call structure were good predictors of habitat use: e.g. three of the five gap species were fast flying molossids, typified by long, narrow wings and long, narrowband FM calls. All five gap species also foraged in the neighbouring eucalypt woodland.

Fullard *et al.* (1991) found that seven species of insectivorous bats in the Perup forest of south-western Australia formed loose clusters of clutter, edge, and open habitat foragers, with substantial interspecific overlap (Fig. 7.10).

WL, AR, and call structure correlated well with foraging zone classification. They also noted the flexibility shown by most species—six of the seven foraged in a wide range of microhabitats, and a wide variety of insects were taken by most species. The study was carried out in the dry season, when insects are less abundant. The authors suggest that some species could be more selective in the wet season, and I hope the idea is being followed up.

Kalko (1995), observed foraging emballonurids in Panama with night vision goggles and recorded echolocation call structure. The results are summarised in Fig. 7.11, which

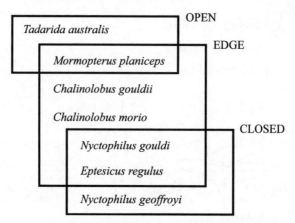

Fig. 7.10. Overlap of foraging niches in another Australian bat community (from Fullard *et al.*, 1991).

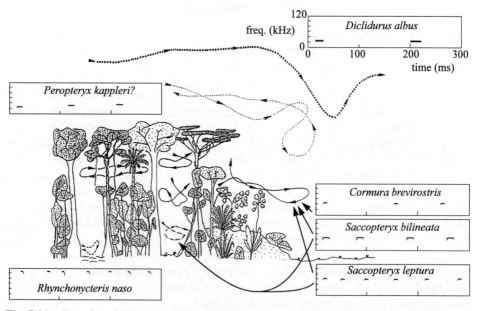

Fig. 7.11. Foraging niches and echolocation call structures of six emballonurid bats in Panama (adapted from Kalko, 1995).

shows foraging microhabitats, typical flight paths, and search phase echolocation call structure. The two species feeding in the open had low frequency, quasi-CF search phase pulses around 24–32 kHz. At the other extreme, the tiny *Rhynchonycteris naso*, which foraged over small streams in the vegetation, had a high frequency call (100–105 kHz), with a steep FM tail to most of its short CF pulses. The three species feeding in gaps in the forest understorey had intermediate frequency (42–56 kHz) pulses, with FM sweeps either side of a quasi-CF pulse. The two *Saccopteryx* species also fed close to the ground, and often emitted pulses in pairs. Evidence for microhabitat partitioning is clear, but there is overlap in both niche and call structure, particularly in the three species feeding in the understorey.

The consensus is thus for partitioning of resources (i.e. foraging microhabitat), but with appreciable overlap between species within a guild, and considerable flexibility of foraging style in many species. However, there are many factors which have yet to be taken into account—we need more precise information about the time of feeding, prey preference, capture methods, and seasonal variation in prey, to name just a few. As yet, there is little evidence for partitioning on the basis of prey taken. Findley and Black (1983) examined the morphology and stomach contents of nine insectivorous species captured outside a cave in Zambia. Morphology and diet were closely related. On the basis of multivariate analysis they proposed a community with a cluster of invariant specialists, and a smaller number of species with more variable morphology and diet. Heller and Helversen (1989) studied 12 syntopic *Rhinolophus/Hipposideros* species in the Krau Game Reserve, Malaysia. The narrowband echolocation calls of these species were significantly more evenly distributed than predicted by chance, a result not due to differences in bat size. There was also evidence for a minimum frequency separation between species. These results could be interpreted as evidence for partitioning of prey on the basis of size: higher frequencies are better at detecting smaller prey, but over shorter distances (see Chapter 3). However, call separation of this nature could also have a role in communication. We need more information before we can determine the relative importance of the two hypotheses.

When species other than insectivores are examined, the situation gets more complex. Humphrey *et al.* (1983) studied guild structure in nine species of 'surface-gleaning', omnivorous phyllostomids in Panama. Multivariate analysis suggested a single guild, with beetles as a major dietary component of all species. A large number of factors were responsible for guild structure, including at least five food types (insects, vertebrates, nectar, pollen, and fruit), food size, and microhabitat.

An interesting example of possible resource partitioning comes from a study of the pallid bat, *Antrozous pallidus* in the south-western United States and northern Mexico, by Herrera *et al.* (1993). Carbon stable-isotope ratios (see Chapter 6, p. 194) suggest that although the pallid bat and the California leaf-nosed bat, *Macrotus californicus*, both feed on large arthropods, primarily by gleaning, only the pallid bat regularly feeds at cactus and agave flowers. Incidentally, although it is unlikely that the bat is feeding on nectar, it does appear to be an effective pollinator: are we looking at an early stage in the evolution of nectarivory?

There are a number of issues I have not addressed, but which should not be forgotten. One thing to remember is that similarity of form, and hence foraging style and niche occupation, may arise through phylogenetic constraints: related bats are usually morphologically similar. The part phylogeny plays in guild/community structure will often be difficult to measure. We should also remember that other resources may be important in determining community structure, such as roosting requirements. For example, for species using bamboo culms, or furled leaves, roosting requirements are so specific that they will determine the presence or absence of the species in a community. Humphrey (1975) found that increased topographic diversity in the environment (primarily trees and buildings) led to an increase in the species richness and diversity of colony forming bats. Findley (1993) cites evidence in support of a similar trend in Europe, but suggests this factor may be much less important in the tropics. More detailed discussions of this subject can be found in Kunz (1982) and Findley (1993).

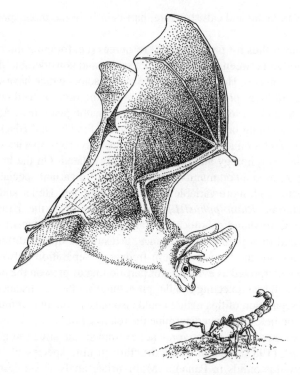

Pallid bat, *Antrozous pallidus*, taking a scorpion

PREDATORS AND PREY

Bats as predators

Bats feed on a wide range of animals, but I know of no published study which investigates the effects bats have on community dynamics. The few species feeding on vertebrates are unlikely to have a major effect on the community of which they are a part. On the other hand, the enormous concentrations of insectivorous microbats found in many parts of the world must have a significant impact on insect population dynamics, and in turn are likely to influence other parts of their ecosystem. It has been estimated from the mean increase in bat weight after foraging that 13 000 tonnes of insects were eaten by a colony of 20 million Mexican free-tailed bats, *Tadarida brasiliensis*, in a single summer. Control of fruit-eating bats and vampires in several countries has been crude and indiscriminate, killing microbats too, and increases in local insect pests have been reported, but they lack scientific corroboration. Until rigorous studies are carried out, an enormously difficult task, we can only guess at the effects insectivorous bats have on community structure. However, we can say rather more about the interaction between bats and their prey at the individual level.

The arms race: bats versus insects

Most insectivorous bats locate and capture their prey by using echolocation. However, many insects can hear ultrasound: species from at least six orders (Coleoptera,

Dictyoptera, Diptera, Lepidoptera, Neuroptera, and Orthoptera) possess auditory organs capable of detecting sounds at frequencies >20 kHz (Michelson and Larsen, 1985; Yager and Hoy, 1986; Spangler, 1988; Robert *et al.*, 1992). These tympanic ears have evolved from a variety of organs, and are located on the abdomen, thorax, head, legs, or even the wings, depending upon the insect. The ears of moths, the best studied group, are tuned to the frequencies emitted by the bats which are known to, or are most likely to, prey upon them (Fullard, 1987) and from 50 to over 90% of moth species in a given locality may be able to hear (Fenton and Fullard, 1979; Waters, 1993). It is now widely accepted, at least in the case of moths, that hearing evolved as a defence against predation by bats (e.g. Roeder, 1965; Miller, 1975; Yager *et al.*, 1990; Fullard and Yack, 1993). In other insects, a bat-evasion function may have evolved in ears used primarily for intraspecific communication (Fullard and Yack, 1993). Yager *et al.* (1990) suggest that hearing has evolved independently at least eight times in the insects, three times in the Lepidoptera alone.

Sound reception generally produces a two-stage evasive reaction. Low intensity ultrasound causes moths (and some other insects studied) to fly away from the sound: high intensities induce complex spirals, loops, and dives, or cessation of flight, to quickly take the moth out of a bat's flight path (Roeder, 1964). There is evidence to suggest that moths and mantids gain information about the proximity of bats from the increased pulse repetition rates of the feeding buzz (Fullard, 1992; Yager and May, 1990). Roeder and Treat (1961) estimated that these strategies reduced the chance of capture in the field by about 40%. Later field studies also suggest that insects with ears have a significantly greater chance of survival (e.g. Acharya, 1992; Rydell, 1992). Some species of Arctiidae emit loud clicks in response to very loud bat ultrasound calls, and these can impair the performance of attacking bats (Miller, 1991). Fullard *et al.* (1994) suggest that the late emission of the clicks, during the bat's terminal feeding buzz, will maximise this jamming/startle effect. The click may also be a warning to predators that the moth is unpalatable (e.g. Acharya and Fenton, 1992). Bates and Fenton (1990) found that naive big brown bats (*Eptesicus fuscus*) are startled by arctiid clicks, but individuals learn to associate the clicks with unpalatability.

The evolution of ears by moths, together with adaptive behavioural responses to bat echolocation calls, can be thought of as the second step in an evolutionary arms race: a response to the first step, predation by bats using ultrasound. The term arms race is very graphic, but it has been criticised on the grounds that there must be evidence of response and counter-response if it is to be appropriate. An arms race may be occurring between bats and moths, since there is evidence that bats have taken step three, and evolved ways of avoiding detection by moths with ears. (However, work in progress by G. Jones and colleagues suggests an alternative view.)

There is widespread evidence that moths with ears make up a significant part of the diet of many bats, despite the moths' defences, and in some cases this is due to one of several apparently adaptive responses by the bats. The first response has been the evolution of echolocation calls of very high frequency, that is above the 20–50 kHz to which moths' ears are sensitive. High frequency calls are used by a number of bats known to feed largely on moths (see Fullard, 1987 for review). The highest frequency calls ever recorded were by the bat *Cloeotis percivali*, at 212 kHz (Fenton and Bell, 1981): several years earlier, Whitaker and Black (1976) had noted that it fed exclusively on moths. Fullard (1987) suggests that such a strategy could only persist if the bats using high frequency ultrasound were a small component of the bat fauna, otherwise, moths would ulti-

mately evolve higher frequency hearing. Waters (1993) broadcast real ultrasound recordings of three FM and two high frequency CF bat species at tympanic preparations of two
species of noctuid moth. The high frequency calls of *Rhinolophus hipposideros* (peak
frequency 110 kHz) were significantly less apparent to the moths than those of the other
species (peak frequencies 49–83 kHz). Bats could of course use calls below the best
hearing range of their prey: *Tadarida teniotis*, the European free-tailed bat, uses a narrowband call of 11–12 kHz, and large moths and Neuroptera make up 90% of its diet
(Rydell and Arlettaz, 1994).

An alternative response is to use very low intensity, short duration calls, e.g. *Myotis
evotis* and *M. septentrionalis* (Faure *et al.*, 1990; Faure *et al.*, 1993). *Plecotus auritus*
uses similar calls in Europe, but Waters (1993) found its calls to be just as audible to
moths as FM bats with more intense calls. However, Anderson and Racey (1991) have
shown that in captivity this bat switches off its echolocation, and uses prey-generated
sound to locate its prey. This is a strategy used by a number of other species, including
Trachops cirrhosus, *Tonatia sylvicola* (Tuttle *et al.*, 1985), and *Myotis evotis* (Faure and
Barclay, 1992). Other species achieve essentially the same effect during the feeding buzz,
by reducing call intensity and duration.

Finally, some insectivorous species are known to use vision to locate prey when sufficient
light is available, e.g. the California leaf-nosed bat, *Macrotus californicus* (Bell, 1985).

The arms race: bats versus frogs

Evidence also exists for an arms race between the phyllostomid bat, *Trachops cirrhosus*,
and its prey. Although this species commonly takes insects and a range of small vertebrates, the population studied by Tuttle and Ryan (1981), on Barro Colorado Island in
Panama, took large numbers of frogs. *Trachops* preyed on males of *Physalaemus pustu-
losus* at breeding ponds, and capture rates were significantly higher when male frogs were
calling to attract females. By playing recordings of frog calls to bats in enclosures and in
the field, Tuttle and Ryan were able to show that the bats preferred the calls of *P. pustulo-
sus* to those of a local poisonous species and another species too large for the bats to
handle. The frogs alter the complexity of their call, a whine followed by up to six chucks,
by increasing the number of chucks in response to the calls of other males. The chucks
carry information on the size of the male, and females prefer the more complex calls.
Why don't the males use complex calls all the time? Probably because it increases the
predation risk—*Trachops* has been shown to prefer complex calls too (Ryan *et al.*, 1982).
Bats are typically most sensitive to the range of sound frequencies used in their echolocation calls, and are rarely sensitive to low frequencies (see Chapter 3). *Trachops'* sensitivity to sound is high at frequencies greater than 15 kHz and falls in the range 15–5 kHz as
expected, but then increases again from 5–0.2 kHz: the dominant frequency range in the
frogs' mating calls (Ryan *et al.*, 1983).

Carnivores—hunting by sight, sound, and echolocation

Those bats which feed on other vertebrates as part of their diet also have the problem of
alerting prey with their echolocation calls. To overcome this, some appear to have a very
flexible foraging strategy, combining echolocation with the use of prey-generated sound
and vision. Echolocation calls are typically broadband FM, and suited to the cluttered

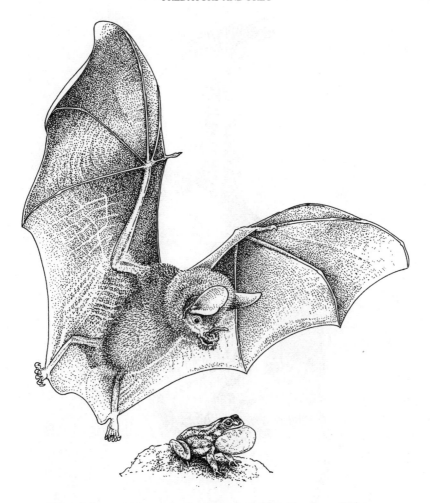

Frog being preyed upon by the fringe-lipped bat, *Trachops cirrhosus*

environment in which the bats hunt, but they are also low intensity, possibly to reduce the likelihood of detection by prey (Norberg and Fenton, 1988). Several species are known to make use of prey-generated sound e.g. the Indian false vampire, *Megaderma lyra* (Fiedler, 1979), and the large ears characteristic of insectivorous bats which make use of this strategy are found in most of the known carnivores. Although it has not been investigated, I suspect the large eyes of many carnivorous bats are used to detect prey—some insectivores certainly use vision (e.g. Bell, 1985). The large, forward pointing eyes of the Australian ghost bat, *Macroderma gigas*, are almost owl-like.

Bats as prey

Evidence for predators (other than humans) having a significant effect on bat populations is sparse. Few predators specialise on bats, but a largely anecdotal literature includes

Indian false-vampire, *Megaderma lyra*, with rodent

many occasional bat-eaters: monkeys, a loris, mustelids, racoons, opossums, cats, bats themselves, raptors, snakes, frogs, fish, and a few large arthropods, mainly spiders. Only birds and snakes appear to be regular predators, and those likely to have an effect on bat populations. At least five snakes in Central and South America and Africa are known to take bats roosting in caves and trees (Hill and Smith, 1984), and sometimes in flight as they leave caves. The brown tree snake, *Boiga irregularis*, introduced to Guam in the late 1940's is having a very significant and worrying effect on the population of the rare *Pteropus mariannus* by taking young (see Mickleburgh *et al.* 1992). Owls, hawks, and falcons take bats throughout the world (Gillette and Kimbourgh, 1970), but I know of

Bat falcon, *Falco rufigularis*

African harrier hawk, *Polyboroides typus*, and molossid bats

only one attempt to estimate their impact on bats. Speakman (1991) calculated that although bats made up a very small component of the diets of owls, the only important avian predators of bats in Britain, they could account for 10% of the annual bat mortality. This figure could be higher in mainland Europe (see Julian and Altringham, 1994). Individual owls occasionally take large numbers of bats, and could have a significant local effect on populations (Julian and Altringham, 1994).

Raptors versus bats

The benefits of roosting in colonies were discussed in the last chapter, and I also mentioned some of the potential costs, one of which was predation. Bats are particularly vulnerable to aerial predation as they leave the roost: they often emerge in large numbers, over a relatively short period and at a time which can be predicted by predators. Several raptors are known to predate emerging bats, and large numbers hunt at some of the vast colonies of Mexican free-tailed bats (*Tadarida brasiliensis*) in the southern United States. Fenton *et al.* (1994) recently studied the behaviour of both bats and birds at roosts in South Africa. Whalberg's eagle (*Aquila wahlbergi*) and hobby (*Falco subbuteo*) stooped on free-tailed bats (*Tadarida pumila* and *T. condylura*), emerging from roosts in buildings and bridges. The African goshawk (*Accipiter tachiro*) pursued bats in flight. The raptors appeared at dusk, and either flew close to the roosts or perched nearby until the bats began to earlier. Some birds were also present for the dawn return of the bats. Half the attempted attacks were successful, and handling time (0.5–5 min) was the major factor influencing overall predation rate, given the short emergence time (10–30 min). Bats were usually taken to a perch to be eaten, but some birds reduced their handling time by eating in flight. A successful bird could meet more than 50% of its daily food requirements. Bats appeared to use three strategies to minimise risk: late departure from the roost at small colonies, emergence in clusters, and roost switching. Large colonies emerged earlier than small ones, perhaps gaining from the safety in numbers factor. Since insect populations peak in the early evening, early emergence is desirable, but increases the risk of predation by diurnal predators: the actual emergence time is probably a compromise between these conflicting factors (Jones and Rydell, 1994). Clustering may have functions of greater or equal importance to predator avoidance, particularly where aerial predators are less common. In some cases, clustering behaviour may be related to foraging strategy. Evening bats (*Nycticeius humeralis*) leave the roost within 10 s of each other far more often than predicted by chance: females unsuccessful at foraging earlier that evening follow other bats to increase their chances of feeding (Wilkinson, 1992). Some degree of social interaction is evident in the emergence patterns of pipistrelles, *Pipistrellus pipistrellus* (Altringham and Park, 1996.). On leaving the roost, bats flew in the same direction as the preceding bat far more often than predicted by chance and clusters of up to seven consecutive bats flying in the same direction occurred more often that predicted. This behaviour may be related to foraging strategy and/or predator avoidance.

BATS AND PLANTS

Heithaus (1982) has written a review on co-evolution and other aspects of the interaction between bats and plants, with an emphasis on the New World. The Old World has been dealt with by Marshall (1983). Fleming (1982) has discussed foraging strategies in plant-visiting bats, and has also written a book on the short-tailed fruit bat (1988), which covers many aspects of the subject in considerable detail.

Adaptive radiation: in the bats

Over 250 species of bat eat one plant product or another, ranging from obligate frugivores or nectarivores, through versatile omnivores, to insectivores which take a little fruit when gleaning insects. Megabats are known to feed on plants from 188 genera, phyllostomids from 146 genera (Marshall, 1983; Heithaus, 1982). The transition to frugivory in one form or another has been a major factor in the adaptive radiation of the phyllostomids. For example, three of the six subfamilies of the Phyllostomidae appear to have

Megaloglossus woermanni, African long-tongued fruit bat

undergone their major radiations following their independent evolution of frugivory (van der Pijl, 1972).

Adaptive radiation: in the plants

In turn, the bats have had their effect on the adaptive radiation of the plants. Vogel (1969) suggests that bat pollination has arisen independently in at least 27 New World plant families, affecting over 500 species. Similarly, the use of bats as major seed dispersers also appears to have arisen independently on many occasions.

Pollination and seed dispersal

We can safely assume that since so many plants are adapted to exploit bats as pollinators and seed dispersers, then the process is an important one to the plants: bats must have some influence on the density and distribution of many plant species, and possibly a significant effect on the ecosystem of which they are a part. Bats can transfer pollen over several kilometres, an important factor for those plants which are randomly spaced at low density, and also important in maintaining a large breeding population (Heithaus, 1982). Plants must evolve characteristics which attract potential pollinators and seed dispersers. The degree to which this has been achieved varies with the plants and bats involved, and depends to a large extent on the specificity of the interaction between the species. Only those plants which have evolved close and specific relations with particular bats are likely to have fine tuned their bat-attracting qualities. In fact, plants rarely depend entirely on one species of bat, or even on bats alone. Similarly, the bat may feed on many species of plant. Some bats even eat many of the flowers they are pollinating, or groom the pollen from their fur before it can be transferred to another plant. Furthermore, different bats may respond to the same plant in different ways. The large *Phyllostomus discolor* and the small *Glossophaga soricina* both feed on the nectar of *Bauhinia pauletia*. *P. discolor* empties the flower in a single visit, and forages in flocks, possibly to reduce the chance of an individual bat visiting a flower that has already been emptied. *G. soricina* forages along traplines, taking only a little nectar at each flower, and it can return to a single flower many times (Heithaus *et al.*, 1974). In terms of the quantity of nectar provided, the distribution of food is perceived differently by the two bats, and they have evolved different strategies to exploit it. The plant, faced with this diversity, must evolve a nectar producing strategy which is a compromise between the needs of these and perhaps other pollinators.

By evolving mechanisms to disperse its seeds, a plant can gain in several ways, through increased gene exchange, enhanced colonisation of new sites, reduced competition, and reduced seed predation. Those bats which transport large numbers of seeds long distances without damaging them are thus likely to be beneficial to plants. Many megabats and phyllostomids fall into this category. Morrison (1978) calculated that *Artibeus jamaicensis* disperses at least 7% of the annual fig crop on Barro Colorado Island in Panama, and pteropodids consume large numbers of fruit before commuting up to 50 km to their day roosts. Bonaccorso *et al.* (1980) found that of the 16 species of mammal (including four bats) that ate the fruits of *Dipteryx* on Barro Colorado Island, only the phyllostomid *Artibeus lituratus* was a 'high-quality' disperser. Interestingly, one of the other bats, *Carollia perspicillata*, which is too small to disperse *Dipteryx* seeds, is the principal disperser for several *Piper* species and *Solanum hayesii* (Heithaus and Fleming, 1978). If a plant depends on several pollinators pressures on the evolution of fruit size and shape may be conflicting: large bats can carry fruit away from the parent tree, promoting seed dispersal, but a small bat may need to eat the fruit at the parent tree, and uneaten seeds will fall below it. If gut transit times are short, as is often the case, few seeds may be dispersed in the faeces. On the other hand, the damage done to seed cases in their passage through the bat, and the nutrient content of the faeces in which they are deposited, may improve germination. Old World fruits eaten by bats tend to be large, whereas smaller fruits are usually eaten by the smaller phyllostomids of the New World. It should be said that the size of the bat is not always a reliable indicator of whether fruit is carried away to be eaten. Predator avoidance, and male defence of females and territory, are among the many additional factors which influence foraging behaviour.

Megabats and Pacific island floras

The depauperate faunas of many Pacific islands include few pollinators of the native flora: *Pteropus* species are the only indigenous, frugivorous mammals on most islands, and many islands have few pollinating birds, and even insects, relative to continental areas. The role bats play in maintaining the diversity of the native flora, and in turn the fauna, may be crucial (Cox *et al.*, 1991). Many Pacific island bats are endemic to single or small groups of islands, and are under threat from hunting and habitat destruction. At least one species has become extinct in recent years, and populations of several other species are probably too low for them to be effective pollinators and dispersers. Unless conservation measures are effective, we may see a graphic, and perhaps catastrophic, natural experiment unfold, which tells us just how important the bats are to these ecosystems.

Coevolution?

The obvious mutual dependence that exists between some bats and plants has led to the suggestion that coevolution has occurred in many instances. Strictly speaking, the term should be used to describe only the process by which one species is the source of the selective forces which determine the evolution of another, with the changes (morphological, physiological, or behavioural) in one inducing changes in the other. In time, the association may become so specialised that the two species are mutually and totally dependent upon each other for their existence. It would appear that true coevolution is much rarer than once believed, and its very importance as a major evolutionary force has been questioned (Nitecki, 1983; Futuyma and Slatkin, 1983). Many examples may now be explained in terms of diffuse coevolution or preadaptation. Diffuse coevolution occurs when more than one species, and often many, are involved on the two sides of the interaction. The degree of specificity and mutual dependence in the interaction between any two species is therefore likely to be low. Preadaptation is when one species is able to interact with another simply because independent evolutionary pressures have by chance given it the attributes which enable it to do so. The evolution of bat/plant interactions appears to have been driven primarily by diffuse coevolution and preadaptation.

The Old World megabats have always been frugivores, and coevolution, true or diffuse, would have to start with the plants. The first microbats to evolve frugivorous habits, the phyllostomids of the neotropics, probably did so in association with plants which were either preadapted to bats, either by visitations from other neotropical, nocturnal vertebrates (Sussman and Raven, 1978), or through evolution from megabat pollinated ancestors in the Old World (Baker, 1973). The first steps into coevolution in the New World must have been made by the bats. Baker (1973) highlights the danger of too readily using coevolution as an explanation for bat/plant relations. *Ceiba* and *Parkia* species, bat-pollinated plants which have been used to define bat flowers, must have existed in both the Old and the New Worlds before the evolution of either megabats or phyllostomids. To become the principle pollinators of these plants, in both Worlds, they must have displaced other pollinators.

Bat plants

The flowers of plants have to evolve mechanisms which attract bats, and ensure that pollen is deposited on the bat for transfer to the next flower. Bat-pollinated flowers are generally white, creamy, or greenish, with a musky, even 'batty', odour. They frequently open only at night (and perhaps only for one night), and sometimes only for a limited time after dusk.

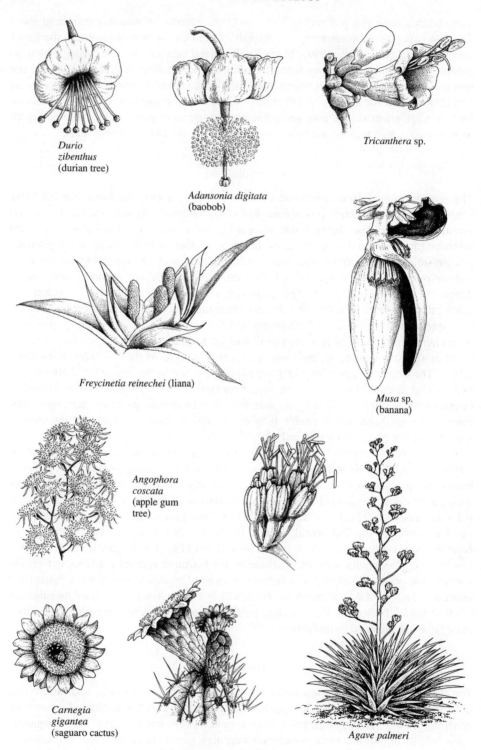

Durio
zibenthus
(durian tree)

Adansonia digitata
(baobob)

Tricanthera sp.

Freycinetia reinechei (liana)

Musa sp.
(banana)

Angophora
coscata
(apple gum
tree)

Carnegia
gigantea
(saguaro cactus)

Agave palmeri

Fig. 7.12. Bat plants.

They may be quite large and bell-like, with their large nectaries deep in the bowl of the flower, or 'shaving brushes', with nectaries exposed (Fig. 7.12), and some flowers have landing platforms. A nectary may hold 5–10 ml of nectar when full. The stamens are placed to leave pollen on the bat—from a heavy covering over much of the body, to a strategic dab on the top of the head. Bat plants are usually trees and vines, and several characteristics increase access to bats. For example, the flowers are often pendulous, they are typically held free of obstruction, say on the periphery of the tree, and the tree may be leafless during flowering (Vogel, 1969). Temporal differences in flowering and fruiting patterns are also important, and can be characterised by the two extremes seen (Heinrich and Raven, 1972; Gentry, 1974; Heithaus, 1982). Some plants exhibit 'big-bang' reproduction, producing vast numbers of flowers over just a few days, attracting many opportunistic foragers including bats, other mammals, insects, and birds. Flower shape and nectar production are such that few potential pollinators are excluded. At the other extreme are the 'steady state' plants which produce just a few flowers each night over a long period. Pollinators have time to memorise the location of flowering trees and visit repeatedly, often by trap-lining, but because there are few flowers per tree, they must visit several trees, improving pollination success. Flower shape may restrict access to these regular visitors and discourage opportunistic foragers. Between the two extremes there are many other patterns, including the 'multiple-bang'. To some extent these patterns must reflect co-evolution between a plant and its pollinator(s).

Bat–plant interactions: coevolution and mutualism

The relationships which have evolved are too numerous and complex to describe here, and the reader should go to the references I gave at the beginning of this section for information on particular bats and plants. I want to look at a couple of examples which perhaps come closest to true coevolution.

Is coevolution evident in the relationship between the tree *Oroxylum iridicum* and a small pteropodid, *Eonycteris spelaea* (Gould, 1978)? This species roosts in caves, and migrates long distances to its feeding grounds, arriving well after dark. The tree's flowers do not open until 2.5 h after dusk, and drop before dawn, giving time for *E. spelaea* to arrive, but preventing earlier feeders from getting the nectar. The flower initially opens only sufficiently wide to allow *E. spelaea* in, and the nectar is in exactly the right spot for it to reach it with its long tongue, when the head and shoulders are wedged into the flower. The flower has to be tipped on its rigid stem before the nectaries charge the tuft of hairs which the bat feeds from. The flower cannot be tipped by a bat smaller than *E. spelaea*. Only a little nectar is given up each time, so the bat needs to move repeatedly from flower to flower—something larger megabats rarely do. The bottom line is that no other bat species feed at this tree. However, although the plant's dependence on the bat is possibly total, the bat feeds on many other tree species, and there is no direct evidence that *E. spelaea* has made specific evolutionary responses to *Oroxylum*—it simply has the long muzzle and tongue, and other characteristics, common to many nectar-feeding bats.

Leptonycteris curasoae (sanborni) is a nectar-eating phyllostomid, feeding on a broad range of plants in Central America and the south-western United States, but it may depend primarily on a single species at certain times of the year. Howell (1979), studied its interaction with the agave, *Agave palmeri*, in the Arizona summer. Flowers of the agave produce most of their nectar early in the evening, with minimal production in the second half of the night. Flocks of *L. curasoae* must feed at the flowers of at least four plants in one night to optimise their own energy budgets. The optimal foraging strategy is to switch plants before completely exhausting the nectaries, and to move on to previously unvisited plants, rather than return to those visited earlier in the night. The pattern of nectar production ensures cross-pollination, since this plant is not intrafertile. The heads and shoulders of the bats are covered in pollen after feeding, the pollen clinging to specially adapted hairs. Much of it is groomed off and eaten, and its amino acid composition appears to be matched to the physiological needs of the bat (Howell, 1974). Again however, the dependence is not absolute for either partner. The agave is also pollinated to a limited extent by sphinx moths and carpenter bees, as are other bat-pollinated succulents like the saguaro cactus. Seed set losses are respectively only 16% and 28% lower when the saguaro is pollinated by moths and bees, rather than by *L. curasoae* (McGregor *et al.*, 1962). As already stated, *L. curasoae* is a generalist, feeding on a wide range of plants, presumably specialising on *A. palmeri* only when it is energetically advantageous. Close, mutual dependence between just two species is an unstable situation, since a decline in one species (even temporarily) will inevitably lead to a decline in both, possibly to extinction (May, 1981). This may be why such systems are hard to find in nature, and why mutualisms are generally more diffuse: dependence between species is not absolute, and more than two species are involved. Begon *et al.* (1990), provide an excellent summary, and suggest that the study of mutualisms addresses one of the most fundamental ecological questions: 'Do whole communities of organisms in nature represent more or less tightly coevolved relationships?' Ecologists and ecology textbooks have concentrated on competition and predator–prey relations. More attention could perhaps be given to the study of mutualisms in the context of community ecology.

Finally, a fascinating example has recently come to light. The endemic *Dactylanthus taylorii* is New Zealand's only completely parasitic plant. It has large, dull flowers on unisexual plants which produce lots of nectar and a strong odour. The only real candidate

Fig. 7.13.   A New Zealand short-tailed bat, *Mystacina tuberculata*, feeding on the nectar of *Dactylanthus*. See text for details.

for its principle pollinator is another endemic species, the short-tailed bat, *Mystacina tuberculata*. It has been seen to make up to 40 visits per night to take nectar, over a four week period (Ecroyd, 1993). *Mystacina* is the only microbat outside the phyllostomids known to feed on plant products. In this relationship we have one of the world's most unusual and possibly endangered bats in a mutualistic relationship with an unusual and endangered plant. The study of this interaction may be crucial to the survival of both species.

8 Conservation

WHY CONSERVE BATS?

Why conserve bats? First and foremost, for a reason we do not see stated as often as we should in conservation arguments: because they have a right to a place on this planet. Bats are part of the global ecosystem, with a part to play in its survival and evolution.

Whether we study bats as professional biologists or as amateur naturalists, or simply watch them in our gardens or on television wildlife programmes, they enrich our lives. They are another facet of the natural world to marvel at and to try to understand. The study of the natural world, and the transfer of what we learn to a wider public, is an end in itself: a part of our culture. As I hope this book shows, when we study bats we also learn more about the ways in which the natural world works. This study often has medical or economic benefits, frequently unsuspected, and basic research leads on to strategic research. However, we often place too little value on our natural heritage and the study of how it works. Wilson (1994) argues powerfully and eloquently on the need to study life's diversity.

If you have already read the later chapters in this book, you will appreciate the ecological importance of bats: as predators of arthropods, as prey to other vertebrates, and as seed dispersers and pollinators. In some ecosystems their role may be a key one, crucial to the maintenance of the system. There is now increasing evidence to suggest that through seed dispersal, bats play an important role in tropical forest regeneration.

Bats as pests and as benefactors

To many people, if an animal has no economic value it is not worth protecting, and if it is perceived as a pest, then they believe it should be eradicated. Most of the claims that bats are vermin, as carriers of disease or as destroyers of buildings and crops, are either false or exaggerated: bats are rarely a significant problem to humans. They are involved in the transmission of a small number of diseases, most seriously rabies and histoplasmosis. However, they are responsible for a very small number of cases. Histoplasmosis is a respiratory disease caught by inhaling a species of fungus found in soil rich in organic matter—for example under large roosts of birds or bats. Infections are rare and fatalities even rarer. The fungus is found in the southern United States, South America, and Africa, with isolated reports from some other parts of the world. Most recorded infections are in people who enter tropical caves with large bat populations. Rabies is a widespread and serious disease. Only one bat, the common vampire, is a major vector, and it is responsible for the death of many domestic cattle in South and Central America. Vaccination programmes have led to a much lower incidence of rabies in domestic livestock, but it still remains a problem. Rabies infection of humans by vampires was once relatively high in some part of the New World, but cases are increasingly rare due to improved public health. Rabies is no more prevalent in other bats than in most other animal-eating mammals, and since people do not encounter bats very often, they are far more likely to catch rabies from domestic or wild carnivores. In a single year, an American is more likely to be killed by a dog, a bee, or a lawn-mower, than by rabies in 30 years. Bats do carry other diseases, as do all animals, but none are a significant threat to humans. Roosting bats can occasionally cause a nuisance when they form large colonies in buildings, particularly in the tropics. The biggest problems are noise and odour due to the accumulation of droppings. However, these rarely constitute a health hazard. In temperate regions, problems are far less frequent and usually easily overcome without cost to humans or bats.

On the positive side, insectivorous bats must be important as a natural control of insects including many medical and agricultural pests. Unfortunately there is no quantitative evidence to show just how important. The large deposits of guano which build up under bat colonies have been exploited for centuries and in many tropical countries it is still an economically important agricultural fertiliser. An anticoagulant protein isolated from vampire saliva dissolves potentially dangerous blood clots twice as fast as any substance currently in clinical use.

Damage to fruit crops by bats can be severe but even this is generally overestimated. When costs have been assessed objectively they are frequently low and must be offset against the positive gains of improved pollination success. The durian fruit alone, from a bat-pollinated tree, adds $120 million to local economies in South East Asia. Bats may also be important in maintaining wild populations of fruit plants through pollination and seed dispersal. Wild strains are important in plant breeding, to ensure a constant supply of healthy and disease-resistant commercial strains. Fruit-eating bats in the New World have recently been identified as a vital factor in forest regeneration after timber operations, since they are the most important dispersers of the seeds of 'coloniser' tree species. Unfortunately, as natural habitat is destroyed, and replaced with commercial fruit crops, bats are forced to turn to these crops for food

THREATS TO BATS

There is now considerable evidence that bat populations in many parts of the world are in decline, the range of many species has contracted. Eight species have not been recorded for 50 years or more, and a further four have almost certainly been driven to extinction more recently (Groombridge, 1994).

Arguably the single biggest threat to bats, one common to very many plants and animals, is habitat destruction. This directly destroys their food sources and natural roost sites. Once destroyed or degraded beyond a certain stage, many habitats cannot regenerate, or do so only slowly. New management practises, or the use of herbicides or pesticides can seriously degrade a habitat which superficially still looks healthy. Reduction in habitat area can also have serious consequences. Individual patches must be large enough to sustain viable populations, and habitat corridors may be necessary between patches to enable bats and other organisms to move around.

Destruction of roosts (in addition to those lost through forest clearing) has also been a major problem, from the wholesale mining of cave systems to insensitive renovation of buildings. Caves and similar sites in the tropics can be year-round homes to vast colonies of bats. In temperate countries large numbers may gather in caves and mines to hibernate, and buildings often house the most important maternity roosts. Although bats can cause problems in buildings, typically through noise or the accumulation of dropping, these can generally be overcome. In the United Kingdom, largely due to the activities of volunteer enthusiasts, the majority of householders with roosts have learned not only to accept their bats but to cherish them. In the United States, bats have successfully adopted artificial roosts provided as an alternative.

Bats are eaten in several parts of the world, but this rarely constitutes a threat. However, in Guam, megabats are eaten in large numbers, and with the demise of the island's own bats they have been imported from other Pacific islands. Since many of these islands have endemic bats, or species with very limited distributions, several are under serious threat. Import/export control has been difficult despite the CITES Agreement (Convention on International Trade in Endangered Species of Wild Fauna and Flora).

Roost disturbance has been a factor at sites where bats are hunted, or where guano is collected. Ironically, insensitively conducted tours to watch bats leave their roosts to forage has led to reductions in colony size, and in the past, the activities of biologists studying the bats themselves has probably had a similar effect.

Finally, deliberate persecution is a problem. Superstition and ignorance can lead to declines, either through direct killing of the bats, or through destruction of their roost: some species do not appear to be able to establish themselves in new sites quickly. Control of vampires or bats believed to be crop pests not only kills the bats in question, but frequently many other species which share their roosts.

BAT CONSERVATION ORGANISATIONS

The following two organisations are charities specifically set up to promote bat conservation. Both seek the active involvement of the public as members and participants in their work, and are an enthusiastic mixture of professionals and amateurs. They support a wide range of activities including education, practical conservation, survey work, and research. They have been responsible for some major legislation and conservation projects, and the successful promotion of a more informed and publicly acceptable image for bats. Both produce a quarterly newsletter in addition to booklets and leaflets, reports on specific projects, conservation plans, guides to survey techniques, manuals for bat house construction and siting, etc. Slide packs, education packs, and identification guides to bats are also produced.

IUCN—the World Conservation Union's Species Survival Commission has a Chiroptera Specialist Group, a network of about 100 authorities of the world's bats. The group acts on particular conservation issues and prepares broad policies and strategies for bat conservation.

The Bat Conservation Trust, 15 Cloisters House, 8 Battersea Park Road, London, SW4 4BG, UK. Tel. 0171 627 2629.

Bat Conservation International, PO Box 162603, Austin, Texas 78716, USA. Tel. 512 327 9721.

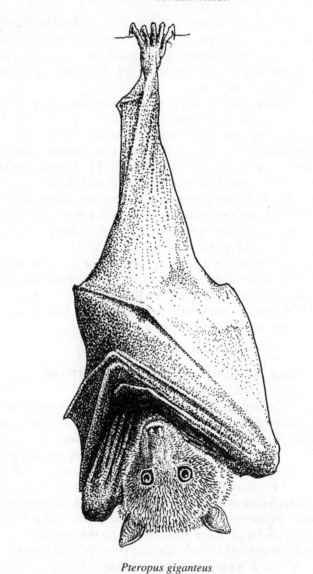

Pteropus giganteus

References

Acharya, L. (1992) Are ears valuable to moths flying around lights? *Bat Res. News* **33**, 47.

Acharya, L. and Fenton, M.B. (1992) Echolocation behaviour of vespertilionid bats (*Lasiurus cinereus* and *Lasiurus borealis*) attacking airborne targets, including arctiid moths. *Can. J. Zool.* **70**, 1292–1298.

Aldridge, H.D.J.N. (1986) The flight kinematics of the greater horseshoe bat, *Rhinolophus ferrumequinum*. In: *Biona Rep. 5, Bat flight-Fledermausflug*, edited by W. Nachtigall, pp 127–138. Gustav Fischer Verlag, Stuttgart.

Aldridge, H.D.J.N. and Rautenbach, I.L. (1987) Morphology, echolocation and resource partitioning in insectivorous bats. *J. Anim. Ecol.* **56**, 763–778.

Alexander, R.McN. and Young, I.S. (1992) Dynamic models of breathing. *S.E.B. Seminar Series* **51**: *Oxygen transport in biological systems*, edited by S. Egginton and H.F. Ross. Cambridge University Press, Cambridge.

Altenbach, J.S. and Hermanson, J.W. (1987) Bat flight muscle function and the scapulo-humeral lock. In: *Recent advances in the study of bats*, edited by M.B. Fenton, P.A. Racey and J.M.V. Rayner, pp 100–118. Cambridge University Press, Cambridge.

Altringham, J.D. and Park, K.J. (1996) Why do bats emerge from roosts in clusters? In preparation.

Altringham, J.D. and Young, I.S. (1991) Power output and the frequency of oscillatory work in mammalian diaphragm muscle: the effects of animal size. *J. exp. Biol.* **157**, 381–389.

Ammerman, L.K. and Hillis, D.M. (1992) A molecular test of bat relationships: monophyly or diphyly? *Syst. Biol.* **41**, 222–232.

Anderson, M.E. and Racey, P.A. (1991) Feeding behaviour of captive brown long-eared bats, *Plecotus auritus. Anim. Behav.* **42**, 489–493.

Anthony, E.L.P. and Kunz, T.H. (1977) Feeding strategies of the little brown bat, *Myotis lucifugus*, in southern New Hampshire. *Ecology* **58**, 775–786.

Archer, M. (1984) The Australian marsupial radiation. In: *Vertebrate zoogeography and evolution in Australasia*, edited by M. Archer and G. Clayton, pp 633–808. Hesperian Press, Carlisle, W. Australia.

Au, W. (1993) *The sonar of dolphins*. Springer-Verlag, Berlin.

Audet, D. and Fenton, M.B. (1988) Heterothermy and the use of torpor by the bat *Eptesicus fuscus* (Chiroptera: Vespertilionidae): a field study. *Physiol. Zool.* **61**, 197–204.

Audet, D., Krull, D., Marimuthu, G., Sumithran, S. and Bala Singh, J. (1991) Foraging behaviour of the Indian False Vampire Bat, *Megaderma lyra* (Chiroptera: Megadermatidae). *Biotropica* **23**, 63–67.

Audley-Charles, M.G. (1983) Reconstruction of eastern Gondwanaland. *Nature* **306**, 48–50.

Avery, M.I. (1985) Winter activity of pipistrelle bats. *J. Anim. Ecol.* **54**, 721–738.

Baagøe, H.J. (1987) The Scandinavian bat fauna: adaptive wing morphology and free flight in the field. In: *Recent advances in the study of bats*, edited by M.B. Fenton, P.A. Racey and J.M.V. Rayner, pp 57–74. Cambridge University Press, Cambridge.

Bailey, W.B. (1991) *Acoustic behaviour of insects: an evolutionary perspective* (Chapter 10, Avoiding predation). Chapman and Hall, London.

Bailey, W.J., Slightom, J.L. and Goodman, M. (1992) Rejection of the 'flying primate hypothesis' by phylogenetic evidence from the ϵ-globin gene. *Science* **256**, 86–89.

Baker, H.G. (1973) Evolutionary relationships between flowering plants and animals in American and African forests. In: *Tropical forest ecosystems in Africa and South America: a comparative review*, edited by B.J. Meggers, E.S. Ayensu, and W.D. Duckworth, pp 145–159. Smithsonian Institute Press, Washington.

Baker, R.J., Novacek, M.J. and Simmons, N.B. (1991) On the monophyly of bats. *Syst. Zool.* **40**, 216–231.

Balasingh, J., Suthakar Isaac, S. and Subbaraj, R. (1993) Tent-roosting of the frugivorous bat *Cynopterus sphinx* (Vahl 1797) in southern India. *Curr. Sci.* **65**, 418.

Balcombe, J.P. (1990) Vocal recognition of pups by mother Mexican free-tailed bats, *Tadarida brasiliensis mexicana. Anim. Behav.* **39**, 960–966.

Balcombe, J.P. and McCracken, G.F. (1992) Vocal recognition in Mexican free-tailed bats: do pups recognise mothers? *Anim. Behav.* **43**, 79–88.

Barbour, R.W. and Davis, W.H. (1969) *Bats of America*. University Press of Kentucky, Lexington.

Barclay, R.M.R. (1982) Interindividual use of echolocation calls: eavesdropping by bats. *Behav. Ecol. Sociobiol.* **10**, 271–275.

Barclay, R.M.R. (1985) Long- versus short-range foraging strategies of hoary (*Lasiurus cinereus*) and silver-haired (*Lasionycteris noctivagans*) bats and the consequences for prey selection. *Can. J. Zool.* **63**, 2507–2515.

Barclay, R.M.R. (1986) Foraging strategies of silver haired (*Lasionycteris noctivagans*) and hoary (*Lasiurus cinereus*) bats. *Myotis* **23–24**, 161–166.

Barclay, R.M.R. (1991) Population structure of temperate zone insectivorous bats in relation to foraging behaviour and energy demand. *J. Anim. Ecol.* **60**, 165–178.

Barclay, R.M.R. (1995) Constraints on reproduction by bats: energy or calcium? In: *Ecology, evolution and behaviour of bats*, edited by P.A. Racey and S.M. Swift. *Symp. Zool. Soc. Lond.* **67**, pp 245–258. Oxford University Press, Oxford.

Barclay, R.M.R. and Brigham, R.M. (1991) Prey detection, dietary niche breadth and body size in bats: why are aerial insectivorous bats so small? *Amer. Nat.* **137**, 693–703.

Bartholomew, G.A., Dawson, W.R. and Lasiewski, R.C. (1970) Thermoregulation and heterothermy in some of the smaller flying foxes (Megachiroptera) of New Guinea. *Zeitsch. fur Vergl. Physiol.* **70**, 196–207.

Bates, D.L. and Fenton, M.B. (1990) Aposematism or startle? Predators learn their responses to prey. *Can. J. Zool.* **68**, 49–52.

Bateman, G.C. and Vaughan, T.A. (1974) Night activities of mormoopid bats. *J. Mammal.* **55**, 45–65.

Bay, F.A. (1978) Light control of the circadian activity rhythm in mouse-eared bats (*Myotis myotis*). *J. Interdiscipl. Cycle Res.* **9**, 195–209.

Beasley, L.J. (1986) Seasonal cycles of pallid bats (*Antrozous pallidus*): proximate factors. *Myotis* **23–24**, 115–123.

Beasley, L.J., Pelz, K.M. and Zucker, I. (1984) Circannual rhythms of body weight in pallid bats. *Am. J. Physiol.* **246**, R955–R958.

Beasley, L.J., Smale. L. and Smith, E.R. (1984) Melatonin influences the reproductive physiology of male pallid bats. *Biol. Reprod.* **30**, 300–305.

Beer, J.R. and Richards, A.G. (1956) Hibernation of the big brown bat. *J. Mammal.* **37**, 31–41.

Begon, M., Harper, J.L. and Townsend, C.R. (1990) *Ecology: Individuals, populations and communities*. 2nd edition. Blackwell, Oxford.

Bell, G.P. (1982) Behavioural and ecological aspects of gleaning by a desert insectivorous bat, *Antrozous pallidus* (Chiroptera: Vespertilionidae). *Behav. Ecol. Sociobiol.* **10**, 217–223.

Bell, G.P. (1985) The sensory basis of prey location by the California leaf-nosed bat, *Macrotus californicus* (Chiroptera: Phyllostomidae). *Behav. Ecol. Sociobiol.* **16**, 343–347.

Bell, G.P. and Fenton, M.B. (1984) The use of Doppler-shifted echoes as a flutter detection and clutter rejection system: the echolocation and feeding behaviour of *Hipposideros ruber. Behav. Ecol. Sociobiol.* **15**, 109–114.

Belwood, J.J. and Fenton, M.B. (1976) Variation in the diet of *Myotis lucifugus* (Chiroptera: Vespertilionidae). *Can. J. Zool.* **54**, 1674–1678.

Bennett, M.B. (1992) Structural modifications involved in the fore- and hind limb grip of some flying foxes (Chiroptera: Pteropodidae) *J. Zool. Lond.* **229**, 237–248.

Berger, M. and Hart, J.S. (1974) Physiology and energetics of flight. In: *Avian biology,* Vol. 4, edited by D.S. Farner and J.R. King. Academic Press, London.

Bloedel, P. (1955) Observations on the life histories of Panama bats. *J. Mammal.* **36**, 232–235.

Bonaccorso, F.J. (1979) Foraging and reproductive ecology in a Panamanian bat community. *Bull. Fla. State Mus. Biol. Ser.* **24**, 359–408.

Bonaccorso, F.J., Glanz, W.E. and Sandford, C.M. (1980) Feeding assemblages of mammals at fruiting *Dipteryx panamensis* (Papilionaceae) trees in Panama: seed predation, dispersal, and parasitism. *Rev. Biol. Trop.* **28**, 61–72.

Brack, V. and Twente, J.W. (1985) The duration of the period of hibernation of three species of vespertilionid bats. I. Field studies. *Can J. Zool.* **63**, 2952–2954.

Bradbury, J.W. (1977a) Social organisation and communication. In: *Biology of bats*, Vol. 3, edited by W.A. Wimsatt, pp 1–72. Academic Press, New York.

Bradbury, J.W. (1977b) Lek mating behaviour in the hammer-headed bat. *Z. Tierpsychol.* **45**, 225–255.

Bradbury, J.W. and Emmons, L.H. (1974) Social organisation of some Trinidad bats. I. Emballonuridae. *Z. Tierpyschol.* **36**, 137–183.

Bradbury, J.W. and Vehrencamp, S.L. (1976a) Social organisation and foraging in emballonurid bats. I. Field studies. *Behav. Ecol. Sociobiol.* **1**, 337–381.

Bradbury, J.W. and Vehrencamp, S.L. (1976b) Social organisation and foraging in emballonurid bats. II. A model for the determination of group size. *Behav. Ecol. Sociobiol.* **1**, 383–404.

Bradbury, J.W. and Vehrencamp, S.L. (1977a) Social organisation and foraging in emballonurid bats. III. Mating systems. *Behav. Ecol. Sociobiol.* **2**, 1–17.

Bradbury, J.W. and Vehrencamp, S.L. (1977b) Social organisation and foraging in emballonurid bats. IV. Parental investment patterns. *Behav. Ecol. Sociobiol.* **2**, 19–29.

Brigham, R.M. (1987) The significance of winter activity by the big brown bat (*Eptesicus fuscus*): the influence of energy reserves. *Can. J. Zool.* **65**, 1240–1242.

Brigham, R.M. (1991) Flexibility in foraging and roosting behaviour by the big brown bat (*Eptesicus fuscus*). *Can. J. Zool.* **69**, 117–121.

Brooke, A.P. (1990) Tent selection, roosting ecology and social organisation of the tent-making bat, *Ectophylla alba*, in Costa Rica. *J. Zool. Lond.* **221**, 11–19.

Brooke, A.P. (1994) Diet of the fishing bat, *Noctilio leporinus* (Chiroptera: Noctilionidae). *J. Mammal.* **75**, 212–218.

Brosset, A. (1962a) The bats of central and western India. Part I. *J. Bombay Nat. Hist. Soc.* **59**, 707–746.

Brosset, A. (1962b) The bats of central and western India. Part II. *J. Bombay Nat. Hist. Soc.* **59**, 583–624.

Brosset, A. (1962c) The bats of central and western India. Part III. *J. Bombay Nat. Hist. Soc.* **59**, 1–57.

Brosset, A. (1966) *La biologie des chiroptères*. Masson, Paris.

Brosset, A. (1976) Social organisation of the African bat, *Myotis bocagei. Z. Tierpsychol.* **42**, 50–56.

Bruns, V. (1976) Peripheral auditory tuning for fine frequency analysis by the CF-FM bat, *Rhinolophus ferrumequinum*. II. Frequency mapping in the cochlea. *J. Comp. Physiol.* A. **106**, 87–97.

Buchler, E.R. (1980) The development of flight, foraging and echolocation in the little brown bat (*Myotis lucifugus*). *Behav. Ecol. Sociobiol.* **6**, 211–218.

Buchler, E.R. and Childs, S.B. (1981) Orientation to distant sounds by foraging big brown bats (*Eptesicus fuscus*). *Anim. Behav.* **29**, 428–432.

Buchler, E.R. and Childs, S.B. (1982) Use of post-sunset glow as an orientation cue by the big brown bat (*Eptesicus fuscus*). *J. Mammal.* **63**, 243–247.

Caple, G., Balda, R.P. and Willis, W.R. (1983) The physics of leaping animals and the evolution of preflight. *Am. Nat.* **121**, 455–467.

Carpenter, R.E. (1985) Flight physiology of flying foxes. *J. exp. Biol.* **114**, 619–647.

Carpenter, R.E. (1986) Flight physiology of intermediate sized fruit bats (Pteropodidae). *J. exp. Biol.* **120**, 79–103.

Cervený, J. and Bürger, P. (1989) Density and structure of the bat community occupying an old park at Zihobce (Czechoslovakia). In: *European bat research 1987*, edited by V. Hanák, I. Horácek and J. Gaisler, pp 475–488. Charles University Press, Praha.

Charles-Dominique, P. (1993) Tent-use by the bat *Rhinophylla pumilio* (Phyllostomidae: Carolliinae) in French Guiana. *Biotropica* **25**, 111–116.

Choe, J.C. (1994) Ingenious design of tent roosts by Peter's tent-making bat, *Uroderma bilobatum* (Chiroptera: Phyllostomidae). *J. Nat. Hist.* **28**, 731–737.

Clutton-Brock, T.H. (1989) Mammalian mating systems. *Proc. R. Soc. Lond.* B **236**, 339–372.

Coles, R.B., Guppy, A., Anderson. M.E. and Schlegel, P. (1989) Frequency sensitivity and directional hearing in the gleaning bat, *Plecotus auritus* (Linnaeus 1758). *J. Comp. Physiol.* A. **165**, 269–280.

Cox, P.A., Elmqvist, T., Pierson, E.D. and Rainey, W.E. (1991) Flying foxes as strong interactors in south Pacific island ecosystems: a conservation hypothesis. *Cons. Biol.* **5**, 448–454.

Crome, F.H.J. and Richards, G.C. (1988) Bats and gaps: microchiropteran community structure in a Queensland rain forest. *Ecology* **69**, 1960–1969.

Daan, S. (1973) Activity during natural hibernation in three species of vespertilionid bats. *Neth. J. Zool.* **23**, 1–71.

Dal Piaz, G. (1937) I mammiferi dell'Oligocene Veneto. *Archaeopteropus transiens. Mem 1st Geol. Univ. Padova* **11** **(6)**, 1–8.

Daniel, M.J. (1990) Order Chiroptera. In: *The handbook of New Zealand mammals*, edited by C.M. King, pp 114–137. Oxford University Press, Auckland.

Darwin, C. (1859) *The origin of species.* John Murray, London.

Davis, R.B. and Cockrum, E.L. (1962) Repeated homing exhibited by a female pallid bat. *Science* **137**, 341–342.

Davis, R.B., Herreid, C.F. and Short, H.L. (1962) Mexican free-tailed bats in Texas. *Ecol. Monogr.* **32**, 311–346.

Dwyer, P.D. (1963) The breeding biology of *Miniopteris schreibersii blepotis* (Temminck) (Chiroptera) in north-eastern New South Wales. *Aust. J. Zool.* **11**, 219–240.

Dwyer, P.D. (1966) The population pattern of *Miniopterus schreibersii* (Chiroptera) in north-eastern New South Wales. *Aust. J. Zool.* **14**, 1073–1137.

Dwyer, P.D. (1968) The little bent-winged bat—evolution in progress. *Aust. Nat. Hist.* **1968**, 55–58.

Dwyer, P.D. (1970a) Latitude and breeding season in a polyestrous species of *Myotis*. *J. Mammal.* **51**, 405–410.

Dwyer, P.D. (1970b) Social organisation in the bat *Myotis adversus*. *Science* **168**, 1006–1008.

Dwyer, P.D. (1971) Temperature regulation and cave-dwelling in bats: an evolutionary perspective. *Mammalia* **35**, 424–453.

Dwyer, P.D. and Hamilton-Smith, E. (1965) Breeding caves and maternity colonies of the bent-winged bat in south-eastern Australia. *Helictite* **4**, 3–21.

Dwyer, P.D. and Harris, J.A. (1972) Behavioural acclimatisation to temperature by pregnant *Miniopterus* (Chiroptera) *Physiol. Zool.* **45**, 14–21.

Ecroyd, C. (1993) In search of the wood rose. *Forest and Bird* **Feb.**, 24–28.

Ewing, W.G., Studier, E.H. and O'Farrell, M.J. (1970) Autumn fat deposition and gross body composition in three species of *Myotis*. *Comp. Biochem. Physiol.* **36**, 119–129.

Faure, P.A. and Barclay, R.M.R. (1992) The sensory basis of prey detection by the long-eared bat, *Myotis evotis*, and the consequences for prey selection. *Anim. Behav.* **44**, 31–39.

Faure, P.A., Fullard, J.H. and Barclay, R.M.R. (1990) The response of typmanate moths to the echolocation calls of a substrate gleaning bat, *Myotis evotis*. *J. Comp. Physiol.* A **166**, 843–849.

Faure, P.A., Fullard, J.H. and Dawson, J.W. (1993) The gleaning attacks of the northern long-eared bat, *Myotis septentrionalis*, are relatively inaudible to moths. *J. exp. Biol.* **178**, 173–189.

Feng, A.S. Simmons, J.A. and Kick, S.A. (1978) Echo detection and target-ranging neurons in the auditory system of the bat *Eptesicus fuscus*. *Science* **202**, 645–648.

Fenton, M.B. (1985) *Communication in the Chiroptera*. Indiana University Press, Bloomington.

Fenton, M.B. (1990) The foraging behaviour and ecology of animal-eating bats. *Can. J. Zool.* **68**, 411–422.

Fenton, M.B. (1992) Wounds and the origin of blood-feeding in bats. *Biol. J. Linn. Soc.* **47**, 161–171.

Fenton, M.B. and Bell, G.P. (1981) Recognition of species of insectivorous bats by their echolocation calls. *J. Mammal.* **62**, 233–243.

Fenton, M.B. and Fullard, J.H. (1979) The influence of bat hearing on bat echolocation strategies. *J. Comp. Physiol.* **132**, 77–86.

Fenton, M.B., Rautenbach, I.L., Smith, S.E., Swanepoel, C.M., Grosell, J. and Jaarsveld, J. van. (1994) Raptors and bats: threats and opportunities. *Anim. Behav.* **48**, 9–18.

Fiedler, J. (1979) Prey catching with and without echolocation in the Indian false vampire bat (*Megaderma lyra*). *Behav. Ecol. Sociobiol.* **6**, 155–160.

Findley, J.S. (1993) *Bats: a community perspective*. Cambridge University Press, Cambridge.

Findley, J.S. and Black, H.L. (1983) Morphological and dietary structuring of a Zambian insectivorous bat community. *Ecology* **64**, 625–630.

Findley, J.S. and Jones, C. (1964) Seasonal distribution of the Hoary bat. *J. Mammal.* **45**, 461–470.

Findley, J.S. and Wilson, D.E. (1974) Observations on the neotropical disk-winged bat, *Thyroptera tricolor*. *J. Mammal.* **55**, 562–571.

Fleming, T.H. (1982) Foraging strategies of plant-visiting bats. In: *The ecology of bats*, edited by T.H. Kunz, pp 287–325. Plenum Press, New York.

Fleming, T.H. (1986) Opportunism vs. specialization: the evolution of feeding strategies in frugivorous bats. In: *Frugivores and seed dispersal*, edited by A. Estrada and T.H. Fleming, pp 105–118. W. Junk, Dordrecht, The Netherlands

Fleming, T.H. (1988) *The short-tailed fruit bat: a study in plant-animal interactions*. University of Chicago Press, Chicago.

Fleming, T.H. (1993) Plant-Visiting Bats. *Amer. Sci.* **81**, 460–467.

Fleming, T.H., Breitwisch, R. and Whitesides, G.H. (1987) Patterns of tropical vertebrate frugivore diversity. *Ann. Rev. Ecol. System.* **18**, 91–109.

Fleming, T.H., Hooper, E.T. and Wilson, D.E. (1972) Three Central American bat communities: Structure, reproductive cycles and movement patterns. *Ecology* **53**, 555–569.

Fleming, T.H., Nunez, R.A. and Sternberg, L. da S. L. (1993) Seasonal changes in the diets of migrant and non-migrant nectarivorous bats as revealed by carbon stable isotope analysis. *Oecologia* **94**, 72–75.

Foster, M.S. (1992) Tent roosts of Macconnell's bat (*Vampyressa macconnelli*). *Biotropica* **24**, 447–454.

Freeman, P.W. (1981) Correspondence of food habits and morphology in insectivorous bats. *J. Mammal.* **62**, 166–173.

Fullard, J.H. (1987) Sensory ecology and neuroethology of moths and bats: interactions in a global perspective. In: *Recent advances in the study of bats*, edited by M.B. Fenton, P.A. Racey and J.M.V. Rayner, pp 244–272. Cambridge University Press, Cambridge.

Fullard, J.H. (1992) The neuroethology of sound production in tiger moths (Lepidoptera, Arctiidae) I. Rhythmicity and central control. *J. Comp. Physiol.* A **170**, 575–588.

Fullard, J.H., Barclay, R.M.R. and Thomas, D.W. (1993) Echolocation in free-flying atiu swiftlets (*Aerodramus sawtelli*). *Biotropica* **25**, 334–339.

Fullard, J.H. and Yack, J.E. (1993) The evolutionary biology of insect hearing. *T.R.E.E.* **8**, 248–252.

Fullard, J.H., Koehler, C., Surlykke, A. and McKenzie, N.L. (1991) Echolocation ecology and flight morphology of insectivorous bats (Chiroptera) in south western Australia. *Aust. J. Zool.* **39**, 427–438.

Fullard, J.H., Simmons, J.A. and Saillant, P.A. (1994) Jamming bat echolocation: the dogbane tiger moth *Cynia tenera* times its clicks to the terminal attack calls of the big brown bat *Eptesicus fuscus*. *J. exp. Biol.* **194**, 285–298.

Futuyma, D.J. and Slatkin, M. (1983) Editors. *Coevolution*. Sinauer Associates. Sunderland, Mass.

Fuzessery, Z.M., Buttenhof, B., Andrews, B. and Kennedy, J.M. (1993) Passive sound localisation of prey by the pallid bat (*Antrozous pallidus*). *J. Comp. Physiol.* A. **171**, 767–777.

Gaisler, J., Hanák, V. and Dungel, J. (1979) A contribution to the population ecology of *Nyctalus noctula* (Mammalia, Chiroptera). *Acta Sci. Nat. Brno* **13**, 1–38.

Gall, L.F. and Tiffney, B.H. (1983) A fossil noctuid moth egg from the late Cretaceous of eastern North America. *Science* **219**, 507–509.

Gentry, A.H. (1974) Flowering phenology and diversity in tropical Bignoniaceae. *Biotropica* **6**, 64–68.

Gerell, R. and Lundberg, K. (1985) Social organisation in the bat *Pipistrellus pipistrellus*. *Behav. Ecol. Sociobiol.* **16**, 177–184.

Gillette, D.D. and Kimbourgh, J.D. (1970) Chiropteran mortality. In: *About bats*, edited by B.H. Slaughter and D.W. Waiton, pp 262–281. Dallas Southern Methodist University Press, Dallas.

Goodwin, G.G. and Greenhall, A.M. (1961) A review of the bats of Trinidad and Tabago. *Bull. Am. Mus. Nat. Hist.* **122**, 187–302.

Gould, E. (1978) Foraging behaviour of Malaysian nectar-feeding bats. *Biotropica* **10**, 184–193.

Greenhall, A.M. and Stell, G. (1960) Bionomics and chemical control of free-tailed house bats (*Molossus*) in Trinidad. *Spec. Sci. Rep. Wildl. Serv.*, Washington D.C.

Griffin, D.R. (1958) *Listening in the dark*. Yale University Press, New Haven, Conn. (Reprinted 1986).

Griffin, D.R. (1970) Migration and homing of bats. In: *Biology of Bats*, Vol. I, edited by W.A. Wimsatt, pp 233–246. Academic Press, New York.

Griffin, D.R. Webster, F.A. and Michael, C.R. (1960) The echolocation of flying insects by bats. *Anim. Behav.* **8**, 141–154.

Griffiths, J.R. and Varne, R. (1972) Evolution of the Tasman Sea, Macquarie Ridge and Alpine Fault. *Nature Phys. Sci.* **235**, 83–86.

Grinnell, A.D. (1963) The neurophysiology of audition in bats: intensity and frequency parameters. *J. Physiol.* **167**, 38–66.

Grinnell, A.D. and Griffin, D.R. (1958) The sensitivity of echolocation in bats. *Biol. Bull.* **114**, 10–22.

Groombridge, B. (1993) The 1994 IUCN Red List of Threatened animals. IUCN, Gland, Switzerland.

Guppy, A. and Coles, R.B. (1988) Acoustical and neural aspects of hearing in the Australian gleaning bats *Macroderma gigas* and *Nyctophilus gouldi*. *J. Comp. Physiol.* **162**, 653–668.

Gustin, K. and McCracken, G.F. (1987) Scent recognition in the Mexican free-tailed bat, *Tadarida brasiliensis mexicana*. *Anim. Behav.* **35**, 13–19.

Habersetzer, J. and Storch, G. (1992) Cochlea size in extant Chiroptera and middle Eocene Microchiropterans from Messel. *Naturwiss.* **79**, 462–466.

Hall, J.S. (1962) A life history and taxonomic study of the Indiana bat, *Myotis sodalis. Sci. Pub. Reading Pub. Mus. Art Gall.* **12**, 1–68.

Hamilton, I.A. and Barclay, R.M.R. (1994) Patterns of daily torpor and day-roost selection by male and female big brown bats (*Eptesicus fuscus*). *Can. J. Zool.* **72**, 744–749.

Hamilton, W.D. (1971) Geometry for the selfish herd. *J. Theor. Biol.* **31**, 295–311.

Hays, G.C., Speakman, J.R. and Webb, P.I. (1992) Why do brown long-eared bats (*Plecotus auritus*) fly in winter? *Physiol. Zool.* **65**, 554–567.

Hayward, B.J. and Cross, S.P. (1979) The natural history of *Pipistrellus hesperus* (Chiroptera: Vespertilionidae). *Office Res. West. N.M.* **3**, 1–36.

Heinrich, B. and Raven P.H. (1972) Energetics and pollination. *Science* **176**, 597–602.

Heithaus, E.R. (1982) Coevolution between bats and plants. In: *The ecology of bats*, edited by T.H. Kunz, pp 327–367. Plenum Press, New York.

Heithaus, E.R. and Fleming, T.H. (1978) Foraging movements of a frugivorous bat, *Carollia perspicillata* (Phyllostomidae). *Ecol. Monog.* **48**, 127–143.

Heithaus, E.R., Opler, P.A. and Baker, H.G. (1974) Bat activity and pollination of *Bauhinia pauletia*: plant–pollinator coevolution. *Ecology* **55**, 412–419.

Heller, K.-G., Achmann, R. and Witt, K. (1993) Monogamy in the bat *Rhinolophus sedulus. Z. Saug.* **58**, 376–378.

Heller, K.-G. and Helversen, O. V. (1989) Resource partitioning of sonar frequency bands in rhinolophid bats. *Oecologia* **80**, 178–186.

Hennig, W. (1966) *Phylogenetic systematics*. University of Illinois Press, Urbana.

Henson, O.W. (1965) The activity and function of the middle ear muscles in echolocating bats. *J. Physiol.* **180**, 871–887.

Herreid, C.F. (1963) Temperature regulation and metabolism in Mexican free-tailed bats. *Science* **142**, 1573–1574.

Herreid, C.F. (1967) Temperature regulation, temperature preference and tolerance, and metabolism of young and adult free-tailed bats. *Physiol. Zool.* **40**, 1–22.

Herrera, L.G., Fleming, T.H. and Findley, J.S. (1993) Geographic variation in carbon composition of the pallid bat, *Antrozous pallidus*, and its dietary implications. *J. Mammal.* **74**, 601–606.

Hill, J.E. (1974) A new family, genus and species of bat (Mammalia: Chiroptera) from Thailand. *Bull. Brit. Mus. (Nat. Hist.), Zoology* **32**, 29–43.

Hill, J.E. and Smith, J.D. (1984) *Bats: a natural history*. British Museum (Natural History). London.

Honeycutt, R.L. and Adkins, R.M. (1993) Higher level systematics of eutherian mammals: An assessment of molecular characters and phylogenetic hypotheses. *Ann. Rev. Ecol. Syst.* **24**, 279–305.

Hooper, J.H.D. and Hooper, W.H. (1956) Habits and movements of cave-dwelling bats in Devonshire. *Proc. Zool. Soc. Lond.* **127**, 1–26.

Howell, D.J. (1974) Bats and pollen: physiological aspects of the syndrome of Chiropterophily. *Comp. Biochem. Physiol.* **48**, 263–276.

Howell, D.J. (1979) Flock foraging in nectar-feeding bats: advantages to the bats and to the host plants. *Amer. Nat.* **114**, 23–49.

Howell, D.J. and Hartl, D.L. (1980) Optimal foraging in Glossophagine bats: when to give up. *Am. Nat.* **115**, 696–704.

Hughes, P.M. and Rayner, J.M.V. (1993) The flight of pipistrelle bats *Pipistrellus pipistrellus* during pregnancy and lactation. *J. Zool. Lond.* **230**, 541–555.

Hughes, P.M., Ransome, R.D. and Jones, G. (1989) Aerodynamic constraints on flight ontogeny in free-living greater horseshoe bats, *Rhinolophus ferrumequinum*. In: *European Bat Research 1987*, edited by V. Hanák, I. Horácek and J. Gaisler, pp 255–262. Charles University Press. Praha.

Humphrey, S.R. (1975) Nursery roosts and community diversity in nearctic bats. *J. Mammal.* **56**, 321–346.

Humphrey, S.R., Bonaccorso, F.J. and Zinn, T.L. (1983) Guild structure of surface-gleaning bats in Panama. *Ecology* **64**, 284–294.

Humphrey, S.R., Richter, A.R. and Cope, J.B. (1977) Summer habitat and ecology of the endangered Indiana bat, *Myotis sodalis. J. Mammal.* **58**, 334–346.

James, R.S., Altringham, J.D. and Goldspink D.F. (1994) The mechanical properties of fast and slow skeletal muscles of the mouse in relation to their locomotory function. *J. exp. Biol.* **198**, 491–502.

Janzen, D.H. (1976) Why tropical trees have rotten cores. *Biotropica* **8**, 110.

Jepson, G.L. (1966) Early Eocene bat from Wyoming. *Science*, **154**, 1333–1339.

Jepson, G.L. (1970) Bat origins and evolution. In: *Biology of bats*, Vol. I, edited by W.A. Wimsatt, pp 1–64. Academic Press, New York.

Johnson-Murray, J.L. (1977) Myology of the gliding membranes of some petauristine rodents (genera: *Glaucomys, Pteromys, Petinomys* and *Petaurista*). *J. Mammal.* **59**, 374–384.

Jones, G. (1990) Prey selection by the greater horseshoe bat (*Rhinolophus ferrumequinum*): optimal foraging by echolocation? *J. Anim. Ecol.* **59**, 587–602.

Jones, G. (1994) Scaling of wingbeat and echolocation pulse emission rates in bats: why are aerial insectivores so small? *Funct. Ecol.* **8**, 450–457.

Jones, G. and Ransome, R.D. (1993) Echolocation calls of bats are influenced by maternal effects and change over a lifetime. *Proc. Roy. Soc. Lond.* B **252**, 125–128.

Jones, G. and Rayner, J.M.V. (1988) Flight performance, foraging tactics and echolocation in free-living Daubenton's bats *Myotis daubentonii* (Chiroptera: Vespertilionidae) *J. Zool. Lond.* **215**, 113–132.

Jones, G. and Rayner, J.M.V. (1989a) Foraging behaviour and echolocation of wild horseshoe bats *Rhinolophus ferrumequinum* and *R. hipposideros* (Chiroptera, Rhinolophidae) *Behav. Ecol. Sociobiol.* **25**, 183–191.

Jones, G. and Rayner, J.M.V. (1989b) Optimal flight speed in pipistrelle bats, *Pipistrellus pipistrellus. Eur. Bat Res.* **1987**, 247–253.

Jones, G. and Rayner, J.M.V. (1991) Flight performance, foraging tactics and echolocation in the trawling insectivorous bat *Myotis adversus* (Chiroptera: Vespertilionidae) *J. Zool. Lond.* **225**, 393–412.

Jones, G. and Rydell, J. (1994) Foraging strategy and predation risk as factors influencing emergence time in echolocating bats. *Phil. Trans. Roy. Soc.* B. **346**, 445–455.

Jones, G. and van Parijs, S.M. (1993) Bimodal echolocation in pipistrelle bats: are cryptic species present? *Proc. Roy. Soc. Lond.* B. **251**, 119–125.

Jones, G., Duverge, L. and Ransome, R.D. (1995) Conservation biology of an endangered species: field studies of greater horseshoe bats. In: *Ecology, evolution and behaviour of bats*, edited by P.A. Racey and S.M. Swift, *Symp. Zool. Soc. Lond.* **67**, pp 309–324. Oxford University Press, Oxford.

Jones, G., Hughes, P.M. and Rayner, J.M.V. (1991) The development of vocalizations in *Pipistrellus pipistrellus* (Chiroptera: Vespertilionidae) during post-natal growth and the maintenance of individual vocal signatures. *J. Zool. Lond.* **225**, 71–84.

Jones, K.J. and Genoways, H.H. (1970) Chiropteran systematics. In: *About bats: a chiropteran symposium*, edited by R.H. Slaughter and D.W. Walton, pp 3–21. Southern Methodist University Press, Dallas.

Julian, S. and Altringham, J.D. (1994) Bat predation by a tawny owl. *Naturalist* **119**, 49–56.

Kalko, E.K.V. (1995) Echolocation signal design, foraging habitats and guild structure in six neotropical sheath-tailed bats (Emballonuridae). In: *Ecology, evolution and behaviour of bats*, edited by P.A. Racey and S.M. Swift, *Symp. Zool. Soc. Lond.* **67**, pp 259–273. Oxford University Press, Oxford.

Kallen, F.C. (1977) The cardiovascular system of bats: structure and function. In: *The biology of bats*, Vol. III, edited by W.A. Wimsatt, pp 289–483. Academic Press, New York.

Kick, S.A. (1982) Target detection by the echolocating bat, *Eptesicus fuscus*. *J. Comp. Physiol.* **145**, 431–435.

Kick, S.A. and Simmons, J.A. (1984) Acoustic gain control in the bat's sonar receiver and the neuroethology of echolocation. *J. Neurosci.* **4**, 2725–2737.

Kingdon, J. (1974) *East African Mammals*, Vol. IIA (*Insectivores and bats*). Academic Press, London.

Kleiber, M. (1932) Body size and metabolism. *Hilgardia* **6**, 315–353.

Kobler, J.B., Wilson, B.S., Henson, O.W. and Bishop, A.L. (1985) Echo intensity compensation by echolocating bats. *Hearing Res.* **20**, 99–108.

Krishna, A. (1978) *Aspects of reproduction in some Indian bats*. Unpublished Ph.D. thesis, Banaras Hindu University, Varanasi.

Krzanowski, A. (1961) Weight dynamics of bats wintering in the cave at Pulawy (Poland). *Acta Theriol.* **4**, 249–264.

Kulzer, E. (1967) Die Hertztätigkeit bei lethargischen und winterschlafenden fledermäusen. *Zeitschr. f. vergl. Physiol.* **56**, 63–94.

Kulzer, E. and Storf, R. (1980) Schlaf-lethargie bei dem afrikanischen langzungenflughund *Megaloglossus woermanni* Pagenstecher. *Z. Saugetierk.* **45**, 23–29.

Kunz, T.H. (1973) Population studies of the cave bat (*Myotis velifer*): Reproduction, growth and development. *Occas. Pap. Mus. Nat. Hist. Univ. Kans.* **15**, 1–43.

Kunz, T.H. (1982) Roosting ecology. In: *The ecology of bats*, edited by T.H. Kunz, pp 1–55. Plenum Press, New York.

Kunz, T.H. (1987) Post-natal growth and energetics of suckling bats. In: *Recent advances in the study of bats*, edited by M.B. Fenton, P.A. Racey and J.M.V. Rayner. pp 395–420. Cambridge University Press, Cambridge.

Kunz, T.H. and Stern, A.A. (1995) Maternal investment and post-natal growth in bats. In: *Ecology, evolution and behaviour of bats*, edited by P.A. Racey and S.M. Swift, *Symp. Zool. Soc. Lond.* **67**, pp 123–138. Oxford University Press, Oxford.

Kunz, T.H., August, P.V. and Burnett, C.D. (1983) Harem social organisation in cave roosting *Artibeus jamaicensis* (Chiroptera: Phyllostomidae). *Biotropica* **15**, 133–138.

Kunz, T.H. and Ingalls, K.A. (1994) Folivory in bats: an adaptation derived from frugivory. *Funct. Ecol.* **8**, 665–668.

Kurta, A. and Kunz, T.H. (1987) Size of bats at birth and maternal investment during pregnancy. *Symp. Zool. Soc. Lond.* **57**, 79–106.

LaVal, R.K. amd Fitch, H.S. (1977) Structure, movement and reproduction in three Costa Rican bat communities. *Occas. Pap. Mus. Nat. Hist. Univ. Kans.* **69**, 1–28.

Lawrence, B.D. and Simmons, J.A. (1982a) Measurement of atmospheric attenuation at ultrasonic frequencies and the significance for echolocation by bats. *J. Acoust. Soc. Am.* **71**, 585–590.

Lawrence, B.D. and Simmons, J.A. (1982b) Echolocation in bats: the external ear and perception of the vertical position of targets. *Science* **218**, 481–483.

Lillegraven, J.A. (1974) Biogeographical considerations of the marsupial-placental dichotomy. *Ann. Rev. Ecol. Syst.* **5**, 263–283.

Limpens, H.J.G.A. and Kapteyn, K. (1991) Bats, their behaviour and linear landscape elements. *Myotis* **29**, 39–47

Link, A., Marimuthu, G. and Neuweiler, G. (1986) Movement as a specific stimulus for prey catching behaviour in rhinolophid and hipposiderid bats. *J. Comp. Physiol.* A. **159**, 403–413.

Linnaeus, C. (1758) *Systema naturae per regna tria naturae, secundum classes, ordines, genera, species, cum characteribus, differentiis, synonymis, locis.* Tomus I. Editio Decima, Reformata. Holmiae, Impensis direct. Laurentii Salvii. Stockholm.

Lundberg, K. and Gerell, R. (1986) Territorial advertisement and mate attraction in the bat *Pipistrellus pipistrellus*. *Ethology* **71**, 115–124.

MacArthur, R.H. and Pianka, E.R. (1966) On optimal use of a patchy environment. *Amer. Nat.* **100**, 603–609.

MacArthur, R.H. and Wilson, E.O. (1967) *The theory of island biogeography*. Princeton University Press, Princeton, N.J.

Madhaven, A. (1978) Breeding habits and associated phenomena in some Indian bats. Part V, *Pipistrellus dormeri* (Dobson), Vespertilionidae. *J. Bombay. Nat. Hist. Soc.* **75**, 426–433.

Marimuthu, G. and Neuweiler, G. (1987) The use of acoustical cues for prey detection by the Indian false vampire bat, *Megaderma lyra. J. Comp. Physiol.* **160**, 509–515.

Marshall, A.G. (1983) Bats, flowers and fruit: evolutionary relationships in the Old World. *Biol. J. Linn. Soc.* **20**, 115–135.

Masters, W.M., Moffat, A.J.M. and Simmons, J.A. (1985) Sonar tracking of horizontally moving targets by the big brown bat, *Eptesicus fuscus. Science* **228**, 1331–1333.

May, R.M. (1981) Models for two interacting populations. In: *Theoretical ecology: principles and applications*. Second edition, edited by R.M. May, pp 78–104. Blackwell Scientific Publications, Oxford.

McCracken G.F. (1984) Communal nursing in Mexican free-tailed bat maternity colonies. *Science* **223**, 1090–1091.

McCracken G.F. and Bradbury, J.W. (1977) Paternity and genetic heterogeneity in the polygynous bat, *Phyllostomus hastatus. Science* **198**, 303–306.

McCracken G.F. and Bradbury, J.W. (1981) Social organisation and kinship in the polgynous bat, *Phyllostomus hastatus. Behav. Ecol. Sociobiol.* **8**, 11–34.

McGregor, S.E., Alcorn, S.M. and Olin, G. (1962) Pollination and pollinating agents of the saguaro. *Ecology* **43**, 259–267.

McKenzie, N.L. and Rolfe, J.K. (1986) Structure of bat guilds in the Kimberley mangroves, Australia. *J. Anim. Ecol.* **55**, 401–420.

McManus, J.J. (1976) Thermoregulation. In: *Biology of bats of the New World family Phyllostomidae*. Part I, edited by R.J. Baker, J.K. Jones and D.C. Carter. *Spec. Pubs. Mus. Texas Tech. Univ.* **13**, 281–292. Texas Technical. Press.

McNab, B.K. (1969) The economics of temperature regulation in Neotropical bats. *Comp. Biochem. Physiol.* **31**, 227–268.

McNab, B.K. (1974a) The behaviour of temperate cave bats in a subtropical environment. *Ecology* **55**, 943–958.

McNab, B.K. (1974b) The energetics of endotherms. *Ohio J. Sci.* **74**, 370–380.

McNab, B.K. (1982) Evolutionary alternatives in the physiological ecology of bats. In: *The ecology of bats*, edited by T.H. Kunz, pp 151–200. Plenum Press, New York.

McNab, B.K. (1992) A statistical analysis of mammalian rates of metabolism. *Funct. Ecol.* **6**, 672–679.

McWilliam, A.N. (1987) The reproductive and social biology of *Coleura afra* in a seasonal environment. In: *Recent advances in the study of bats*, edited by M.B. Fenton, P.A. Racey and J.M.V. Rayner, pp 324–350. Cambridge University Press, Cambridge.

Medway, Lord (1971) Observations of social and reproductive biology of the bent-winged bat *Miniopterus australis* in northern Borneo. *J. Zool. Lond.* **165**, 261–273.

Medway, Lord (1972) Reproductive cycles of the flat-headed bats *Tylonycteris pachypus* and *T. robustula* (Chiroptera: Vespertilionidae) in a humid equatorial environment. *J. Linn. Soc. Lond. Zool.* **51**, 33–61.

Medway, Lord and Marshall, A.G. (1970) Roost-site selection among flat-headed bats (*Tylonycteris* spp). *J. Zool. Lond.* **161**, 237–245.

Medway, Lord and Marshall, A.G. (1972) Roosting association of flat-headed bats, *Tylonycteris* species (Chiroptera: Vespertilionidae) in Malaysia. *J. Zool. Lond.* **168**, 463–482.

Menaker, M. (1964) Frequency of spontaneous arousal from hibernation in bats. *Nature* **203**, 540–541.

Michelson, A. and Larsen, O.N. (1985) Hearing and sound. In: *Comprehensive insect physiology, biochemistry and pharmacology*, Vol. 9, edited by G.A. Kerkut and L.I. Gilbert, pp 495–556. Pergamon Press, Oxford.

Mickleburgh, S.P., Hutson, A.M. and Racey, P.A. (1992) *Old World fruit bats: an action plan for their conservation.* I.U.C.N./S.S.C., Gland, Switzerland.

Miller, L.A. (1975) The behaviour of flying green lacewings in the presence of ultrasound. *J. Insect Physiol.* **121**, 205–219.

Miller, L.A. (1991) Arctiid moth clicks can degrade the accuracy of range difference discrimination of echolocating brown bats, *Eptesicus fuscus. J. Comp. Physiol.* A **199**, 571–579.

Möller, J. (1978) Response characteristics of inferior colliculus neurons of the awake CF-FM bat *Rhinolophus ferrumequinum.* II. Two tone stimulation. *J. Comp. Physiol.* A **125**, 227–236.

Morrison, D.W (1979) Apparent male defense of tree hollows in the fruit bat, *Artibeus jamaicensis. J. Mammal.* **60**, 11–15.

Morrison, D.W. (1978) Foraging ecology and energetics of the frugivorous bat, *Artibeus jamaicensis. Ecology* **59**, 716–723.

Morrison, D.W. and Hagen-Morrison, S. (1981) Economics of harem maintenance by a neotropical bat. *Ecology* **62**, 864–866.

Müller, J. (1981) Fossil pollen records of extant angiosperms. *Bot. Rev.* **47**, 1–142.

Myers, P. (1977) Patterns of reproduction of four species of vespertilionid bats in Paraguay. *Univ. Calif. Publ. Zool.* **107**, 1–41.

Nellis, D.W. and Ehle, C.P. (1977) Observations on the behaviour of *Brachyphylla cavernarum* (Chiroptera) in the Virgin Islands. *Mammalia,* **41**, 403–409.

Nelson, J.E. (1965) Behaviour of Australian Pteropodidae (Megachiroptera). *Anim. Behav.* **13**, 544–557.

Neuweiler, G. (1970) Neurophysiologische untersuchungen zum echoortungssystem der grossen hufeisennase, *Rhinolophus ferrumequinum. Z. Zgl. Physiol.* **67**, 273–306.

Neuweiler, G. (1990) Auditory adaptations for prey capture in echolocating bats. *Physiol Rev.* **70**, 615–641.

Nitecki, M.H. (1983) Editor. *Coevolution.* University of Chicago Press, Chicago.

Norberg, U.M. (1970) Functional osteology and myology of the wing of *Plecotus auritus* Linnaeus (Chiroptera). *Arkiv for Zoologi* **22**, 483–543.

Norberg, U.M. (1972) Bat wing structures important for aerodynamics and rigidity (Mammalia, Chiroptera). *Z. Morphol. Tiere* **73**, 45–61.

Norberg, U.M. (1976) Some advanced flight manoeuvres of bats. *J. exp. Biol.* **64**, 489–495.

Norberg, U.M. (1985) Evolution of vertebrate flight: an aerodynamic model for the transition from gliding to active flight. *Am. Nat.* **126**, 303–327.

Norberg, U.M. (1987) Wing form and flight mode in bats. In: *Recent advances in the study of bats,* edited by M.B. Fenton, P.A. Racey and J.M.V. Rayner, pp 43–56. Cambridge University Press, Cambridge.

Norberg, U.M. (1990) *Vertebrate flight.* Springer-Verlag, Berlin

Norberg, U.M. and Fenton, M.B. (1988) Carnivorous bats? *Biol. J. Linn. Soc.* **33**, 383–394.

Norberg, U.M. and Rayner, J.M.V. (1987) Ecological morphology and flight in bats (Mammalia; Chiroptera): wing adaptations, flight performance, foraging strategy and echolocation. *Phil. Trans. Roy. Soc. Lond.* B **316**, 335–427.

Norberg, U.M., Kunz, T.H., Steffensen, J.F., Winter, Y. and von Helversen, O. (1993) The cost of hovering and forward flight in a nectar-feeding bat, *Glossophaga soricina,* estimated from aerodynamic theory. *J. exp. Biol.* **182**, 207–227.

Novacek, M.J. (1985) Evidence for echolocation in the oldest known bats. *Nature* **315**, 140–141.

O'Farrell, M.J. and Studier, E.H. (1970) Fall metabolism in relation to ambient temperatures in three species of *Myotis. Comp. Biochem. Physiol.* **35**, 697–703.

O'Farrell, M.J. and Studier, E.H. (1973) Reproduction, growth and development in *Myotis thysanodes* and *M. lucifugus* (Chiroptera: Vespertilionidae). *Ecology* **54**, 18–30.

O'Neill, W.E. (1987) The processing of temporal information in the auditory systems of echo-locating bats. In: *Recent advances in the study of bats*, edited by M.B. Fenton, P.A. Racey and J.M.V. Rayner, pp 171–199. Cambridge University Press, Cambridge.

O'Neill, W.E. and Suga, N. (1982) Encoding of target range and its representation in the auditory cortex of the moustached bat. *J. Neurosci.* **2**, 17–31.

O'Neill, W.E., Schuller, G. and Padke-Schuller, S. (1985) Functional and anatomical similarities in the auditory cortices of the Old World horseshoe bat and neotropical moustached bat for process-ing of similar biosonar signals. *Assoc. Res. Otolaryn.* **193**, 148.

O'Shea, T.J. (1980) Roosting, social organisation and the annual cycle in a Kenya population of the bat *Pipistrellus nanus. Z. Tierpsychol.* **53**, 171–195.

O'Shea, T.J. and Vaugham, T.A. (1977) Noctural and seasonal activities of the pallid bat, *Antrozous pallidus. J. Mammal.* **58**, 269–284.

Obrist, M.K., Fenton, M.B., Eger, J.L. and Schlegel, P.A. (1993) What ears do for bats: a compara-tive study of pinna sound pressure transformation in chiroptera. *J. exp. Biol.* **180**, 119–152.

Olsen, J.F. and Suga, N. (1986) The auditory thalamus of the moustached bat: convergent input and coincidence of excitation from orientation sound and echo. *Neurosci. Abstr.* **12**, 1272.

Orr, R.T. (1970) Development: Prenatal and postnatal. In: *Biology of bats,* Vol. I, edited by W.A. Wimsatt, pp 217–231. Academic Press, New York.

Pagels, J.F. (1975) Temperature regulation, body weight and changes in total body fat of the free-tailed bat, *Tadarida brasiliensis cynocephala* (LeConte). *Comp. Biochem. Physiol.* **50**, 237–246.

Park, K.J., Masters, E. and Altringham, J.D. (1996) Social structure of three sympatric species of vesper bat. In preparation.

Patterson, C. (1987) Introduction. In: *Molecules and morphology in evolution: conflict or compro-mise?*, edited by C. Patterson, pp 1–22. Cambridge University Press, Cambridge.

Patterson, C., Williams, D.M. and Humphries, C.J. (1993) Congruence between molecular and morphological phylogenies. *Ann. Rev. Ecol. Syst.* **24**, 153–188.

Pennycuick, C.J. (1971) Gliding flight of the dog-faced bat, *Rousettus aegyptiacus*, observed in a wind tunnel. *J. exp. Biol.* **55**, 833–845.

Pennycuick, C.J. (1972) *Animal flight*. Edward Arnold, London.

Pennycuick, C.J. (1989) *Bird flight performance: a practical calculation manual*. Oxford University Press, Oxford.

Peterson, R.L. (1965) A review of the flat-headed bats of the family Molossidae from South America and Africa. *Life Sci. Contr. R. Ont. Mus.* **64**, 3–32.

Pettigrew, J.D. (1985) Echolocation. In: *A dictionary of birds*, edited by B. Campbell and E. Lack. T. &A.D. Poyser, Calton.

Pettigrew, J.D. (1986) Flying primates? Megabats have the advanced pathway from eye to mid-brain. *Science* **231**, 1306–1306.

Pettigrew, J.D. (1991a) Wings or brain? Convergent evolution in the origins of bats. *Syst. Zool.* **40**, 199–216.

Pettigrew, J.D. (1991b) A fruitful, wrong hypothesis? Response to Baker, Novacek and Simmons. *Syst. Zool.* **40**, 231–239.

Pettigrew, J.D. (1994) Flying DNA. *Curr. Biol.* **4**, 277–280.

Pettigrew, J.D. (1995) Flying primates: crashed or crashed through? In: *Ecology, evolution and behaviour of bats*, edited by P.A. Racey, and S.M. Swift, *Symp. Zool. Soc. Lond.* **67**, pp 3–26. Oxford University Press, Oxford.

Pettigrew, J.D., Jamieson, B.G.M., Robson, S.K., Hall, L.S., McAnally, K.I. and Cooper, H.M. (1989) Phylogenetic relations between microbats, megabats and primates (Mammalia: Chiroptera and Primates). *Phil. Trans. Roy. Soc. Lond. B.* **325**, 489–559.

Pierson, E.D., Sarich, V.M., Lownstein, J.M., Daniel, M.J. and Rainey, W.E. (1986) A molecular link between the bats of New Zealand and South America. *Nature* **323**, 60–63.

Pollak, G.D. (1993) Some comments on the proposed perception of phase and nanosecond time disparities by echolocating bats. *J. Comp. Physiol.* A. **172**, 523–531.

Pollak, G.D. and Casseday, J.H. (1989) *The neural basis of echolocation in bats.* Zoophysiology Vol. 25. Springer-Verlag, Berlin.

Pollak, G.D., Bodenhamer, R., Marsh, D.S. and Souther, A. (1977a) Recovery cycles of single neurons in the inferior colliculus of unanaesthetised bats obtained with frequency-modulated and constant frequency sounds, *J. Comp. Physiol.* B. **120**, 215–50.

Pollak, G.D., Marsh, D.S., Bodenhamer, R. and Souther, A. (1977b) Characteristics of phasic on neurons in inferior colliculus of unanaesthetised bats with observations relating to mechanisms for echo ranging. *J. Neurophys.* **45**, 208–26.

Pomeroy, D. (1990) Why fly? The possible benefits for lower mortality. *Biol. J. Linn. Soc.* **40**, 53–65.

Prance, G.T. (1982) Editor: *Biological diversification in the tropics.* Columbia University Press. New York.

Promislow, D.E.L. and Harvey, P.H. (1990) Living fast and dying young: a comparative analysis of life history variation among mammals. *J. Zool. Lond.* **220**, 417–437.

Racey, P.A. (1969) Diagnosis of pregnancy and experimental extension of gestation in the pipistrelle bat, *Pipistrellus pipistrellus. J. Reprod. Fertil.* **19**, 465–474.

Racey, P.A. (1973) Environmental factors affecting the length of gestation in heterothermic bats. *J. Reprod. Fertil. Suppl.* **19**, 175–189.

Racey, P.A. (1982) Ecology of bat reproduction. In: *The ecology of bats*, edited by T.H. Kunz, pp 57–104. Plenum Press, New York.

Racey, P.A. and Swift, S.M. (1981) Variations in gestation length in a colony of pipistrelle bats (*Pipistrellus pipistrellus*) from year to year. *J. Reprod. Fertil.* **61**, 123–129.

Racey, P.A. and Swift, S.M. (1985) Feeding ecology of *Pipistrellus pipistrellus* (Chiroptera: Vespertilionidae) during pregnancy and lactation. I. Foraging behaviour. *J. Anim. Ecol.* **54**, 205–215.

Raikow, R.J. (1985) Locomotor system. In: *Form and function in birds*, edited by A.S. King and J. McLelland, pp 57–147. Academic Press, London.

Ransome, R.D. (1968) The distribution of the greater horseshoe bat, *Rhinolophus ferrumequinum*, during hibernation, in relation to environmental factors. *J. Zool. Lond.* **154**, 77–112.

Ransome, R.D. (1971) The effect of ambient temperature on the arousal frequency of the greater horseshoe bat, *Rhinolophus ferrumequinum*, in relation to site selection and the hibernation state. *J. Zool. Lond.* **164**, 353–371.

Ransome, R.D. (1973) Factors affecting the timing of births of the greater horseshoe bat (*Rhinolophus ferrumequinum*). *Period. Biol.* **75**, 169–175.

Ransome, R.D. (1990) *The natural history of hibernating bats.* Christopher Helm, London.

Rayner, J.M.V. (1981) Flight adaptations in vertebrates. In: *Vertebrate locomotion*, edited by M.H. Day, pp 137–171. Academic Press, London

Rayner, J.M.V. (1986) Vertebrate flapping flight mechanics and aerodynamics, and the evolution of flight in bats. In: *Biona Rep. 5, Bat flight-Fledermausflug*, edited by W. Nachtigall, pp 27–74. Gustav Fischer Verlag, Stuttgart.

Rayner, J.M.V. (1987) The mechanics of flapping flight in bats. In: *Recent advances in the study of bats*, edited by M.B. Fenton, P.A. Racey and J.M.V. Rayner. pp 23–42. Cambridge University Press, Cambridge.

Rayner, J.M.V. (1991) The cost of being a bat. *Nature* **350**, 383–384.

Rayner, J.M.V. (1992) Avian flight evolution and the problem of Archaeopteryx. In: *Biomechanics and evolution*, edited by J.M.V. Rayner and R. Wootton, pp 183–212. S.E.B. Symposium. Cambridge University Press, Cambridge.

Rayner, J.M.V., Jones, G. and Thomas, A. (1986) Vortex flow visualisations reveal change in upstroke function with flight speed in bats. *Nature* **321**, 162–164.

Reite, O.B. and Davis, W.H. (1966) Thermoregulation in bats exposed to low ambient temperatures. *Proc. Soc. Exp. Biol. Med.* **121**, 1212–1215.

Richardson, E.G. (1977) The biology and evolution of the reproductive cycle in *Miniopterus schreibersii* and *M. australis* (Chiroptera: Vespertiliondae). *J. Zool. Lond.* **183**, 353–375.

Rickart, E.A., Heideman, P.D. and Utzurrum, R.C.B. (1989) Tent-roosting by *Scotophilus kuhlii*. *J. trop. Ecol.* **3**, 433–436.

Ridley, M. (1986) *Evolution and classification: the reformation of cladism*. Longman, London

Robbins, L.W. and Sarich, V.M. (1988) Evolutionary relationships in the family Emballonuridae (Chiroptera). *J. Mammal.* **69**, 1–13.

Robert, D., Amoroso, J. and Hoy, R.R. (1992) The evolutionary convergence of hearing in a parasitoid fly and its cricket host. *Science* **258**, 1135–1137.

Roeder, K.D. (1964) Aspects of the tympanic nerve response having significance for the avoidance of bats. *J. Insect. Physiol.* **10**, 529–556.

Roeder, K.D. (1965) Moths and ultrasound. *Sci. Am.* **212**, 94–102.

Roeder, K.D. and Treat, A.E. (1961) The detection and evasion of bats by moths. *Am. Sci.* **49**, 135–148.

Roverud, R.C. (1987) The processing of echolocation sound elements in bats: a behavioural approach. In: *Recent advances in the study of bats*, edited by M.B. Fenton, P.A. Racey and J.M.V. Rayner. pp 152–170. Cambridge University Press, Cambridge.

Roverud, R.C. and Grinnell, A.D. (1985) Echolocation sound features processed to provide distance information in the CF/FM bat *Noctilio albiventris*: evidence for a gated time window utilising both CF and FM components. *J. Comp. Physiol.* A. **156**, 457–469.

Ryan, M.J. and Tuttle, M.D. (1983) The ability of the frog-eating bat to discriminate among novel and potentially poisonous frog species using acoustic cues. *Anim. Behav.* **31**, 827–833.

Ryan, M.J. and Tuttle, M.D. (1987) The role of prey-generated sounds, vision and echolocation in prey localisation by the African bat, *Cardioderma cor. J. Comp. Physiol.* A. **161**, 59–66.

Ryan, M.J., Tuttle, M.D. and Barclay, R.M.R. (1983) Behavioural responses of the frog-eating bat, *Trachops cirrhosus*, to sonic frequencies. *J. Comp. Physiol.* A **150**, 413–418.

Ryan, M.J., Tuttle, M.D. and Rand, A.S. (1982) Bat predation and sexual advertisement in a neotropical frog. *Am. Nat.* **119**, 136–139.

Rydell, J. (1986) Foraging and diet of the northern bat *Eptesicus nilssoni* in Sweden. *Holar. Ecol.* **9**, 272–276.

Rydell, J. (1992) Exploitation of insects around street lamps by bats in Sweden. *Funct. Ecol.* **6**, 744–750.

Rydell, J. and Arlettaz, R. (1994) Low-frequency echolocation enables the bat *Tadarida teniotis* to feed on tympanate insects. *Proc. Roy. Soc. Lond.* **B**. 257, 175–178.

Sahley, C.T., Horner, M.A. and Fleming, T.H. (1993) Flight speeds and mechanical power outputs of the nectar-feeding bat, *Leptonycteris curasoae* (Phyllostomidae: Glossophaginae). *J. Mamm.* **74**, 594–600.

Sales, G. and Pye, D. (1974) *Ultrasonic Communication by Animals*. Chapman and Hall, London.

Savage, D.E. (1951) A Miocene Phyllostomatid bat from Colombia, South America. *Univ. Calif. Pubs in Geol.* **28**, 357–366.

Schaal, S. and Ziegler, W. (1992) Editors. *Messel: an insight into the history of life and of the Earth*. Clarendon Press, Oxford.

Schaffer, J. (1905) Anatomisch-histologische untersuchungen uber den bau der zehen bei fledermausen und einigen kletternden saugeteiren. *Zeitschr. Wissensch. Zool.* **83**, 231–284.

Scherrer, J.A. and Wilkinson, G.S. (1993) Evening bat isolation calls provide evidence for heritable signatures. *Anim. Behav.* **46**, 847–860.

Schmidt, S. (1988) Evidence for a spectral basis of texture perception in bat sonar. *Nature* **331**, 617–619.

Schmidt-Nielsen, K. (1984) *Scaling: Why is animal size so important?* Cambridge University Press, Cambridge.

Schnitzler, H. -U. (1987) Echoes of fluttering insects: information for echolocating bats. In: *Recent advances in the study of bats*, edited by M.B. Fenton, P.A. Racey and J.M.V. Rayner, pp 226–243. Cambridge University Press, Cambridge.

Schnitzler, H. -U. and Ostwald, J. (1983) Adaptations for the detection of fluttering insects by echolocation in Horseshoe bats. In: *Advances in neuroethology*, edited by J.P. Ewart, R.R. Capranica and D.J. Ingle, pp 801–827. Plenum Press, New York.

Schnitzler, H. -U., Menne, D., Kober, R. and Heblich, K. (1983) The acoustical image of fluttering insects in echolocating bats. In: *Neuroethology and behavioural physiology. Roots and growing points*, edited by F. Huber and H. Markl, pp 235–250. Springer-Verlag, Heidelberg.

Schnitzler, H.-U., Kalko, E.K., Kaipf, I. and Grinnell, A.D. (1994) Hunting and echolocation behaviour of the fisherman bat, *Noctilio leporinus*, in the field. *Behav. Ecol. Sociobiol.* **35**, 327–345.

Schoener, T.W. (1986) Overview: kinds of ecological communities—ecology becomes pluralistic. In: *Community ecology*, edited by J. Diamond and T.J. Case, pp 467–479. Harper and Row, New York.

Scholander, P.F., Walters, V., Hock, R. and Irving, L. (1950) Body insulation of some arctic and tropical mammals and birds. *Biol. Bull. mar. biol. lab. Woods Hole* **99**, 225–236.

Scholey, K.D. (1986) The evolution of flight in bats. In: *Biona Rep. 5, Bat flight-Fledermausflug*, edited by W. Nachtigall, pp 1–12. Gustav Fischer Verlag, Stuttgart.

Schumm, A., Krull, D. and Neuweiler, G. (1991) Echolocation in the notch-eared bat, *Myotis emarginatus*. *Behav. Ecol. Sociobiol.* **28**, 255–261.

Simmons, J.A. (1971) Echolocation in bats: Signal processing of echoes for target range. *Science* **171**, 925–928.

Simmons, J.A. (1973) The resolution of target range by echolocating bats. *J. Acous. Soc. Amer.* **54**, 157–173.

Simmons, J.A. (1974) Response of the Doppler echolocation system in the bat *Rhinolophus ferrumequinum*. *J. Acous. Soc. Amer.* **56**, 672–682.

Simmons, J.A. (1979) Perception of echo phase information in bat sonar. *Science* **204**, 1336–1338.

Simmons, J.A. (1993) Evidence for perception of fine echo delay and phase by the FM bat, *Eptesicus fuscus. J. Comp. Physiol.* A. **172**, 533–547.

Simmons, J.A. and Stein, R.A. (1980) Acoustic imaging in bat sonar: echolocation signals and the evolution of echolocation. *J. Comp. Physiol.* **135**, 61–84.

Simmons, J.A. and Vernon, J.A. (1971) Echolocation: discrimination of targets by the bat *Eptesicus fuscus. J. exp. Zool.* **176**, 315–328.

Simmons, J.A., Howell, D.J. and Suga, N. (1975) Information content of bat sonar echoes. *Amer. Sci.* **63**, 204–215.

Simmons, J.A., Kick, S.A., Lawrence, B.D., Hale, C., Bard, C. and Escudie, B. (1983) Acuity of horizontal angle discrimination by the echolocating bat, *Eptesicus fuscus. J. Comp. Physiol.* A **153**, 321–330.

Simmons, N.B., Novacek, M.J. and Baker, R.J. (1991) Approaches, methods, and the future of the chiropteran monophyly controversy: a reply to J.D. Pettigrew. *Syst. Zool.* **40**, 239–243.

Simmons. J.A., Lavender, W.A., Lavender, B.A., Doroshow, C.A., Kiefer, S.W., Livingston, R., Scallet, A.C. and Crowley, D.E. (1974) Target structure and echo spectral discrimination by echolocating bats. *Science* **186**, 1130–1132.

Sluiter, J.W. and van Heerdt, P.F. (1966) Seasonal habits of the noctule bat (*Nyctalus noctula*). *Arch. Neerl. Zool.* **16**, 423–439.

Sluiter, J.W., Voute, A.M. and van Heerdt, P.F. (1973) Hibernation of *Nyctalus noctula. Period. Biol.* **75**, 181–188.

Smith, J.D. and Madkour, G. (1980) Penial morphology and the question of chiropteran phylogeny. In: *Proc. fifth int. bat res. conf.*, edited by D.E. Wilson and A.L. Gardner, pp 347–365. Texas Technical Press, Lubbock.

Smith, J.D. and Storch, G. (1981) New middle Eocene bats from Grube Messel near Darmstadt, W. Germany. *Senckenberg. biol.* **61**, 153–167.

Spangler, H.G. (1988) Moth hearing, defence and communication. *Ann. Rev. Entomol.* **33**, 59–82.

Speakman, J.R. (1991) The impact of predation by birds on bat populations in the British Isles. *Mammal. Rev.* **21**, 132–142.

Speakman, J.R. and Racey, P.A. (1987) The energetics of pregancy and lactation in the brown long-eared bat, *Plecotus auritus*. In: *Recent advances in the study of bats*, edited by M.B. Fenton, P.A. Racey and J.M.V. Rayner, pp 367–393. Cambridge University Press, Cambridge.

Speakman, J.R. and Racey, P.A. (1989) Hibernal ecology of the pipistrelle bat: Energy expenditure, water requirements and mass loss, implications for survival and the function of winter emergence flights. *J. Anim. Ecol.* **58**, 797–813.

Speakman, J.R. and Racey, P.A. (1991) No cost of echolocation for bats in flight. *Nature* **350**, 421–423.

Stebbings, R.E. (1988) *Conservation of European bats*. Christopher Helm, London.

Stewart, C-B. (1993) The powers and pitfalls of parsimony. *Nature* **361**, 603–607.

Stone, G.N. and Purvis, A. (1992) Warm-up rates during arousal from torpor in heterothermic mammals: physiological correlates and a comparison with heterothermic insects. *J. Comp. Physiol.* B. **162**, 284–295.

Strelkov, P.P. (1969) Migratory and stationary bats (Chiroptera) of the European part of the Soviet Union. *Acta Zool. Cracov.* **14**, 393–439.

Studier, E.H. and Howell, D.J. (1969) Heart rate of female big brown bats in flight. *J. Mammal.* **50**, 842–845.

Studier, E.H. and O'Farrell, M.J. (1976) Biology of *Myotis thysanodes* and *M. lucifugus* (Chiroptera: Vespertilionidae). III. Metabolism, heart rate, breathing rate and general energetics. *Comp. Biochem. Physiol.* **54**A 423–432.

Studier, E.H. and Wilson, D.E. (1970) Thermoregulation in some Neotropical bats. *Comp. Biochem. Physiol.* **34**, 251–262.

Studier, E.H. and Wilson, D.E. (1979) Effects of captivity on thermoregulation and metabolism in *Artibeus jamaicensis* (Chiroptera: Phyllostomidae). *Comp. Biochem. Physiol.* **62**, 347–350.

Suga, N. (1970) Echo-ranging neurons in the inferior colliculus of bats. *Science* **170**, 449–452.

Suga, N. (1977) Amplitude spectrum representation in the Doppler shifted CF processing area of the auditory cortex of the moustached bat. *Science* **196**, 64–67.

Suga, N. (1990) Biosonar and neural computation in bats. *Sci. Amer.* **262**, 34–41.

Suga, N. and Jen, P.H.S. (1975) Peripheral control of acoustic signals in the auditory system of echolocating bats. *J. exp. Biol.* **62**, 277–311.

Suga, N. and O'Neill, W.E. (1979) Neural axis representing target range in the auditory cortex of the moustached bat. *Science* **206**, 351–353.

Suga, N. and Schlegel, P. (1972) Neural attenuation of responses to emitted sounds in echolocating bats. *Science* **177**, 82–84.

Suga, N., O'Neill, W.E. and Manabe, T. (1978) Cortical neurons sensitive to combinations of information-bearing elements of bio-sonar signals in the moustached bat. *Science* **200**, 778–781.

Sullivan, W.E. (1982) Neural representation of target distance in auditory cortex of the echolocating bat *Myotis lucifugus*. *J. Neurophys.* **48**, 1011–1032.

Surlykke, A., Miller, L.A., Mohl, B., Andersen, B.B., Christensen-Dalsgaard, J. and Jorgensen, M.B. (1993) Echolocation in two very small bats from Thailand: *Craseonycteris thonglongyai* and *Myotis siligorensis*. *Behav. Ecol. Sociobiol.* **33**, 1–12.

Sussman, R.W. and Raven, P.H. (1978) Pollination by lemurs and marsupials: an archaic coevolutionary system. *Science* **197**, 885–886.

Suthers, R.A. (1967) Comparative echolocation by fishing bats. *J. Mammal.* **48**, 79–87.

Suthers, R.A. and Wenstrup, J.J. (1987) Behavioural discrimination studies involving prey capture by echolocating bats. In: *Recent advances in the study of bats*, edited by M.B. Fenton, P.A. Racey and J.M.V. Rayner, pp 122–151. Cambridge University Press, Cambridge.

Swartz, S.M., Bennett, M.B. and Carrier, D.R. (1992) Wing bone stresses in free flying bats and the evolution of skeletal design for flight. *Nature* **359**, 726–729.

Swift, S.M. (1980) Activity pattern of pipistrelle bats (*Pipistrellus pipistrellus*) in north-east Scotland. *J. Zool. Lond.* **190**, 285–295.

Swift, S.M. and Racey, P.A. (1983) Resource partitioning in two species of vespertilionid bats (Chiroptera) occupying the same roost. *J. Zool. Lond.* **200**, 249–259.

Swift, S.M., Racey, P.A. and Avery, M.I. (1985) Feeding ecology of *Pipistrellus pipistrellus* (Chiroptera: Vespertilionidae) during pregnancy and lactation II diet. *J. Anim. Ecol.* **54**, 217–225.

Thewisen, J.G.M. and Babcock. S.K. (1991) Distinctive cranial and cervical innervation of wing muscles: new evidence for bat monophyly. *Science* **251**, 934–936.

Thomas, D.W. (1993) Lack of evidence for a biological alarm clock in bats (*Myotis* spp.) hibernating under natural conditions. *Can. J. Zool.* **71**, 1–3.

Thomas, D.W. (1995) The physiological ecology of hibernation in vespertilionid bats. In: *Ecology, evolution and behaviour of bats*, edited by P.A. Racey, and S.M. Swift, *Symp. Zool. Soc. Lond.* **67**, pp 233–244. Oxford University Press, Oxford.

Thomas, D.W. and Cloutier, D. (1992) Evaporative water loss by hibernating little brown bats, *Myotis lucifugus. Physiol. Zool.* **65**, 443–456.

Thomas, D.W., Cloutier, D. and Gagne, D. (1990) Arrythmic breathing, apnea and non-steady-state oxygen uptake in hibernating little brown bats (*Myotis lucifugus*). *J. exp. Biol.* **149**, 395–406.

Thomas, D.W., Fenton, M.B. and Barclay, R.M.R. (1979) Social behaviour of the little brown bat, *Myotis lucifugus*. I. Mating behaviour. *Behav. Ecol. Sociobiol.* **6**, 129–136.

Thomas, D.W. and Marshall, A.G. (1984) Reproduction and growth in three species of West African fruit bats. *J. Zool. Lond.* **202**, 265–281.

Thomas, S.P. and Suthers, R.A. (1972) The physiology and energetics of bat flight. *J. exp. Biol.* **57**, 317–335.

Thomas, S.P. (1975) Metabolism during flight in two species of bats, *Phyllostomus hastatus* and *Pteropus gouldii. J. exp. Biol.* **63**, 273–293.

Thomas, S.P. (1987) The physiology of bat flight. In: *Recent advances in the study of bats*, edited by M.B. Fenton, P.A. Racey and J.M.V. Rayner, pp 75–99. Cambridge University Press, Cambridge.

Thomas, S.P. and Suthers, R.A. (1970) Oxygen consumption and physiological responses during flight in an echolocating bat. *Fedn. Proc.* **29**, 265.

Tidemann, C.R., Priddel, D.M., Nelson, J.E. and Pettigrew, J.D. (1985) Foraging behaviour of the Australian ghost bat, *Macroderma gigas* (Microchiroptera: Megadermatidae). *Aust. J. Zool.* **33**, 705–713.

Trappe, M. and Schnitzler, H.-U. (1982) Doppler-shift compensation in insect-catching horseshoe bats. *Naturwissen.* **69**, 193–194.

Tuttle, M.D. (1975) Population ecology of the grey bat (*Myotis grisescens*): Factors influencing early growth and development. *Occas. Pap. Mus. Nat. Hist. Univ. Kans.* **36**, 1–24.

Tuttle, M.D. (1976a) Population ecology of the grey bat (*Myotis grisescens*): factors influencing growth and survival of newly volant young. *Ecology* **57**, 587–595.

Tuttle, M.D. (1976b) Population ecology of the grey bat (*Myotis grisescens*): philopatry, timing and patterns of movement, weight loss during migration, and seasonal adaptive strategies. *Occ. pap. Mus. Nat. Hist. Univ. Kans.* **54**, 1–38.

Tuttle, M.D. (1976c) Collecting techniques. In: Biology of bats of the New World Phyllostomidae. Part 1, edited by R.J. Baker, J.K. Jones and D.C. Carter, pp 71–88. *Spec. Publ. Mus. Texas Tech. Univ. Lubbock* **10**, 1–218.

Tuttle, M.D. (1979) Status, causes of decline, and management of endangered grey bats. *J. Wildl. Manage.* **43**, 1–17.

Tuttle, M.D. and Ryan, M.J. (1981) Bat predation and the evolution of frog vocalisations in the neotropics. *Science* **214**, 677–678.

Tuttle, M.D. and Stevenson, D. (1982) Growth and survival of bats. In: *The ecology of bats*, edited by T.H. Kunz, pp 105–150. Plenum Press, New York.

Tuttle, M.D., Ryan, M.J. and Belwood, J.J. (1985) Acoustic resource partitioning by two species of phyllostomid bats (*Trachops cirrhosus* and *Tonatia sylvicola*). *Anim. Behav.* **33**, 1369–1370.

Twente, J.W. (1955) Some aspects of habitat selection and other behaviour of cavern-dwelling bats. *Ecology* **36**, 706–732.

Twente, J.W. and Twente, J. (1987) Biological alarm clock arouses hibernating big brown bats, *Eptesicus fuscus. Can. J. Zool.* **65**, 1668–1674.

Twente, J.W., Twente, J. and Brack, V. (1985) The duration of the period of hibernation of three species of vespertilionid bats. II. Laboratory studies. *Can J. Zool.* **63**, 2955–2961.

van der Pijl, L. (1972) *Principles of dispersal in higher plants.* Springer-Verlag, New York.

Vater, M. (1982) Single unit responses in the cochlear nucleus of horseshoe bats to sinusoidal frequency and amplitude modulated signals. *J. Comp. Physiol.* A. **149**, 369–388.

Vaughan, T.A. (1959) Functional morphology of three bats: *Eumops, Myotis and Macrotus. Publ. Mus. Nat. Hist. Univ. Kans.* **12**, 1–153.

Vaughan, T.A. (1970) The transparent dactylopatagium minus in phyllostomid bats. *J. Mammal.* **51**, 142–145.

Vaughan, T.A. (1976) Nocturnal behaviour of the African false vampire bat (*Cardioderma cor*). *J. Mammal.* **57**, 227–248.

Vaughan, T.A. and Bateman, M.M. (1980) The molossid wing: some adaptations for rapid flight. *Proc. 5th Int. Bat Res. Conf.*, pp 69–78. Texas Technical Press, Lubboch.

Vaughan, T.A. and O'Shea,T.J. (1976) Roosting ecology of the pallid bat, *Antrozous pallidus. J. Mammal.* **57**, 19–42.

Vehrencamp, S.L., Stiles, F.G. and Bradbury, J.W. (1977) Observations on the foraging behaviour and avian prey of the Neotropical carnivorous bat, *Vampyrum spectrum. J. Mammal.* 469–478.

Vogel, S. (1969) Chiropoterophilie in der neotrophischen flora. *Neue Mitt. II, III. Flora Abt.* B **158**, 185–222, 289–323.

von der Emde, G. and Schnitzler, H.-U. (1990) Classification of insects by echolocating greater horseshoe bats. *J. Comp. Physiol.* A. **167**, 423–430.

Walker, E.P. (1975) *Mammals of the world*, Vol. 1. John Hopkins University Press, Baltimore.

Waters, D.A. (1993) The auditory response of noctuid moths to the echolocation calls of bats. PhD thesis, University of Bristol.

Webster, F.A. (1967) Interception performance of echolocating bats in the presence of interference. In: *Animal sonar systems*, Vol. 1, edited by R.G. Busnel, pp 673–713. Laboritoire de Physiologie acoustique, Jouy-en-Josas.

Wenstrup, J.J. and Suthers, R.A. (1984) Echolocation of moving targets by the fish-catching bat, *Noctilio leporinus. J. Comp. Physiol.* A, **155**, 75–89.

Whitaker, J.O. and Black H.L. (1976) Food habits of cave bats from Zambia, Africa. *J. Mammal.* **57**, 199–204.

Wible, J.R. and Novacek, M.J. (1988) Cranial evidence for the monophyletic origin of bats. *Am. mus. Novit.* **2911**, 1–19.

Wilkinson, G.S. (1984) Reciprocal food sharing in the vampire bat. *Nature* **308**, 181–184.

Wilkinson, G.S. (1985) The social organisation of the common vampire bat. I. Pattern and cause of association. *Behav. Ecol. Sociobiol.* **17**, 111–121.

Wilkinson, G.S. (1987) Altruism and co-operation in bats. In: *Recent advances in the study of bats*, edited by M.B. Fenton, P.A. Racey and J.M.V. Rayner, pp 299–323. Cambridge University Press, Cambridge.

Wilkinson, G.S. (1990) Food sharing in vampire bats. *Sci. Am.* **262**, 64–70.

Wilkinson, G.S. (1992) Communal nursing in the evening bat, *Nycticeius humeralis. Behav. Ecol. Sociobiol.* **31**, 225–235.

Wilkinson, G.S. (1992) Information transfer at evening bat colonies. *Anim. Behav.* **44**, 501–518.

Wilkinson, G.S. (1995) Information transfer in bats. In: *Ecology, evolution and behaviour of bats*, edited by P.A. Racey, and S.M. Swift, *Symp. Zool. Soc. Lond.* **67**, pp 345–360. Oxford University Press, Oxford.

Willig, M.R. and Selcer, K.W. (1989) Bat species density gradients in the New World: a statistical assessment. *J. Biogeog.* **16**, 189–195.

Willig, M.R., Camillo, G.R. and Noble, S.J. (1993) Dietary overlap in frugivorous and insectivorous bats from edaphic cerrado habitats of Brazil. *J. Mammal.* **74**, 117–128.

Wilson, E.O. (1994) *The Diversity of Life*. Penguin, London.

Wilson, D.E. (1971) Ecology of *Myotis nigricans* (Mammalia: Chiroptera) on Barro Colorado Island, Panama Canal Zone. *J. Zool. Lond.* **163**, 1–13.

Wilson, D.E. (1973) Bat faunas: a trophic comparison. *Syst. Zool.* **22**, 14–29.

Wilson, D.E. (1979) Reproductive patterns. In: *Biology of bats of the New World family Phyllostomidae*, Part III, edited by R.J. Baker, J.K. Jones, and D.C. Carter, pp 317–378. *Spec. Publ. Mus. Texas Tech. Univ.* **16**, Lubbock.

Yager, D.D. and Hoy, R.R. (1986) The cyclopian ear: a new sense for the praying mantis. *Science* **231**, 727–729.

Yager, D.D., and May, M.L. (1990) Ultrasound-triggered, flight-gated evasive manoeuvres in the praying mantis *Parasphendale agrionina*. II. Tethered flight. *J. exp. Biol.* **152**, 41–58.

Yager, D.D., May, M.L. and Fenton, M.B. (1990) Ultrasound-triggered, flight-gated evasive escape manoeuvres in the praying mantis, *Paraspenandale agrionina*. I. Free fight. *J. exp. Biol.* **152**, 17–39.

Yalden, D.W. and Morris, P.A. (1975) *The lives of bats*. David and Charles, London.

Young, I.S., Warren, R.D. and Altringham, J.D. (1992) Some properties of the respiratory and locomotory systems of mammals in relation to body size. *J. exp. Biol.* **164**, 283–294.

Index

Bold type indicates illustrations. Drawings of bats, other animals, and plants are indicated by an asterisk.